A TREMOR
IN
THE BLOOD

A TREMOR IN THE BLOOD

Uses And Abuses Of The Lie Detector

David Thoreson Lykken

McGRAW-HILL BOOK COMPANY

New York   St. Louis   San Francisco
Auckland   Bogotá   Düsseldorf   Johannesburg   London   Madrid
Mexico   Montreal   New Delhi   Panama   Paris   São Paulo
Singapore   Sydney   Tokyo   Toronto

Thomas H. Quinn, Michael Hennelly, and Karen Seriguchi were the editors of this book. Christopher Simon was the designer. Teresa F. Leaden supervised the production. It was set in Caledonia with display lines in Trajanus by DataPage, Inc.
Printed and bound by R. R. Donnelley and Sons, Inc.

Library of Congress Cataloging in Publication Data
Lykken, David Thoreson.
  A tremor in the blood.
  Bibliography: p.
  Includes index.
  1. Lie detectors and detection.   I. Title.
HV8078.L94   363.2'54   80–10697
ISBN 0–07–039210–2
1 2 3 4 5 6 7 8 9 RRD RRD 8 1 7 6 5 4 3 2 1

This book is for
JESSE, JOE, and MATTHEW.

Guilt carries Fear always about with it; there is a Tremor in the Blood of a Thief, that, if attended to, would effectually discover him; and if charged as a suspicious Fellow, on the Suspicion only I would always feel his Pulse, and would recommend it to Practice. It is true some are so hardened in Crime that they will boldly hold their Faces to it, carry it off with an Air of Contempt, and outface even a Pursuer; but take hold of his Wrist and feel his Pulse, there you will find his Guilt; . . . a fluttering Heart, an unequal Pulse, a sudden Palpitation shall evidently confess he is the Man, in spite of a bold Countenance or a false Tongue.

—*Daniel Defoe*, An Effectual Scheme for the Immediate Prevention of Street Robberies and Suppressing All Other Disorders of the Night, 1730.

Contents

CHAPTER **1.** **Prologue**   *1*
Who is to Judge?

PART I: **LIE DETECTION: THE CONCEPT**   *7*

CHAPTER **2.** **Mr. Reader Has A Chance To Prove His Innocence**   *11*

CHAPTER **3.** **A Brief History Of Lie Detection**   *23*
William Moulton Marston / Larson and the Berkeley Developments / The Chicago Period / Reid's Contribution: The Clinical Lie Test / Backster and the Polygraphic Lie Test / Voice Analysis / Honesty Tests / The Tools of Diogenes / Science and the Lie Detector

CHAPTER **4.** **The Truth Verifier**   *49*
The Dawning of the Age of Truth / Is There a Truth Verifier? / Current Status of the Specific Lie Response

CHAPTER **5.** **Evaluating The Evidence**   *63*
The Limitations of Expert Opinion / Lykken's Law / Reliability vs. Validity / Reliability / Validity / The Burden of Proof

ix

PART II: **LIE DETECTION: THE METHODS**   *83*

CHAPTER **6.** **The Clinical Lie Test: The Examiner As "Lie Detector"**   *87*

Subjective Scoring and "Behavior Symptoms" / Assumptions of the Clinical Polygraph Examination / Validity of the Clinical Lie Test / Verdict

CHAPTER **7.** **The Relevant/Irrelevant (R/I) Test**   *103*

Assumptions of the R/I Test / Validity of the R/I Test / Verdict

CHAPTER **8.** **The Lie Control Test (LCT)**   *109*

Assumptions of the Lie Control Test / Some Real Life Examples / Validity of the Lie Control Test / Verdict

CHAPTER **9.** **The Truth Control Test (TCT)**   *129*

Assumptions of the Truth Control Test / Verdict

CHAPTER **10.** **The Positive Control Test (PCT)**   *135*

Assumptions of the Positive Control Test / Verdict

CHAPTER **11.** **The Relevant Control Test (RCT)**   *139*

Assumptions of the Relevant Control Test / Validity of the Relevant Control Test / Verdict

CHAPTER **12.** **The   Searching   Peak-Of-Tension   Test (SPOT)**   *145*

Assumptions of the SPOT / Verdict / Summary of Polygraphic Lie Tests

CHAPTER **13.** **Voice Stress Analysis**   *151*

The Tremor in the Voice: The PSE / Does the PSE Measure Stress? / Does the PSE Detect Lying? / Verdict

PART III: **LIE DETECTION: THE APPLICATIONS**   *163*

CHAPTER **14.** **Truth, Ltd.: The Polygrapher As Private Detective**   *167*

The Coker Case / Intra-Mural Crime / A Question of Rights / To Catch a Thief

CHAPTER 15. **Pre- And Post-Employment Screening** *183*

The Case For Polygraphic Screening / The Case Against Polygraphic Screening / Coping with Employee Theft

CHAPTER 16. **Questionnaire Measures Of "Honesty"** *195*

The Prediction of Honesty / Validity of Honesty Questionnaires / Verdict

CHAPTER 17. **The 4th Degree: Polygraphically Induced Confessions** *205*

The Peter Reilly Case / Why Do People Confess? / Confession and the Courts

CHAPTER 18. **The Lie Detector And The Courts** *217*

The Question of Base Rates / The Polygrapher as Expert Witness / How Juries React to Lie Test Evidence / The Psychopathic Liar / The Polygraph in Criminal Investigation

CHAPTER 19. **How To Beat The Lie Detector** *237*

Thumbtacks and Muscle Tension / Legislative Intervention

PART IV: **DETECTING GUILTY KNOWLEDGE** *245*

CHAPTER 20. **Origins Of The Guilty Knowledge Test (GKT)** *249*

The Experiment / The Results

CHAPTER 21. **The Body On The Stairs: A Pedagogical Detective Story** *257*

CHAPTER 22. **Analysis Of The Guilty Knowledge Method** *297*

Validity of the GKT in the Laboratory / Scoring / Counter-Measures / The GKT and the Polygraph / The GKT in the Courtroom / Future Prospects

INDEX *309*

Acknowledgments

Although I was known to be a critic of their industry, officers of the American Polygraph Association and other leading polygraphers have been remarkably generous and helpful in assisting me with the research on which this book is based. I thank them all but especially Norman Ansley, editor of *Polygraph;* Cleve Backster; Dr. Gordon Barland; Robert Brisentine, Jr., vice president of APA; Edward Gelb, president of APA (1979); Dr. Frank Horvath; Raymond Inglin, Los Angeles Police Department; and John Reid. I was especially fortunate in the generosity of my distinguished colleagues—Prof. Leonard Heston, M.D.; William Iacono, Ph.D.; Prof. Paul Meehl, Ph.D.; and Prof. Auke Tellegen, Ph.D.—who read an earlier draft of this manuscript, rent it limb from limb, and materially improved its clarity, its logic, and its accuracy. In the remote eventuality that errors still remain, I shall take credit for them myself. The time and expenses required for this venture were made available to me in the form of a sabbatical leave from the University of Minnesota and a grant from the Law Enforcement Assistance Administration of the U.S. Department of Justice. Neither of these institutions should be held accountable for the contents.

A TREMOR
IN
THE BLOOD

CHAPTER
1

Prologue

It is a pleasure to stand upon the shore, and to see ships tost upon the sea: a pleasure to stand in the windows of a castle, and to see a battle and the adventures thereof below: but no pleasure is comparable to the standing upon the vantage ground of truth (a hill not to be commanded, and where the air is always clear and serene), and to see the errors, and wanderings, and mists, and tempests, in the vale below.

—Francis Bacon

Hundreds of thousands of Americans are subjected (or subject themselves) to lie detector tests each year. The actual total is uncertain, but the number of active polygraphic examiners, multiplied by the average number of tests the typical examiner gives per year, should provide a reasonable estimate. There were from 4,000 to 7,000 polygraphers practicing in the United States in 1979.[1] At least 13 polygraph schools graduate hundreds of new examiners each year from courses of instruction that require six weeks to six months of training. The number of lie tests a polygrapher will administer varies widely, being lowest for police examiners and highest for commercial examiners in private practice. An FBI polygrapher who flies out from Washington to test a suspect at some local FBI office may give only two or three tests in a week. The polygraphers at the Los Angeles Police Department spend three hours on a single examination and average two tests per man per day. Typical commercial examiners finish a test in an hour and deal with perhaps six people each working day. I know of one case in which two commercial polygraphers set up shop in a motel and tested 52 employees of a small-town supermarket in just two days (more than 12 tests per examiner per day at $35 each). The most conservative estimate, assuming a minimum of 4,000 examiners averaging only one test each working day, would indicate that at least *1 million* American citizens are confronted by a lie detector test every year. (Warren Holmes, president of the Florida Polygraph Association, estimates that 100,000 tests are given annually in his state alone, which extrapolates to 4 million nationwide.)[2]

Your turn may come in any one of several ways. You may become a suspect in a criminal investigation; remember that many innocent suspects have been like you, never expecting to find themselves in such a situation. If you are female, you might have the misfortune to be raped and then to discover that your local district attorney or police will not prosecute a rape complaint unless the victim agrees to submit to a lie detector test. Or, you may be a witness in a criminal trial and be requested by counsel to demonstate the veracity of your testimony on some crucial point by means of a polygraph examination. You may become embroiled in civil litigation, either as plaintiff or defendant, in which your version of events conflicts with that given by the other party. Your attorney or your opponent's counsel may suggest that you both take lie tests with each side agreeing in advance that the results will be admissible in court. Perhaps your spouse will come to suspect you of infidelity and one of you will conclude that the only way to settle the matter is by lie detector. Or a business associate may ask you to prove your good faith in a similar way. If you are an executive under consideration for a major promotion, the chairman of the board may require a polygraph examination to explore your company loyalty and the possibility that you might later jump to a competitor with your head full of company secrets. You may work in a government agency whose masters have been driven frantic by unauthorized leaks of information to the press. Or, wherever you may work, an intramural crime may be committed, thievery or sabotage or industrial spying. More and more, in such situations, American management turns not to the police but to internal or private investigators who, in their turn, make increasing use of the polygraph. "You don't have to accept this chance to prove you had nothing to do with the theft. But of course, if the others agree and you don't, well. . . . "

You may be employed by one of the many companies that undertake a periodic screening of all employees in certain categories, perhaps annually or at unpredictable intervals, to determine who might have been dipping in the till, walking off with company property, or behaving in other ways disapproved of by management. If you work for Adolph Coors Brewery, that mandatory lie test may probe into areas that you might consider to be none of management's business.[3] "Are you a Communist?" "Have you ever been involved with homosexuals?" "Have you ever participated in a march or riot or demonstration?" "How much do you owe on your home?" "Is there anything that you know of for which you could be blackmailed?" Although labor unions have been generally opposed to polygraph testing of employees, many union contracts presently in force authorize management use of the lie detector under certain circumstances.

The most common situation in which the average citizen finds him- or herself being connected to a polygraph machine is the ordinary process of applying for a job. Federal security agencies like the CIA or NSA, many state and local police departments, many banks, armored truck or security and guard agencies, diamond merchants, and the like, require job applicants to take a lie detector test. But so do many American companies, large and small, for jobs that could not be described as sensitive or "high security." A recent survey indicated that 20% of the nation's major corporations make use of polygraph testing of employees and about 50% of retail companies, like McDonald's 4,700 hamburger emporiums and Burger Chef's 900 outlets, use pre-employment tests.[4] Many breweries follow Coors' example, as do dozens of retail chains, drugstores and supermarkets, department stores and convenience foodstores, discount houses and stereo equipment shops. Applicants for low echelon positions inevitably are tested in the greatest number, but the polygraph is not intended to be an instrument of class discrimination. As I have suggested, the lie detector finds its way into the executive suite as well. The few jobs that are unlikely to require a lie test as part of the application procedure include those of teachers, journalists, and elected officials. I once commented on this trend in testimony before a committee of the Minnesota State Senate and suggested that, one day, state legislators might be required to pass a lie detector test before being sworn in. An older senator sourly suggested that this might not be a bad idea.

The lie detector industry clearly has become a big business, one of the most important branches of applied psychology both in dollar volume and, especially, in its social consequences. Another field of applied psychology, public opinion polling, may have considerable impact on certain elected officials, on marketing executives or TV show producers, but the outcomes and accuracy of the Harris poll or the Nielsen ratings will not affect the reputation, job security, or police record of a million people in a year. The host of college entrance tests administered annually by the Educational Testing Service has an influence on many individual lives; yet, when one sits down to take a lie detector test, more important things may be at stake than whether one will be admitted into College A rather than having to settle for College B.

The pollsters employ social scientists and statisticians who use techniques based on well-established principles and their product is tested publicly at least at each election. The accuracy of widely used tests of intelligence, aptitude, or personality is subjected to unremitting scrutiny and debate by experts in the field of mental measurement. These experts do not always agree among themselves, but the debate is active and open and can draw upon a large body of published research findings. Polygraphic interrogation techniques, in contrast, have been developed almost entirely by nonscientists and are poorly understood not only by the general public but also by most psychologists. There has been little competent research on the accuracy of lie detection methods and what is available has appeared within the last few years. The sources to which a psychologist, an attorney, a police administrator, business executive, or interested layman might turn for an appraisal of the lie detector industry consist of a few books written by professional polygraphers whose critical detachment falls easy victim to their vested interest.

Who Is To Judge?

Members of a guild, initiates of some mystic order, true believers of whatever persuasion have a natural tendency to resent and disdain evaluation from outside their own ranks. Psychoanalysts have insulated themselves from scientific criticism for generations. Only gradu-

ates of an established psychoanalytic institute who have spent years
in training and in personal analysis are considered fit to offer an
opinion on psychoanalytic doctrine. Few Marxist intellectuals will
waste time in serious discussion with someone who has not mastered
the five-foot shelf of basic dialectic. But few non-Marxists have such
perseverance, and this limits the frequency and quality of critical
debate. Policemen routinely reject proposals for civilian review
boards, claiming that only those familiar with the problems and
stresses of police work from the inside—that is, policemen—can fairly or intelligently evaluate allegations of police misconduct.

Polygraphers, similarly, are inclined to feel that one should not
comment on their art unless one has attended an accredited polygraph school and administered some hundreds of lie detector tests.
Thus, according to polygraphers R. Ferguson and A. Miller:

To permit a psychologist or psychiatrist who is not a trained polygraphist to
express his opinion on the polygraph's validity or reliability is the most
blatant of hearsay and should never be permitted in any court of law. The
mere fact that a person has read a few articles, essays or even books, does
not qualify him as an expert in a field in which he has had no training or
actual experience.

They go on to advise that counsel

should violently object to introduction of opinion testimony by those who
have not trained to become an examiner and who have not conducted live
cases, irrespective of their academic or professional status. To do so would
be somewhat like giving weight to testimony of a doctorate in history criticizing the medical procedure utilized in an appendectomy, simply because
the doctor once read a first-aid book.[5]

While that concluding simile is somewhat baffling, the attitude
expressed in this quotation is understandable—but it cannot be permitted to prevail. It is a Catch 22 position: you cannot criticize unless
you're one of us—and if you're one of us, you will not criticize.

It is true that someone trained in one branch of science may be an
inappropriate critic of research or technology belonging to a different branch. I cannot competently evaluate the evidence on the pro-
phylactic effects of Vitamin C, much less the claims about the latest
quark appearing, say, in *Physical Review*. And I would be dubious of
any biochemist or physicist who presumed to assess the heritability
of intelligence or the utility of the Minnesota Multiphasic Personality
Inventory. But polygraphic interrogation, including lie detection, is

a branch of applied psychology. It is an art that has its roots, however superficially, in the basic science areas of psychophysiology and psychological measurement. Any psychological scientist who is acquainted with these fields of specialization is equipped to understand whatever may be understandable about lie detection. There is no deep mystery here in any case. If this book succeeds in its intention to present the evidence and arguments fairly and clearly, the reader should be able to judge for him- or herself.

Notes

1. The American Polygraph Association estimated in 1974 that there were 4,000 trained polygraphers in the U.S. Perhaps 3,000 additional polygraphers have completed training since 1974 in the 13 or more polygraph schools that operate in the United States. There are, in addition, hundreds of lie test examiners who employ voice stress analyzers instead of polygraphs. Dr. Gordon Barland, an examiner in private practice and an associate editor of *Polygraph*, estimated that there were at least 7,000 active examiners in 1978.
2. Orlando, Florida, *Sentinel Star*, July 2, 1979.
3. *Reign of Terror*, Special report to the AFL/CIO Food and Beverage Trades Department Executive Board, August 6, 1978, pp. 16–18.
4. Belt, J. & Holden, P., Polygraph usage among major U.S. corporations. *Personnel Journal*, 1978, 80–86.
5. Ferguson, R. & Miller, A. *Polygraph for the Defense*. Springfield, Ill: Charles C. Thomas, 1974, pp. 152, 197.

LIE DETECTION:
THE CONCEPT

He who would distinguish the false from the true
must have an adequate idea of what is false and true.

—Spinoza, *Ethics,* 1677

Whenever I lecture on polygraphic interrogation, I like to begin by asking the audience to indicate by show of hands how many would agree to take a lie detector test—and how many would refuse—in some plausible, hypothetical situation that I briefly describe. Among American audiences, a substantial majority acknowledge that they would take the test. European audiences, in marked contrast, indicate that most of them would refuse. The lie detector is almost exclusively an American artifact and, in the United States, it seems firmly entrenched in popular mythology. Many Europeans have never heard of the lie detector but there lurks some vague familiarity with the concept in the mind of nearly every American who can read and wears shoes. The history of this phenomenon has a kind of fascination and will be briefly reviewed in Chapter 3. That chapter also previews the armamentarium available to the modern Diogenes.

But before poisoning your mind with facts and figures, I have arranged to let you experience a lie detector test yourself. Chapter 2 dramatizes what might ensue if you were asked to take a lie detector test administered by a highly competent, professional police examiner under real-life conditions. Chapter 4 considers whether there is or will ever likely be a literal Truth Verifier, a machine that can detect lying. The answer, quite certainly, is negative. There is no lie detector *machine,* but only a form of interview or test employing a machine known as a polygraph, which provides certain data that the examiner uses in reaching his diagnosis of Truthful or Deceptive. But there are several different types of lie detector tests and Chapter 5 discusses the problem of assessing the accuracy of these tests in general: what kind of evidence is relevant to what, and which "evidence" is not relevant at all. Chapter 5 also contains some discussion of elementary statistical concepts. Certain researchers in this field have confused the ideas of "reliability" and "validity" and have interpreted the numbers from research findings incorrectly, so it seems to me essential to set forth the appropriate methods of interpreting data and to show why they are correct. The ideas involved are not difficult and I have tried to present them in such a way that even the number-phobic reader can follow the argument.

2

Mr. Reader Has A Chance To Prove His Innocence

The Polygraph Story: Dedicated to Man's Right to Verify the Truth.

—J. Kirk Barefoot, *American Polygraph Association*

An' what is a lie, tell me? I cud answer mesilf if I always knew what th' thruth was, me boy. A good manny iv th' whoppers I tell ye is th' raysult iv thryin' to take a short cut to th' thruth an' bringin' up just this side iv perjury. Some things that look like lies to me today will seem all r-right in th' presidential year.

—Mr. Dooley

Later on in this book we shall consider polygraphic interrogation from the point of view of the examiner, who wants to produce accurate results, and from the perspective of employers, the police, and the courts, who wish to make decisions based on those results. We shall also examine the lie detector industry from the viewpoint of the citizen and his elected representatives who must be concerned with the impact on American society of the present rapid growth and outreach of this technology. But first, dear Reader, you should try to get a sense of what a lie detector test is like for the person being tested, whom I shall refer to variously as the *subject* or as the *respondent.* Let us set up a scenario in which you are the subject and I am the polygraph examiner. My files are replete with real-life examples we might use; I shall describe a number of these cases in subsequent chapters. But most of these cases have unhappy, or, at best, ambiguous outcomes so that their use would paint an unfair picture of the way the really expert polygraph examiners conduct their business. Therefore, we shall invent a situation for our present purposes.

Let us assume that you are an adult male employed in some white-collar position. Something of value disappears from your place of business; let us say an envelope containing $2,000 in cash is missing from the office safe. There are no signs of breaking and entering. The police consider it to be an "inside job" and suspicion centers on the seven employees who have access to the safe and know the combination. You are one of these seven. Your employer calls you in and explains the situation. The police are asking that each of the potential suspects agrees to take a polygraph examination. You cannot be forced to take the test but, unless you have a contract or belong to a strong union, you might lose your job if you refuse. It is assumed that, if you are innocent, you will welcome this opportunity to prove it. An appointment is made for you to visit my office at police head-quarters at 10 A.M. the next day.

Next morning, in the waiting room, you find among the reading matter books and pamphlets bearing such titles as *Polygraph for the Defense* or *The Polygraph Story: Dedicated to Man's Right to Verify the Truth.* My diplomas and credentials festoon the walls. After some minutes, I come in and introduce myself. I am conservatively dressed and my manner is polite and professional as I usher you into the polygraph room adjoining. This room is carpeted and quiet with a few pastoral prints on the walls. Toward one end you notice an ordinary desk bearing a complicated-looking instrument in an aluminum case, the size of a small suitcase. This is the polygraph. Centered against the front or closed side of the desk is a padded vinyl armchair facing toward the open room. Seated there, the desk and polygraph are behind you. I pull up a chair so that we can talk comfortably.

"Now then, your full name is Robert S. Reader and you live at 123 Sunflower Lane?" I have a clipboard on my lap and make notes as we go. "What was your birthdate, Mr. Reader? Are you married? How long have you been married? Any children? And what are their names and ages?"

Routine questions, breaking the ice; you're beginning to relax a little.

"How long have you been with the Frobischer Company? I see, and you're now the assistant office manager, is that correct? Now, on the day that the money was discovered missing, that would be March 19th, Tuesday, did you come to work as usual? And did you have occasion to open the safe or to take something out or put something in? You did not? Okay. Have you any recollection at all of anything unusual involving that safe during that morning? For example, did you notice that anyone had stepped away from it for a time, leaving it open? I see. So then you have no reason for thinking that someone who didn't know how to unlock the safe might have been able to get into it that morning?

"All right, Mr. Reader. Now I realize that you don't want to get any of your colleagues in trouble but the fact is that this test you're going to be taking might be influenced by any suspicions you have about who might have taken the money or where it is now, even if your doubts don't have any real basis. So I want you to tell me now about any thoughts along these lines you might have so you can get them off your chest before we do the test. Who do you think took that money? . . . You're sure you have no idea at all, no suspicions for any reason?

"Okay. Now I have a list of questions here that I plan to ask you when we've got you hooked up to the polygraph, and I want to go over the list with you first to make sure you understand each question and that you can answer each of them with a simple yes or no. The first one is an irrelevant question that we ask just for calibration purposes. I'll ask you, 'Is today Tuesday?' and you will answer 'Yes.' Then I'll ask you, 'Are you afraid I might ask you about something other than the questions we have already reviewed?' and I want you to be able to answer that one 'No,' okay? Next, I'll ask you, 'Do you know for sure who took the money from the safe?' From what you've told me, I gather you can answer that one 'No' also with a clear conscience, right?

"All right, Mr. Reader, now whoever took this money, it's unlikely that it was the first really dishonest thing that person ever did. Therefore, during the test, I'm going to ask you some questions to find out what kind of a person you are, whether in the past you have ever done anything that might indicate you're the sort of person who would steal money from the office safe. For example, take your income tax returns. I suppose most people make mistakes on their income tax now and then, forget to put something down or exaggerate their expenses. But you haven't been deliberately cheating on your tax returns, have you? If I ask you, 'Over the past five years, have you ever deliberately cheated the government out of more than $100?' you could answer that 'No,' couldn't you?"

Now this might make you begin to feel a little uncomfortable. You're no tax criminal and when you were called in for an IRS audit four years ago you never felt an impulse to skip out of the country. But on the other hand, when you win a few dollars on a football pool or in a poker game, it has never occurred to you to put it down as taxable income. And when you estimate mileage or business expenses, you don't tend to choose the most conservative figures. But you don't want this straight-looking man with his neat haircut to get the wrong idea about you.

"Yes, sure, I could answer that 'No.' "

"That's fine. Then I will ask you, 'Did you take the money from the office safe?' and, of course, you'll answer, 'No,' right? Let's be sure there is no ambiguity about that question; I'm talking about the $2,000 in cash that was in the safe in an envelope and which disappeared on March 19th, okay?

"Now, Mr. Reader, as you may have heard, there was another theft in your office last year that was never solved. Mr. Hodsdon had one of those fancy wrist-watches with a solid gold bracelet that he left either in the washroom or on his desk and when he looked for it, it was gone, and he never got it back. He didn't do anything about it at the time, but he's asked us to inquire about that, too, while we're giving these tests. So, I'm going to ask you, 'Did you take Mr. Hodsdon's gold watch?' Are you comfortable with that question?"

This is the first you've heard anything about a missing watch. There really must be a thief in the office. Funny that old Hodsdon didn't make a fuss about it at the time; he raises hell if his newspaper is missing.

"Sure," you say. "I never even knew about the watch."

"Now we'll have another general honesty question, Mr. Reader. Suppose I ask you, 'From the time you graduated from high school up to two years ago, did you ever steal anything of value?' Would you be able to answer 'No' to that?"

"Oh, well," you protest, "that's pretty tough. Everybody probably takes some little thing that doesn't belong to him once in a while."

I give you a rather searching look. "You say 'some little thing.' Maybe we could change the question to leave the 'little things' out of it. Suppose I say, 'Between high school and two years ago, have you ever stolen anything worth more than $10?' Could you answer 'No' to that?"

You aren't a thief and there is nothing in particular burning in your mind at the moment but you'd hate to stake your life that you won't start thinking of things by this afternoon. "Look," you say, "I can't think of anything right now worth even $10, but you're talking about quite a few years there."

"Mr. Reader, I'm just trying to get a wording that you're comfortable with. It's just a matter of choosing a figure. If you've previously stolen something worth hundreds of dollars, then, of course, we would have to consider that such a person might also steal a watch or some money from the safe. I assume you haven't done that but then you say that $10 might be too low. What sort of figure would you like to have me use in this question?"

You try to remember the dividing line between petty larceny and grand theft. "How about $25? I think I could be comfortable with $25." You walked in here feeling like an assistant office manager on his way up; now you're beginning to feel rather like a petty crook.

"All right, that's the way we'll do it. 'Between high school and two years ago, have you ever stolen anything worth more than $25?' And you will answer 'No' to that. Then I will ask you, 'Regarding that money that was taken from the office safe, did you take that money?' —and, again, you will answer 'No.' Then we have to have one more general honesty question. I'll ask you, 'Between high school and two years ago, did you ever tell a lie to someone in authority in order to stay out of trouble?' What I'm obviously getting at here is whether, when you do make a mistake, you own up to it or whether you're the kind of person who will try to lie his way out of it. Will you be able to answer 'No' to this question?"

"Yes, certainly, no problem about that." Again you have the feeling that some awful contradicting recollection is lurking in the back of your mind, but this man is probably already wondering about you and you don't want to give him a worse impression than you have already.

"Okay, Mr. Reader, that makes nine questions altogether. Now we'll go through this list several times while you're hooked up to the polygraph. I'll pause 15 or 20 seconds between questions and when we get to the end of the list, I'll turn the machine off and you can have a little rest before the next test. I may change the order of the questions, but I won't ask you anything we haven't already agreed on. Or, if I do want to add some new questions, I'll turn off the machine and go over them with you first and make sure that you're agreeable before I use them. Also, when I first hook you up, I'm going to go through a special calibration test in which I'll have you choose a card from a deck and then I'll try to find out which card you've chosen by asking you questions and looking at your polygrams.

"Now, let me explain the polygraph to you. There are four attachments to your body so that the machine can pick up your emotional reactions to the questions. There are these two soft rubber belts that I'll strap around you, one around your stomach and one around your chest. They will measure your breathing. Then there are these two wires with these little attachments on the end. I'll fasten them on the ends of two of your fingers. They measure sweating responses. Finally, I'll wrap this blood pressure cuff around your upper arm here. While I'm running a test, I'll pump up the pressure in the cuff so it will feel tight around your arm and then I'll relax it again between tests. All this is perfectly safe, of course, and none of it will hurt at all."

Now I hand you a printed consent form and explain that you must read and sign it before we can proceed. Most consent forms used by polygraphers are remarkably generous in waiving the rights of the person to be tested while at the same time being rather vague about the responsibilities of the examiner. Since we are trying to run this imaginary test in a professional manner, let us assume that my consent form has been designed with your, the respondent's, rights uppermost in mind.

CONSENT FORM

I hereby consent to a polygraph examination to be administered by (*name of examiner*) on this date of (*date*) and to having the necessary polygraph attachments made to my body as has already been explained to me. I understand that the examination is to be concerned with (*subject of examination*) and that the only questions that will be asked me during any portion of the examination will be discussed with me and approved by me prior to the test. I understand that an audio tape-recording is being made of the entire test, including my discussions with the examiner before and after the actual testing, and that I may obtain a copy of that recording, at my own expense, at any time within six months from the present date. I hereby authorize the examiner to communicate the results of the examination to the police officer in charge of the investigation of the above-named matter and also to (*enter name or 'no other person'*).

(Signature of respondent.)

"This 'no other person,' " you ask, "Does this mean that you won't even tell my boss how I did on this test?"

"That's right, Mr. Reader. This test is for police purposes and police use only." I do not explain it in detail but the fact is that this is an important protection for you. Suppose you fail this test while your six colleagues pass theirs. And suppose you continue to protest your innocence and the police are unable to find any evidence against you. You cannot be convicted, indicted, or even arrested just on the basis of a lie detector test, not in this jurisdiction. But if the results are given to your employer, you will very probably be fired. You will be punished, your career perhaps permanently blighted, with no vestige of due process. If I were a private examiner, hired by Frobischer, Inc., then you would have to take your chances. But (in this scenario) I am a police examiner and my job is to assist a criminal investigation in an orderly and legal fashion.

Now I apply the polygraph attachments and you begin to feel uncomfortable again, exposed in a curious way, those four pens behind you scratching out their squiggly lines which presumably reveal what's going on inside you, your emotional reactions, almost reading your mind. It is years since you've felt as self-conscious as you feel right now. You think of a time when your fourth-grade teacher accused you of some misdemeanor that you hadn't committed and, although innocent, you could feel yourself blushing under her hard gaze and you knew you looked guilty. You begin to wonder whether this machine can tell an honest emotion from a guilty one.

I take a deck of playing cards out of the desk, shuffle them, and fan them out in front of you face down. "Choose a card, look at it, and then put it in your pocket without letting me see it."

Your card is the queen of hearts. You tuck it away in your shirt pocket.

"All right, Mr. Reader, I'm going to ask you some questions about the card you have in your pocket. I want you to answer 'No' to each question, no matter what the true answer might be. Put both feet on the floor and sit there quietly until I tell you you can move. I'll pump up the pressure on the arm cuff now. Remember to answer 'No' to each question. Here we go."

"About the card in your pocket, is it a red suit?"

"No," you answer.

"Well, that looks like a deceptive response," I say after a few seconds of watching the polygraph behind you. "I'm going to assume that it is a red suit. Is the card in your pocket a diamond?"

"No."

Another pause. "Is it a heart?"

"No."

"All right, I think the suit must be hearts. Is the card in your pocket a face card?"

"No."

Ten or 15 seconds elapse after each answer. The cuff on your right arm seems tight. Your nose itches and you would like to shift your weight in the chair but you are not supposed to move.

"Well, I think this is going to be an easy one. You're a good responder, Mr. Reader. Your card is a face card all right. Is the card in your pocket the king of hearts?"

"No."

Another pause. "Is it the queen of hearts?"

"No." You have a feeling that the jig is up.

"Okay, Mr. Reader, I'll release the pressure on your arm now and you can move in your chair if you want to. We're done with this calibration test. Your card is the queen of hearts—right?" You hand it over to me. "Now I know what your chart looks like when you're telling the truth and what it looks like when you're lying. So now in just a minute or two we'll get started with the first test."

This little demonstration has been quite effective. You still feel a bit naked, connected to that machine, but it does seem to work. Nevertheless, you'll be glad when this is over. I pump up the arm cuff again and proceed to work through the question list, just as we had discussed it earlier. This takes about four minutes. It is a relief when I release the cuff pressure again and you can flex your arm and restore circulation. During this rest period, I stay behind you looking at the output of the machine and I don't say much.

"We got a good record that time, Mr. Reader. You're sitting nice and quietly and you give good responses. Settle down now and we'll go through the questions again."

This time I change the order of some of the questions but there aren't any new ones. The two questions about the money from the safe and the one about old Hodsdon's watch continue to alternate with what I called the "general honesty" questions. I give you another two-or three-minute rest after this set while I stand behind you at the polygraph making notes on the charts.

"Now for this next test, I want you to listen carefully to each question but I don't want you to answer. Don't say anything at all. Just sit there quietly and listen to the questions. Here we go."

Let us get out of the scenario for a moment while you consider how you think you might be feeling at this stage of the polygraph test. The nine questions are collected together for easy reference in Table 2–1. Those polygraph charts that I am studying behind your back will probably show some sort of reaction to each of the questions. What I am looking for is differences in the strength of reaction from one question to another. What would you predict I'll find? The first question, "Is today Tuesday?" is innocuous enough although you might show some small response since, being first, that question signals the start of the series. How might you have reacted to the questions about the money stolen from the safe? These, after all, are the reasons you are taking this test in the first place. The money *was* stolen,

TABLE 2–1   **Questions used on your polygraph examination.**

1. Is today Tuesday?

2. Are you afraid I might ask you about something other than the questions we have already reviewed?

3. Do you know for sure who took the money from the safe?

4. Over the past five years, have you ever deliberately cheated the government out of more than $100 on your income tax?

5. Did you take the money from the office safe?

6. Did you take Mr. Hodsdon's gold watch?

7. Between high school and two years ago, have you ever stolen anything worth more than $25?

8. Regarding that money that was taken from the office safe, did you take that money?

9. Between high school and two years ago, did you ever tell a lie to someone in authority in order to stay out of trouble?

you can open the safe, you are a legitimate suspect. On the other hand, you are innocent; you did not take the money and you do not know who did. There is no logical reason for you to be upset by—to react emotionally to—these questions, is there? Remember that fourth-grade teacher looking down at you accusingly; you hadn't thrown the eraser but you blushed anyway. The polygraph is registering internal blushes; what will it find in you?

Then there is Hodsdon's gold watch. You never even knew the thing was missing. What will the pens indicate when I ask you if you stole that watch? Now consider the "general honesty" questions, the ones about previous thefts, cheating on your income tax, lying to stay out of trouble. I told you I wanted to find out whether you were the kind of person who might be inclined to steal money from a safe and those questions bothered you some when we first talked about them. You weren't absolutely sure that your "No" answers were strictly true. What do you think the polygraph has had to say about your reactions to those questions as compared to the ones about the money in the safe or the watch?

What you would not have known, unless you had read this book or some other discussion of lie detection methods, is that I am going to evaluate your test by comparing your reactions to the relevant questions, the ones about the stolen money, with your reactions to the "general honesty" questions, which polygraphers would call "control" questions. If you consistently respond more strongly to the relevant questions, then I will conclude that you are lying about the stolen money and you will fail the test; my diagnosis will be "Deception indicated." If you respond consistently more strongly to the control questions, I will report "No deception indicated." In the few cases where the two sets of reactions are about equal, I will score the test as "Inconclusive." How did you do? Did you pass? How will you do next time, now that you know how it works?

But let us return to that polygraph room because the test isn't over yet. When I release the cuff pressure after the last question on the third or "silent answer" test, there is quite a long silence while I stand there behind you, studying the charts.

"Look, Mr. Reader, on the matter of the gold watch, there doesn't seem to be any problem there. But on the questions about the money, I'm getting reactions to both of those. I'm wondering if there is anything about those two questions that might account for what I'm getting? Anything about the way they're worded? Maybe something about some previous experience with something from a safe or something stolen from the office or some currency you might have taken some other time? In other words, is there anything you haven't already told me about that might explain why you're reacting this way to those two questions?"

This is alarming news to say the least. No, you don't have any obsession about safes that you know of. You've never absconded with any handful of banknotes just as you didn't take this envelope of money from the office safe.

"No, I can't think of any reason. Except, after all, I do know that this money was stolen and that I'm a suspect and I can't help feeling concerned about that."

"But what is there to be concerned about, as long as you didn't take the money?" I ask politely. "I tell you what, Mr. Reader, I'm going to give you a few minutes to collect yourself and maybe you'll think of some reason why I'm getting these reactions. You just sit there quietly and think about it and I'll be back in a few minutes."

I walk out of the room leaving you to stew. That large picture of a Swiss valley at the end of the room is actually a one-way mirror. In the darkened observation room on the other side of that wall I settle down to watch you squirm. Like most other polygraphers, I remember that marvelous case in Cincinnati a few years ago.[1] A private examiner, testing an employee in connection with a theft of a few hundred dollars, had employed this same technique. The respondent, obviously upset, kept glancing back at the polygraph charts covered with their apparently damning hieroglyphics. Suddenly, as the examiner watched unbelieving from the next room, the subject reached back, tore the charts from the machine and proceeded to eat them, bit by bit, all six feet of paper six inches wide. After this bizarre meal was completed, the examiner returned as if nothing had happened and began to prepare for the next test. Suddenly he leaned his ear down to the polygraph and said,

"What's that? He *ate* them?!"

"My God, you mean the thing can *talk*, too?" expostulated the respondent, who then proceeded to confess that he had taken the money.

You don't do anything so dramatic. You just sit there, fidgeting from time to time. When I return, you have nothing to report, no explanation for those worrisome reactions to the critical questions. We do another test just like the first one. You are really nervous now; each time your heart beats you can see a slight movement of your shirt front and your voice sounds strange in your ears as you give your replies, "No," "No." When this fourth test is finished, I proceed to remove the polygraph attachments without saying anything. Then I sit down and look at you for a moment.

"Mr. Reader, we seldom have any criminals in this room. Just ordinary people who may have made a mistake, usually for a good reason. People who were pushed too far or tempted too much and then slipped up. And when ordinary decent people make a mistake, the thing for them to do—the only sensible thing to do—is to admit it, get it off their chests, make amends as best they can. Then they not only feel better about it, but the consequences of their mistakes will be minimized. Look at it from our point of view. A confession saves all kinds of time and hassle and we appreciate that. When somebody with a good record admits that he made a mistake, we appreciate that kind of cooperation, we think it shows a good attitude, and we try to arrange things in a way that makes minimum trouble for everybody. Now, have you anything you want to tell me about this matter? Anything at all?"

Let us cut off the narrative at this point before you say something you'll regret later. Let *me* make a confession instead. I was simply trying to give you an opportunity to confess, in case you had something *to* confess, and I might have done so no matter what your polygraph charts had looked like. As we shall see later, perhaps the major utility of the lie detector is its extraordinary capacity for eliciting confessions. That story about Mr. Hodsdon's gold watch was pure invention, what we call a "guilt complex" question. I wanted to see how you would react to a question about a crime you could not have committed since it never happened. And one other thing. That deck of cards that we were using earlier? I bought that deck at a magic store. All 52 cards in the deck are queens of hearts.

Notes

1. Hold the Mustard. *Cincinnati Inquirer,* July 1, 1975.

CHAPTER 3

A Brief History
Of Lie Detection

Lord, Lord, how this world is given to lying.

—Falstaff in *Henry V, Part 1*

All th' wurruld is busy deceivin' its neighbor an itsilf. Th' poor are poor because they are poor liars an' th' rich are men that've accumylated a large stock iv non-assissable, inthrest-bearin' lies or inherited th' same fr'm their indulgent an' mendacyous fathers. That's what they tell me.

—Mr. Dooley

Some of the most amusing lies on record have been told in connection with the Lie Detector itself.

—W. M. Marston

Natural history is full of guile. From the lowly insects to our primate cousins, animals have evolved a wide variety of methods for deceiving other animals, their enemies, their conspecifics or, most commonly, their prey. Some of these deceptions are structural in character; the animal has become a walking (swimming, flying) lie.

The praying mantis that stands like a dry stick, the angler fish whose luminous uvula lures its small victims right into its jaws, the moth whose markings simulate a bitter-tasting relative. Higher animals practice behavioral deception. They creep and hide, stalk from down-wind, simulate injury to lure the predator from their vulnerable nesting place, double back on their own trails, freeze and then pounce. But a lie, Webster tells us, is a falsehood acted or uttered with the intention to deceive and we would commit the sin of anthropomorphic inference if we attributed intentionality to that poor mother quail hopping away from her nest dragging one wing. The liar intends to communicate a false belief to his victim and this intention presupposes a rule-governed system of veridical communication between them. To lie is to break those rules and lying works because the rules are usually obeyed.

To understand why we are such frequent and fluent liars, it is helpful to adopt the perspective of the new science of sociobiology. Just as man's anatomical and physiological characteristics represent a distillation of those ancestral traits that conferred the most survival value, so too many of our social (and other) behavior tendencies may have resulted from the evolutionary sieving. For our hominid ancestors, the ability to mislead or deceive probably carried an evolutionary advantage just as did fleetness of foot or the possession of an opposable thumb. George Steiner puts it this way:

Fiction was disguise: from those seeking out the same waterhole, the same sparse quarry, or meagre sexual chance. To misinform, to utter less than the truth was to gain a vital edge of space or subsistance. Natural selection would favor the contriver. Folk tales and mythology retain a blurred memory of the evolutionary advantage of mask and misdirection. Loki, Odysseus, are very late, literary concentrates of the widely diffused motif of the liar, of the dissembler as flame and water, who survives.[1]

Ann and David Premack, psychologists who have devoted 20 years to teaching a language-like system of communication to the chimpanzee, have recently made an effort to induce their chimps to lie.[2] The animals know how to tell their trainer where to find a banana hidden outside the cage and they can also tell him that they would like to eat the banana when he finds it. Confronted now with an unreliable trainer, one who they know from past experience is likely to eat the banana himself, will they misdirect his search or pretend that there is no banana? At last report, these honest chimps had not yielded to prevarication in spite of their contaminating contact with

humankind. They hide their hands behind them, striving painfully
not to communicate at all, but that is as far as they will go. Yet one
knows that this laboratory Eden has its serpent, that this innocence
cannot endure. From language to lying, the primrose path is short
and ineluctable.

If man learned to lie not long after he acquired language, we may
assume that the first attempts at lie detection soon made their appearance. In this respect, ontogeny does recapitulate phylogeny. The
child learns first to talk, then to dissemble, then to detect when his
or her own leg is being pulled. We are all human lie detectors; we
must be to survive in our mendacious society. Those who are least
skillful in this respect we call gullible or credulous. Our slang is rich
with names for these trusting innocents; we call them cullys, cat's-
paws, dupes, greenhorns, gulls, jays, mugs, pigeons, and there are
plenty of them, one born every minute. It is interesting that there
seems to be no English term for the other end of this dimension, the
unusually skillful lie detector. (There is a German word, *Menschenkenner,* that comes close: one who can see into, and perhaps see
through, other people. "Skeptic" implies a biased attitude rather
than a discerning separation of the false from the true; adjectives like
"perceptive" and "astute" are too broad.) If language reflects a society's interests and concerns, as their 14 words for snow reflect the
Eskimos' preoccupation with that substance, then this plethora of
names for the inept human lie detector—synonyms for "sucker"—
may confirm that we are a deceitful and predatory race.

Early societies evolved a variety of exotic methods for getting at
the truth, reviewed in detail by several authors, notably J. A. Larson.[3]
Torture has always been a favorite technique. Statements uttered on
the rack or at the point of death were given more credibility than
they deserved, an attitude retained in the common law that attaches
special weight to dying declarations. Trials by ordeal generally rested
on a religious or magical premise. The innocent would be stronger
in combat; the truthful person would be helped by the gods to hold
his arm longer in boiling water or the bleeding from a ritual incision
would stop more quickly for the honest man than for the liar. A
method worth the attention of modern marriage counselors was
employed in medieval Germany to settle allegations of infidelity.
The man's left arm was bound behind him and he stood in a tub
sunken waist deep in the ground, a short club in his right hand. The
woman wore only a chemise having one sleeve longer than the other
and in this sleeve was sewn a rock. The procedure required that the

wife dance about the tub attempting to brain the husband with the rock while at the same time avoiding the swings of his club. Since it is not recorded how the outcome of this contest was supposed to settle the allegations brought before the court, it may be conjectured that the method was intended to discourage litigation altogether.

In other ordeals, the stress imposed was more psychological than physical. The ancient Hindus required a suspect to chew a mouthful of rice and then attempt to spit it out upon a leaf from the sacred Pipal tree. A man who successfully spat out the rice was considered truthful but, if instead the grains stuck to his tongue and palate, he was adjudicated guilty. During the Inquisition, the Roman Church adapted this technique for testing the veracity of clergy. Instead of rice, a piece of barley bread and cheese were placed on the altar in front of the suspect priest and prayers were offered that, should he be guilty of the offense charged against him, God should send His angel Gabriel to stop his throat. Thereupon the priest attempted to consume the bread and cheese. According to Mackay's *Memoirs of Extraordinary Popular Delusions,* "There is no instance upon record of a priest having been choked in this manner." These alimentary techniques have often been identified as precursors of modern lie detector methods, depending as they do on the subject's faith in the procedure, on his fear of being found out if he is lying, and on the physiological reactions that this fear may bring about. In the rice test, for example, fear leads to activity of the sympathetic branch of the autonomic nervous system controlling salivation. The saliva diminishes in volume and becomes viscid in consistency; the rice sticks in the mouth.

The ancients made use of other physiological indicants—sweating, blushing, trembling, the unsteady gaze, the racing pulse. Lombroso, the 19th century Italian criminologist, and his student, Mosso, adapted the plethysmograph, a device for measuring changes in the volume of a limb, to produce continuous records of pulse and blood pressure changes in their subjects' records very similar to those obtained on the "cardio" channel of a modern interrogation polygraph.[4] A. R. Luria, the distinguished Russian psychologist, measured finger tremor and reaction time during the interrogation of criminal suspects.[5] Sir Francis Galton experimented with the technique of word association; asked to associate to words presented orally, guilty suspects were inclined to show disturbances in the speed or nature of their responses to words related to their crime.[6] But instrumental lie detection—polygraphic interrogation—is a 20th century phenomenon and as American as apple pie.

William Moulton Marston

A Harvard professor of psychology, Hugo Münsterberg, surveyed all these possibilities in his 1908 book, *On the Witness Stand,* which advocated greater forensic attention to the techniques of experimental pyschology. It was William M. Marston, J.D., Ph.D., a student of Münsterberg's at Harvard, whose alleged discovery of a specific lie response, in Marston's own modest appraisal, "marked the end of man's long, futile striving for a means of distinguishing truth-telling from deception."[7] Marston was an avid publicist and either coined the graphic phrase "lie detector" himself or else adopted the expression from one of the reporters to whom he described the wonders of his method. Immediately after the sensational kidnapping of the Lindbergh baby, Marston wrote to Col. Lindbergh, "placing the Lie Detector and my experience with it at his disposal."[8] Lindbergh did not reply but, nothing daunted, Marston approached Bruno Hauptmann's defense counsel and the governor of New York with a proposal to test Hauptmann in his death cell as well as "Jafsie," the self-appointed intermediary between Lindbergh and the kidnapper. Rebuffed again, Marston lamented that, "the secret knowledge of the crime that Hauptmann had locked in his brain died with him." More positively, "I hope, even yet, to find a living human being whose mind contains information about the Lindbergh kidnapping. If such a person exists, his secret knowledge can be read like print by the Lie Detector."[9]

Marston not only invented modern lie detection but was among the first to appreciate its commercial possibilities. An article in *Look Magazine* described his use of the polygraph in marital counseling; a wife's reaction to her husband's kiss is compared with her response to the kiss of an attractive stranger.[10] Marston and his machine appeared in full-page ads for razor blades. Finally hitting upon the ideal outlet for his fertile imagination, Marston—under the nom de plume "Charles Moulton"—created the comic strip character Wonder Woman.[11]

Because of his extravagant claims and uninhibited conduct, Marston was repudiated by serious students of polygraphic interrogation. In a scathing review of his 1938 book, Professor Fred Inbau concluded, "It can only bring ridicule upon the subject matter and disrespect for its author." Nonetheless, Marston might be called the grandfather ("foxy grandpa?") of polygraphy because of the early reports of his work, published prior to 1921, and their impact on Chief August Vollmer of the Berkeley, California, police department and especially upon one of Vollmer's police officers, John A. Larson.

Larson and the Berkeley Developments

Larson, who subsequently attended Rush Medical College in Chicago and later became a forensic psychiatrist, began experimenting with measurement of blood pressure and respiratory changes during questioning. Encouraged by Chief Vollmer, Larson assembled the first continuous-recording interrogation polygraph, and it happened that some of its first practical applications were outstandingly successful. A female college student had been shoplifting in a local store. The shop clerk knew only that the culprit lived in a certain dormitory but could not identify her further. Larson was able to question all 38 residents of that dormitory (in one 16-hour day!) using what later came to be called the relevant/irrelevant or R/I technique, a mixture of irrelevant questions ("Are you sitting down?" "Is your name Sarah?") and relevant ones ("Have you taken items from Katz's store without paying for them?"). One of the 38 young women responded much more strongly to the relevant questions, as compared to the irrelevant ones, than did any of the other 37, and she subsequently made a full confession.[12]

One can imagine Chief Vollmer's reaction to this episode—a seemingly hopeless case solved as by divination! Not only did the polygraph pick out the culprit from among 38 candidates but the experience so impressed the woman herself that she confessed, sparing further costly efforts, possibly futile, to locate admissible evidence. Larson's reaction was apparently more complex and, indeed, he remains a somewhat enigmatic figure. One gets the impression that he was uncomfortable with words and abstractions, especially so for a psychiatrist. It is difficult to find quotable passages in Larson's writings, clear and succinct statements of his views. His 1932 book, the first thorough-going study of lying and its detection, was a major scholarly effort that brought together in its 400 pages a mass of relevant material, ancient and modern. But oddly, this work is almost entirely quotation, an introductory sentence or two by Larson followed by pages of text from the cited authorities. The difficulty of assessing Larson's own position can be illustrated by considering his Chapter 8, which is concerned with methods of interrogation used by the police of that period. Of the 26 pages in this chapter, at least 20 are devoted to extended quotations from 16 different sources, some piously denying any impropriety in police methods while others catalog examples of confessions extorted by intimidation, threats, starvation, beatings, and confinement in the "sweat box." When he speaks for himself, Larson sometimes appears to defend the police, and yet ends by saying, "So long as ignorant officials are employed by the police or in the district attorney's office, there will be cases in which a false confession has been obtained by brutal methods."[13] The main point of the chapter seems to be to motivate the use of polygraphic interrogation as an alternative to the brutality that Larson reluctantly admits and obviously deplores.

Another puzzle is why Larson agreed to write a complimentary introduction for Marston's self-aggrandizing pot-boiler in 1938. In a paper of his own published rather obscurely that same year, Larson insisted that "there is no disturbance graphic or in quantitative physiological terms specific for deception,"[14] that is, that there is no specific lie response, although the opposite claim is Marston's central thesis. Larson devoted a 12-page chapter to Marston's work in 1932, one page in Larson's words and eleven of quotation, but he did point out even then that Marston based his approach "upon the assumption, not necessarily always true, that there is an increase of blood pressure during deception." And one wonders how Larson could have condoned Marston's incredible claims about the accuracy of his method, when he was at the same time concluding his own 1938 paper with the warning, "Because of the errors of interpretation, and these have been found to be large, a deception test alone should never be used as court evidence."[15]

In view of the boundless enthusiasm and extravagant claims of his associates and successors, Larson's persisting attitude of scientific skepticism seems especially noteworthy. During the first *half-century* after 1915, when Marston's "lie detector" was becoming entrenched in American folklore, Larson was the only investigator to report an objective study of the accuracy of the diagnosis of deception using polygraph recordings obtained from criminal suspects. In the same 1938 paper quoted above, he tells of examining 62 suspects, whose records were then independently evaluated by nine psychologists. The number of records classified by the different judges as indicating deception ranged from 5 to 33, although 61 of the 62 suspects were in fact truthful. Most recently, Larson has said:

I originally hoped that instrumental lie detection would become a legitimate part of professional police science. It is little more than a racket. The lie detector, as used in many places, is nothing more than a psychological third-degree aimed at extorting confessions as the old physical beatings were. At times I'm sorry I ever had any part in its development.[16]

The Chicago Period

It should be emphasized that Larson's experience and at least some of his disillusionment was focused on the relevant/irrelevant test format and that other interrogation techniques, notably the control-question lie test and the guilty knowledge test, were developed later. Until about 1950, the R/I procedure was standard in the field and even now continues to be taught by one of the major schools of polygraphy and to be used by many of the older examiners. It was promulgated especially by two of Larson's associates in the Berkeley Police Department, C. D. Lee and Leonarde Keeler. Lee, formerly a captain of detectives in Berkeley, developed and manufactured a portable field polygraph and wrote a textbook for polygraphic examiners.[17] Keeler began as a high school student, assisting Larson in his early work. He also developed a portable instrument, the Keeler Polygraph, and then in 1930 moved to join the staff of the new Scientific Crime Detection Laboratory of the Northwestern University School of Law in Chicago. That laboratory, which later became a unit of the Chicago Police Department, was an outgrowth of public concern stimulated by the celebrated St. Valentine's Day Massacre in that city. It was in Chicago's bracing atmosphere that polygraphy's seedling, planted in Boston, nourished in Berkeley, finally took root and flourished. There Keeler met Fred Inbau, professor of criminal law at Northwestern and later director of the Chicago Crime Laboratory. Inbau was an expert on criminal interrogation. There too he met John Reid, another young polygraphy enthusiast who also had his own machine, the Reid Polygraph. It was in Chicago that Keeler and Reid established competing schools of polygraph technique and substantially all of the 4,000 to 7,000 polygraphic examiners now practicing can trace their lineage to these two men.

Keeler played an important role both in developing polygraphy and in publicizing the technique. Apparently it was Keeler who invented the card test, used to enhance the subject's faith in the procedure; he also developed the important idea of the Peak of Tension test, which will be considered later. And in the movie *Northside 777*, it was Keeler himself who administered a R/I lie test to Richard Conte in Joliet Prison, proving what reporter Jimmy Stewart had suspected all along, that Conte was innocent of the crime for which he was imprisoned.

Reid's Contribution: The Clinical Lie Test

But a still more important role in the development of polygraphy must be acknowledged for John E. Reid. His school became the Reid College of Detection of Deception, accredited by the State of Illinois to award a master's degree to the graduates of its six-month course of instruction. His private firm, John E. Reid and Associates, operates branches in several cities. His textbook with Fred Inbau, now in its second edition, has become the standard in the field.[18] Two of Reid's early students, Richard O. Arther and Cleve Backster, have established active schools of their own. Most important of all, Reid developed three new ideas about polygraphic interrogation, the concepts of the "guilt complex" question, the "control" question, and the systematic appraisal of "behavior symptoms."

In a 1947 paper, Reid first described what he then called the "comparative response" question, later elaborated and renamed the "control" question in his textbook.[19] This was a response to the dawning awareness of the inadequacies of the relevant/irrelevant format. After 30 years, polygraphers were coming to realize that questions like "Did you take the money?" or "Did you kill George Fisbee?" must sometimes generate stress or emotional reactions in criminal suspects even when the suspects are innocent and their denials truthful. Reid proposed adding to the list of questions some that were not directly concerned with the crime under investigation but that were calculated to induce an emotional reaction. Specifically, the control questions should be ones to which the subject's answers will be probably untrue. Questions like "Have you ever cheated on your income tax?" or "Have you ever stolen anything?" may be answered "No" and, if they are, these answers are unlikely to be literally true. Reid's idea was to use the subject's responses to the control questions as standards against which to measure his reactions to the relevant questions. Backster later provided a psychological rationale for this approach together with other refinements so that Reid's method, in one form or another, has come to be the standard technique used by most modern examiners in dealing with "specific issue" cases, as in criminal investigation situations.

Reid's proposal to use a "guilt complex" question was, in my view, a much sounder idea than the control question notion, but it is more difficult to implement and never really caught on. In the latest edition of their textbook, even Reid and Inbau treat it as an ancillary technique to be used only in rare and special situations. The idea is, when interrogating about the subject's possible involvement in Crime X, to pretend to be equally interested in whether he might also have been guilty of some fictitious crime, Crime Y. If this fiction can be made convincing, then the subject's response to "Did you commit Crime Y?" provides a good prediction of how that subject ought to respond to the relevant question, about X, if he is being truthful in denying X. Thus, the guilt complex question, properly presented, provides a genuine control in the scientific sense of that term whereas the control questions actually used in every Lie Control Test do not. These theoretical issues will be discussed in detail later on in this book and are mentioned here just to illustrate the importance of Reid's role in the evolution of polygraphy.

Reid's advocacy of the use of behavior symptoms as supplementary criteria in the scoring of polygraph examinations has been especially controversial and, indeed, has led to a persisting schism among modern examiners. This proposal grew out of a study, published by Reid and Arther in 1953,[20] tabulating behavior symptoms which, it was alleged, were exhibited during polygraph examinations only by deceptive subjects, together with another list of symptoms said to be characteristic only of the truthful individual. To a psychologist, these tabulations seem at the same time plausible and yet excessively naive. It is plausible that a lying subject might try to postpone his examination, be late for his appointment, be "very worried and highly nervous" in the examination room, and want to leave promptly when the test is over. But the thought that these and other listed "symptoms of lying" will be systematically totted up and then contribute to the final diagnosis gives one pause. Since the beginning, polygraph examiners had used "global scoring"; the same individual reads the case file, conducts the pretest interview, formulates the questions, administers the test, observes the "behavior symptoms," evaluates the polygraph charts, and then reaches the final diagnosis of Deceptive or Truthful. Reid's school and especially Arther's emphasize the clinical evaluation of behavior symptoms, insisting that the examiner constitutes the real lie detector, guided by his training, judgment, and experience. Yet neither of these two leaders of the global scoring tradition show any apparent appreciation of the profound psychometric difficulties inherent in their approach, a can of worms we shall have to open in a later chapter devoted to the clinical lie detector test.

Backster and the Polygraphic Lie Test

We have already seen that a diminishing proportion of polygraph examiners still employ the relevant/irrelevant test format while some form of control question test is used by the majority. This larger group, in turn, is split into two factions, one of which relies on the Reid-Arther practice of global scoring (also used by adherents of the R/I test). The remaining faction, which I believe includes the most professional of modern-day polygraphers, follows the lead of Reid's other influential student, Cleve Backster.

Backster achieved considerable celebrity some years ago in connection with his experiments with plants. Popular accounts had it that Backster had connected his philodendron to a lie detector but what he actually did was to clamp a plant leaf between the two electrodes of the electrodermal channel, the part of the polygraph normally used to measure electrical changes in the skin produced by palmar sweating. One can imagine his excitement when the polygraph pen first began to trace out what appeared to be responses from the leaf, changes in electrical resistance not unlike those shown by human subjects. Further experiments persuaded him that these botanical reactions were related to events in the laboratory, even to the experimenter's unspoken *thoughts* concerning what he planned to do next to the plant! Backster went on to study, in a similar way, the reactions of fertile chicken eggs and, finally, aggregations of living human cells, including spermatozoa. His experiments along these exotic lines generated sufficient interest in scientific circles to lead to an invitation to present his findings at the 1975 meetings of the American Association for the Advancement of Science. Other investigators have been unable to repeat Backster's findings, and he is currently attempting to develop an experimental technique robust enough to work consistently in other people's hands.

Backster's contributions to human polygraphy include the "zone of comparison" format, in which adjacent relevant and control responses are compared so as to compensate for changes in the subject's reactivity over the course of the test. Most important of all, Backster initiated the practice of numerical scoring of the polygraph charts. Using rather specific rules and criteria, adjacent control and relevant responses are compared separately for each polygraph channel. Scores are awarded, ranging from $+1$ to $+3$ if the control response is larger and from -1 to -3 if the relevant response is the larger. Summing these scores over all channels and all repetitions of the same question list to get a total score, the test is then classified as Deceptive if the total is negative and sufficiently large, as Truthful if the total is sufficiently high and positive, or as Indeterminate if the total falls in some range about zero. There is no use of behavior symptoms, case facts, or other extraneous considerations; the test outcome is intended to be based entirely on the polygraph findings. Moreover, this systematic numerical scoring procedure makes it less likely that the examiner's preconceptions about the subject's honesty will influence his interpretation of the polygraph record. The evidence indicates that competent examiners trained in this method can achieve high levels of agreement when they independently score the same set of charts.

The importance of Backster's innovation lies in the fact that, for the first time, a polygraph examination conducted in this fashion could lay claim to being called a "test" in the accepted sense of that term. As Professor Meehl has pointed out, a psychological test has four cardinal properties: (1) standardized method of administration (all polygraph methods stretch this requirement since all require questions tailored to the respondent); (2) immediate recording of behavior (the polygraph records immediately, but the examiner's clinical impressions may not jell until the interview is over); (3) objective scoring (the clinical lie "test" is intractably subjective); and (4) external validity criteria (we shall see that there are no clear validity data on the clinical lie test).

Examinations administered by adherents of the Keeler, Reid, or Arther schools are interrogations, not tests. They are semistandardized methods of clinical observation in which the examiner has the opportunity to collect relevant data. When it is the examiner who is the "lie detector," then it becomes especially difficult to assess the accuracy of the technique in any general way. The Backster technique also depends heavily upon the skill of the examiner, especially in his selection of the specific questions to be used. But at least the fruit of the examination, the test results, can be localized in the polygraph charts and we can expect different examiners to score the same charts with reasonably good agreement.

Voice Analysis

During the 1960s the American military became increasingly interested in the possibilities of covert lie detection and sponsored various R&D efforts in that direction. Lt. Col. Allan Bell, an Army intelligence officer, together with Lt. Col. Charles McQuiston, an Army polygrapher, designed an instrument intended to measure microtremor in the human voice, a low-frequency warble thought to be related to emotional arousal or stress. In 1970, Bell and McQuiston resigned from the Army and set up a private company called Dektor Counterintelligence and Security to manufacture their machine, known as the Psychological Stress Evaluator, or PSE. A New Jersey company, Law Enforcement Associates, markets a competing device called the Mark II Voice Analyzer, which was also developed with Army funding. Both machines cost upwards of $4,000, but one might also consider the Hagoth, which claims to reveal voice stress through a pattern of flickering lights rather than a tracing on a paper chart, and costs only $1,500. Or one could wait for a promised wristwatch size device that will sell for under $100.

Voice analyzers operate on tape recordings of the subject's speech and therefore can be used covertly, wherever hidden microphones might be employed, and can even be turned to historical research. They have already been used to "show" that Lee Harvey Oswald was truthful when he denied killing President Kennedy, that Bruno Hauptmann was innocent of kidnapping the Lindbergh baby (the researcher here employed a smuggled recording of Haptmann's courtroom testimony; how envious Marston would have been!) and to assess the veracity of President Nixon, John Dean, and other televised notables.[21] It should be emphasized that none of these voice analyzers are claimed to be able to detect deception directly. Like the polygraph, they are said to measure variations in emotional stress; whether a particular statement is deceptive is inferred from a comparison of the "stress" associated with that and other utterances by the same respondent. It must be admitted that some voice analysts, like some polygraphers, operate as if lying is the only reasonable explanation for an emotional reaction to a question, thus committing themselves to the simplistic assumptions of the relevant/irrelevant test format. The polygraph does measure variations in nonspecific emotional arousal (except when the subject knows how to produce misleading reactions by means of self-stimulation). The problem with various methods of polygraphic interrogation is whether deception can plausibly be inferred when the subject is more aroused by one question than by another. Voice analyzers confront the same problem as do all other proposed methods for recording stress—using skin temperature, changes in pupil diameter, even body odors. If a given type of voice analyzer *can* measure emotional arousal, then it could be used for lie detection no less but no more accurately than the traditional polygraph. As we shall see, the voice analyzers have yet to cross this first hurdle; there is no convincing evidence that any of them even measure stress.

Honesty Tests

The principal application for the polygraph or the voice analyzer is in the screening of job applicants to determine whether they were in the habit of stealing from previous employers or whether they were truthful in answering the questions on their application forms; in short, to determine whether the applicant is likely to be a reliable, trustworthy employee. An alternative approach is to administer a paper-and-pencil "honesty test" like the Reid Report or the Stanton Survey or the Personnel Security Inventory, multiple-choice questionnaires that are easy and inexpensive to administer and that are claimed to be able to select honest employees. The Reid Report, the first honesty test on the market and typical of the group, was developed by the John Reid organization of Chicago for sale to those of its business clients who were unable or unwilling to use the more costly polygraph screening. The close connection between the honesty tests and the methods of instrumental interrogation already described is highlighted by the fact that the evidence offered for the validity of these questionnaires consists mainly of correlations with the polygraph. For example, when the Stanton Survey was administered to a group of applicants who were also given a polygraph test, nearly two-thirds of the applicants "failed" both tests. We shall discuss the implications of such remarkable findings in Chapter 16.

The Tools of Diogenes

Thus we can see that the modern Diogenes has many tools at his disposal, and it is my purpose in this book to examine each of them critically. There are honesty tests and there are methods of instrumental interrogation. The interrogation methods may employ a voice analyzer device or a conventional polygraph. One experimental method of polygraphic interrogation attempts to determine whether the respondent possesses "guilty knowledge," whether he recognizes facts, scenes, or objects that he could identify only if he were guilty of the crime in question and had been present at the scene. Most instrumental interrogation now used in the field, however, is intended to detect lying, to determine whether the respondent's answers to certain relevant questions are deceptive or truthful. Whatever instrument is used, the lie detector examiner may employ one of several question formats. Each of these question formats requires a different set of assumptions if deception (or truthfulness) is to be inferred from the polygraphic responses. Whatever format the examiner uses—and whichever instrument he employs for recording the subject's reaction—he may arrive at his final judgment either through clinical evaluation or through objective numerical scoring of the polygraph (or voice analyzer) records alone. Examiners who use clinical evaluation allow themselves to be influenced not only by the instrumental findings but also by the respondent's demeanor and behavior symptoms, the case facts, and other sources of intuitive insight.

After 50 years of virtual neglect, there has been recently a wholesome increase of critical discussion of this truth technology and its potential impact upon our society. But much of this discussion, both in law journals and in the popular press, has treated these varied techniques in an undiscriminating way, as if they were all equally valid or equally absurd, equally useful or equally pernicious. Among polygraphers, proponents of one method scrupulously avoid criticizing other methods, at least in print, perhaps in fear of providing ammunition to critics from without. Although their business is flourishing, the truth merchants are sensitive to outside criticism and quickly close ranks in bristling solidarity. Some see polygraphy as in a Cold War and adopt the tactics of that period. Richard Arther, in his text *The Scientific Investigator*, exemplifies this approach:

Obviously, from our [foreign] enemies' viewpoint the only way to stop their exposure is to stop the polygraph. That is the reason for most of the anti-polygraph articles in the press and a great deal of the legislation being introduced in some of our states by Communist dupes and fellow travelers.[22]

Another reason why proponents of the truth technology tend to be less discriminating than they should be is, I think, ideological. Many polygraphers and many of their clients are concerned about what they see as a breakdown of law and order and are tolerant of almost any development intended to help stem this seeming tide of anarchy. Listen again to polygraphers Ferguson and Miller:

Permissiveness, lack of conformity to the accepted rules and regulations long governing moral conduct in this country, has already deprived the order and right of the sincere majority for the sake of pacifying a few depraved, warped minds. This is the epitome of misguided humanitarianism at best. At worst, it approximates social suicide, twisting liberty into license from law. Due to our legislative and court-affected complacency, we have seen our cities convulsed with mindless destruction in the name of *civil rights*, universities bomb blasted or shut down by self-styled revolutionaires in the name of *academic rights*, sedition and draft evasion by cowards and overeducated milque-toasts in the name of *morality*, militants and radicals openly advocating guerrilla warfare and anarchy in order to disrupt the democratic process and overthrow the government in the name of *freedom*, a youth culture anesthetized and sustained by drugs in the name of *self-expression*, hippies and flower children aimlessly wandering and littering the streets in the name of *peace*, an increase of gonorrhea and syphilis in the name of *free love*, and finally a shambles of primitive lawlessness in the name of the *right to equal shares for everybody*.

This kind of complacency and toleration, with respect to crime and moral conduct, is the deadliest of diseases. If a deadly disease is not checked, death results—in this case, the death of a nation. No matter how hard it is to accept, a democracy such as ours, like less libertarian systems, cannot grant all freedoms to individuals and leave none for itself to use in the interest of its own preservation.[23]

Not all polygraphers share this menacingly authoritarian outlook. But the great majority of them come from a background in police work or military intelligence and they are not always ardent supporters of those various rights and freedoms that Ferguson and Miller deprecate.

Ideology aside, however, it seems unwise for examiners of the Keeler-Reid-Arther persuasion to be defensive about the Polygraphic Lie Test or make extravagant claims about what can be read in the charts since, if that relatively objective method had really high accuracy, then their clinical evaluation, using behavior symptoms and other subjective evidence, would be contraindicated because it could only serve to lower the overall accuracy of their results. Adherents of the Backster method of numerical scoring, conversely, whose approach is specifically designed to avoid the subjectivity and bias of clinical evaluation, only compromise themselves by supporting those who argue that it is the examiner who is the lie detector. Every polygrapher who has been taught to use some form of control question format has had it explained by his instructors that the relevant/irrelevant method is outmoded, naive, and invalid. For them to support colleagues wedded to the R/I method is not only disingenuous but impugns the credibility of their own approach.

Opponents of the truth technology tend to emphasize issues like the right to privacy and the dignity of man and seem to take the position that all these techniques should be proscribed on the basis of the same set of libertarian principles. Thus, Robert Ellis Smith, editor of *Privacy Journal* asserts,

Even if polygraphs were regarded as totally reliable, I would still oppose their use as lie detectors, just as I oppose the use of wiretaps. Wiretaps, after all, are totally reliable, but they still violate individual privacy.[24]

Note that this is a false analogy. When he refers to the "reliability" of the polygraph, Mr. Smith has in mind the accuracy of the lie detector test. Because it is not a test, a wiretap can be neither accurate nor inaccurate in that sense. Or consider the splendid fulminations of law professor E. A. Jones:

If the lie-detecting polygraph were indeed to be what it is *not*—a monument to technological infallibility—if it were a chrome-plated, flickery-lighted, superefficient computerized conduit of discovery, linked to the sweaty wrist and breath-gulping, heaving chest of an evasive, guilt-worried, fault-smothering, self-excusing human being, which is surely descriptive of what each of us has become on some occasions in the course of our lives, I would still come down on the side of exclusion. Each of us is too imperfect and fragile a creature to sustain such rigorous thrusts of suspicion and rejection into our being and yet maintain that sense of personal worth and higher purpose— and recurrent resolve to do better—which is indispensable to dignity and accomplishment. I think it is far preferable that a fellow human, concededly imperfect in the capacity to perceive calculated falsehoods, be the assessor of credibility than to achieve a mechanical perfection akin to Orwell's *1984* and Huxley's *Brave New World.*[25]

Although I respect both these writers and share their values and concerns, I believe that their approach is mistaken both substantively and tactically. This book is anti-Luddite in its conviction that these tools of Diogenes will be used if they work and that they cannot effectively be opposed merely because they are new or employ the trappings of technology. If there is or could be a method to infallibly detect lying, then I shall argue that such a resource would be irresistible, that it would come to be used widely and would produce a social revolution to which these principles of privacy and dignity would have to accommodate themselves. A method of lie detection that is invalid, based on deceit, or tainted by examiner bias can more confidently be opposed for those reasons than on the basis of abstractions with respect to which public opinion is widely divided, whatever the Constitution may be interpreted to say. Many Americans, for example, do not really object to warrantless search by the police (until it happens to themselves) because "if you have nothing to hide, you have nothing to fear." Such citizens are unlikely to support a ban on lie detectors because they "intrude into man's interior domain"—the basis on which Pope Pius XII condemned the lie detector in 1958[26] —but they probably would support a ban if the lie detector can be shown to be biased or inaccurate.

Between these two extremes of chance accuracy and near infallibility there remains a wide range to be discriminated. If an instrumental method for affixing guilt could be shown to be, not infallible, but able on the average to make only half as many errors as our criminal courts make now, who would want to reject that method out of hand? In assessing credibility or predicting honesty, certain methods such as physical abuse or intimidation are intrinsically intolerable, but barring these, is not the accuracy of the method more important than its nature? Employers *will* attempt to predict the trustworthiness of a job applicant. Is it better that they should do this intuitively from interviews and background checks even if a questionnaire or a brief, standardized polygraph interrogation could be shown to be objective, unbiased, and more accurate? I do not mean to argue that questions of privacy, human dignity, or constitutional principle are less important than questions of the accuracy and reliability of this new technology. On the contrary, my thesis is that these higher principles are better served if their consideration is deferred until one is quite clear about what these various techniques are like, how accurate they are in identifying the culpable, what price is paid in misidentifying the innocent, and thus how strong a case can reasonably be made in favor of their use.

It will therefore be apparent that this book is not written by a lawyer. I once examined a 15-year-old boy who had been adjudicated guilty of murder by a juvenile court and referred for pre-sentence evaluation. Convinced that this lad was psychologically incapable either of the killing itself or of behaving as he did afterwards if he had been guilty, I studied the state's case against him, even going so far as to hire a private investigator to look into the matter, and then explained in my report to the court why I believed that the facts denied his guilt. After being severely admonished by the judge for "meddling in evidentiary matters," I came to realize that the legal and the scientific mind differ in subtle and unexpected ways, their diverging concepts of the nature of (and professional claims upon) "evidence" being only one example. Judges who scrupulously administer the established rules of evidence can be astonishingly credulous in respect to certain psychological inferences. Judge Jerome Frank reveals

absurd rules-of-thumb some trial judges use, such as these: A witness is lying if, when testifying, he throws his head back; or if he raises his right heel from the floor; or if he shifts his gaze rapidly; or if he bites his lip. Every psychologist knows how meaningless as signs of prevarication any such behavior may be. . . . Not very long ago, a federal judge, toward the end of his long career on the bench, publicly revealed for the first time that he had always counted as a liar any witness who rubbed his palms while testifying. That judge must have decided hundreds of cases in which he arrived at his [findings of fact] by applying that asinine test for detecting falsehoods.[27]

An article in the *New York University Law Review* begins by explaining that the authors do not intend to consider the "scientific reliability of polygraph evidence" but will rather assume "that the lie detector test results are scientifically reliable enough for some evidentiary purposes."[28] They then proceed with a 30-page discussion of precedents, constitutional issues, and surprisingly, a section on "Weighing the Probative Value of Polygraph Evidence," although how one can usefully discuss the "probative value" of a test without considering the evidence for the validity of the test is hard to understand for one not learned in the law.

A psychologist, therefore, especially admires those legal scholars who seem to think like scientists. Attorney Lee M. Burkey[29] and law professor Jerome H. Skolnick[30] are highly recommended for this reason. Another law professor, Edgar A. Jones,[31] has provided an analysis of the psychology of both the polygraph examiner and the examinee that is brilliantly perceptive. Enough of his admirable prose will be quoted herein to tempt the reader to read Jones's chapter, intended for contract arbitrators and other triers-of-fact, but accessible to any interested person. I was especially impressed by a Canadian Supreme Court justice, the Honorable Donald R. Morand, who was appointed in 1975 to preside over a Royal Commission to investigate the practices of the Toronto metropolitan police. Polygraph evidence had been offered concerning the veracity of various witnesses in this matter and, noting that American enthusiasm for polygraphy was tending to drift north across the border, Justice Morand determined to seize this opportunity for a thorough study of the matter. Many days of testimony, comprising 11 volumes of the Commission record, were obtained from leading polygraphers and a number of interested scientists. A full chapter of the Commission's 1976 report is devoted to an appraisal of this record.[32] Inevitably, Justice Morand looks first at legal precedents, but it becomes quickly apparent that he is primarily concerned with the concrete nature of these techniques, the plausibility of the assumptions on which they are based, and the independent evidence available concerning their reliability. Some of this judge's trenchant observations will be quoted in the following pages.

Science and the Lie Detector

None of the major figures in the development of instrumental interrogation methods have had credentials as scientists. The Backster form of polygraph examination is a psychological test. Physiological reactions are used as a basis on which to draw inferences about the psychological state of the respondent: Was he more aroused by this question than by that one? Was he lying? The Reid or Keeler forms of examination are not strictly tests but their objective, similarly, is that of making a psychological diagnosis. And yet Reid and Inbau are lawyers, not psychologists; Keeler, Backster, and Arther had no professional psychological or scientific training; Lee and even Larson, during the main period of his work in polygraphy, were policemen. At the present time, perhaps ten of the thousands of practicing examiners might meet requirements for licensure as consulting psychologists. In view of the extravagant and discredited claims of W. H. Marston, with his Ph.D. in psychology from Harvard, it might be held that this conspicuous lack of participation by professional psychologists in the development of polygraphy has been all to the good.

The creator of Wonder Woman notwithstanding, the fact that this major area of applied psychology has such tenuous roots in psychological science is cause for concern. There is a great body of knowledge and theory concerning psychological testing in that branch of psychology known as psychometrics or psychological assessment, a data base with which only a handful of polygraphers are able to make contact. The use of physiological responses as indicators of psychological states or events also is a subdiscipline of academic psychology, the field known as psychophysiology. Again, only a handful of polygraphers have had significant basic-science training in this area. Psychologists specializing in psychometrics or in clinical psychology know something about the perils and pitfalls of psychological assessment, the factors that diminish test accuracy, and they understand how to measure the reliability and the validity of a test in an objective and credible fashion. Academic psychologists know (or should know) how to conduct, report, and interpret scientific research.

Finally, and this is especially important, academic psychologists maintain the archival literature of their discipline, scientific journals in which appear only those research reports that have survived a screening process of peer review. If I wish to publish an article about lie detection in *The Journal of Applied Psychology* or in *Psychophysiology,* my contribution must first be read by the editor and by at least two editorial consultants, scientists knowledgeable about the substance and methods involved in my work, and my article will not be published unless or until these individuals are satisfied that it makes both a valid and a useful contribution to knowledge. This screening process is by no means infallible. I have had brilliant(!) papers rejected by pig-headed reviewers and other researchers have managed to slip flawed or trivial manuscripts past the half-closed eyes of sleepy or incompetent editors. But the scientific peer-review process is nonetheless enormously important, as can be inferred from the fact that perhaps 80% of the papers submitted to these journals are rejected altogether while a high proportion of the remainder appear in print only after more or less extensive revision to remove ambiguities, overstatements, and downright errors detected by the editors.

People are inclined to think that books are more substantial and authoritative than mere journal articles. A book is undeniably harder to write (as I have discovered toiling at this one) but even scientific books are seldom subjected to really serious peer review before publication. The handful of books on polygraphy (this book has in fact been screened by a number of experts) represent the view of the author, screened only by himself, and the reader must be his or her own judge of the logic of the arguments and the quality of the evidence presented. A substantial proportion of the literature of polygraphy over the past 40 years has appeared in law journals, especially the *Journal of Criminal Law, Criminology and Police Science* (of which Reid's collaborator, Professor Inbau, was for many years managing director and then editor), in police journals such as *Police, Journal of Police Science and Administration, Military Police Journal,* or *Law and Order,* or in trade journals like *Polygraph, Journal of Polygraph Studies, Security World,* or *Banker's Monthly.* These all may be perfectly respectable publications of their type, but they are not scientific journals and none of them requires their contributors to pass the scrutiny of sharp-eyed scientific editorial review. For someone attempting, as I am here, a fair and reasonably comprehensive critical survey of this literature, the vast bulk of which has not had such preliminary screening, this situation is a kind of nightmare. I would expect that anyone with a scientific background who attempted to read critically all of the 1700 references cited in Ansley and Horvath's bibliography of polygraphy, *Truth and Science,*[33] might risk serious psychiatric consequences. I have read widely but selectively, emphasizing the scientific literature, the major books in the area, many of the law journal articles, plus *Polygraph,* the official journal of the American Polygraph Association.

The scientific literature relating to polygraphy totals perhaps 80 titles in this century, about 40 published since 1950. A handful of scientifically trained investigators are currently active, notably Dr. J. Kubis at Fordham, Dr. Martin Orne and his associates at the University of Pennsylvania, Drs. G. Ben-Shakar, S. Kugelmass, and I. Lieblich at the Hebrew University of Jerusalem, Dr. A. Suzuki and associates in Japan, Dr. D. Raskin at the University of Utah, Dr. G. Barland of Salt Lake City, Dr. S. Abrams of Portland, Oregon, and Dr. F. Horvath at Michigan State University. Abrams, Barland, Horvath, and Raskin, as well as the Japanese group, are practicing polygraphic examiners either full-time or part-time, a fact that helps to explain their interest in these problems. Fewer than 0.03% of the accredited psychologists in the United States have contributed to the polygraphy literature; it is doubtful if 46 of the 46,000 members of the American Psychological Association know enough about the topic to offer an informed opinion. Yet polygraphic interrogation is unquestionably one of the most important areas of applied psychology in the United States, whether measured as a multimillion dollar industry or in terms of its wide social impact. And polygraphy is an interesting and challenging problem scientifically as well as in its public policy aspects. It seems to me that this neglect by psychologists and psychophysiologists is unfortunate, baffling, and somewhat scandalous. A similar situation prevailed in respect to the subject of hypnosis in 1934, when the eminent psychologist Clark L. Hull published his survey of that topic and Hull was similarly baffled and scandalized. Perhaps hypnosis then and the lie detector now carries a taint of sensationalism which threatens to embarrass the respectable scientist. Psychologists rather should be embarrassed about their ignorance of this important and burgeoning development.

The lie detector is currently used in criminal investigation and security applications in Canada, Israel, Japan, South Korea, Mexico, Pakistan, the Philippines, Taiwan, and Thailand. Many foreign examiners have been trained at the Army Polygraph School at Fort McClelland, Alabama. Employee screening applications are almost exclusively North American. Western European police agencies remain skeptical about the value of the polygraph. Scotland Yard, for example, have reviewed the matter and concluded that the polygraph does not fit in with their methods and policies. Like Coca-Cola and the snowmobile, the lie detector has become a distinctive feature of contemporary American culture. We shall decide later whether this fact is a reason for chauvinism or chagrin.

Notes

1. George Steiner, *After Babel*, London: Oxford University Press, 1975.
2. Professor David Premack, University of Pennsylvania; personal communication, 1977.
3. Larson, J. A. *Lying and its Detection*, Chicago: University of Chicago Press, 1932.
4. Lombroso, C. *L'Homme Criminel* (2nd French edition, 1895); cited in P. V. Trovillo, A history of lie detection. *Journal of Criminal Law, Criminology and Police Science*, 1939, *30*, 848–881.

5.   Luria, A. R. *The Nature of Human Conflicts* (translated and edited by Horsley Gannt, 1932).

6.   Galton, F. Psychometric experiments. *Brain*, 1979, *2*, 162.

7.   Marston, W. M. *The Lie Detector Test*, New York: Richard R. Smith, 1938, p. 45.

8.   *ibid.* p. 81.

9.   *ibid.* p. 87.

10. *Look,* December 6, 1938, pp. 16–17.

11. Linehan, J. G. Lie detection pioneer profiles. *Polygraph*, 1978, *7*, 95–100.

12. Larson, J. A. *op. cit.,* p. 333.

13. *ibid.* p. 121.

14. Larson, J. A. The lie detector polygraph: Its history and development. *Journal of the Michigan State Medical Society*, 1938, *37*, 893–897.

15. Larson, J. A. *The Lie Detector Test,* p 191.

16. Cited in Skolnick, J. H. Scientific theory and scientific evidence: An analysis of lie-detection. *The Yale Law Journal*, 1961, *70*, 694, 728.

17. Lee, C. D. *The Instrumental Detection of Deception: The Lie Test,* Springfield, Ill.: Charles C. Thomas, 1953.

18. Reid, J. E. & Inbau, F. E. *Truth and Deception, The Polygraph ("Lie Detector") Technique,* 2nd Ed. Baltimore: Williams & Wilkins, 1977.

19. Reid, J. E. A revised questioning technique in lie-detection tests. *Journal of Criminal Law and Criminology*, 1947, *37*, 542–547.

20. Reid, J. E. & Arther, R. O. Behavior symptoms of lie detector subjects. *Journal of Criminal Law and Criminology*, 1953, *44*, 104–108.

21. Rice, B. The new truth machines. *Psychology Today*, 1978, June, 61–78.

22. Arther, R. O. *The Scientific Investigator,* Springfield, Ill.: Charles C. Thomas, 1965.

23. Ferguson, R. J. & Miller, A. L. *Polygraph for the Defense,* Springfield, Ill.: Charles C. Thomas, 1974, pp. 36–37. This is by no means an isolated example. A past-president of the American Polygraph Association inveighs against "the do-gooders, the bleeding hearts, and the civil libertarians . . . [who] see no reason why a person who elects a life of crime should not enjoy absolute privacy to continue his career unmolested" (R. J. Weir, Jr., *Polygraph*, 1974, *3*, 125). The editor of the *APA Newsletter* warns his readers of a State Department initiative to admit into the U.S. 500 political prisoners from Chile and Argentina. Referring to these refugees as "terrorists, communists, and revolutionaries," he suggests that polygraphers called upon to give pre-employment tests to such persons should "take a refresher course in communism, Marxism, and terrorism" (May-June issue, page 25). In a letter attacking me for an article opposing pre-employment screening, H. M. Hanson of Scientific Security Systems in Phoenix comments: "You, not being responsi-

ble for meeting a payroll or overhead, would not and cannot understand why employers do not wish to have . . . ex-convicts or 'hypes'
(those on narcotics) on our payrolls, even though various bureaucratic
agencies and obviously liberal colleges permit this to exist within their
organizations. I have always felt that the University of Minnesota was
a rather conservative and certainly highly respected university in the
academic world. Obviously the likes of Humphrey and other liberals
have changed the image at Minnesota" (January 8, 1975).

24. Smith, R. E. *Privacy: How to Protect What's Left of It,* Garden City,
    N.Y.: Anchor Press/Doubleday, 1979, p. 255.
25. Jones, E. A., Jr. "Truth" when the polygraph operator sits as arbitrator
    (or judge): The deception of "detection" in the "Diagnosis of truth and
    deception." In J. Stern & B. Dennis, Eds. *Truth, Lie Detectors, and
    Other Problems,* (31st Annual Proceedings, National Academy of Arbi-
    trators, 1979, 75–152), p 133.
26. *ibid.,* footnote 108, p. 133.
27. Frank, J. *Courts on Trial,* Princeton, N.J.: Princeton University Press,
    1949, pp. 247–335.
28. Editors. Pinocchio's new nose. *New York University Law Review,* 1973,
    339–361, p. 340.
29. Burkey, L. M. Privacy, property and the polygraph. *Labor Law Jour-
    nal,* 1967, *18,* 79.
30. Skolnick, J. H. Scientific theory and scientific evidence: An analysis of
    lie detection. *Yale Law Journal,* 1961, *70,* 694–728.
31. Jones, E. A., Jr. *op cit.*
32. Morand, Justice D. R. *The Royal Commission into Metropolitan Toron-
    to Police Practices,* Toronto, Canada: 1976.
33. Ansley, N. & Horvath, F. *Truth and Science,* Linthicum Heights, Md.:
    American Polygraph Association, 1977.

CHAPTER

4

The Truth Verifier

To unmask falsehood and bring truth to light.

—Shakespeare

No normal human being wants to hear the truth.

—H. L. Mencken

It seems natural to believe that a machine can detect lying, a machine not so simple as a smoke detector, perhaps, but more like the cardiac monitor that is connected to intensive care patients in hospitals and that turns on an alarm when heart action strays beyond normal limits. The familiar term "lie detector" conjures such an image, a machine that rings a bell each time the subject tells a lie. A moment's reflection makes clear that such a device could exist only if everyone produced some distinctive physiological response when attempting to deceive, a response never produced, for example, when telling the truth but feeling frightened or afraid that he or she may not be believed. As Dr. Marston correctly pointed out, "It is necessary to test for some emotion which will not be present unless a person is lying. . . . some *one* bit of behavior which would *always* mean a person was lying. Early in the twentieth century this long-sought symptom of deception was discovered."[1] As we shall see, Marston's claims of discovery were premature. But if there were such a specific lie response, then modern psychophysiological techniques would probably allow us to detect it and the dream of a genuine "lie detector" would be a reality. It will be instructive to consider how society as we know it might be changed by the existence of such an instrument.

The Dawning of the Age of Truth

In 1961, a conference was convened in Washington, D.C., by the Institute for Defense Analyses (IDA) to discuss potential contributions of the polygraph to national security. IDA is a kind of think-tank operated by the U.S. Department of Defense. Attending the conference were most of the American scientists then living who had done research on polygraphic interrogation, a total of eight people altogether. One of the topics for discussion was whether use of the lie detector might not be incorporated into the nuclear test ban agreement then being negotiated with the Soviets. In those days the skies were not yet filled with Russian and American spy satellites, and the physical scientists could not promise to detect more than 20% of any nuclear weapons testing done in violation of the treaty. Perhaps each side could be permitted to administer polygraph tests at regular intervals to key officials of the other government? But this raised the possibility that the Soviets (or we) would keep one set of figurehead officials ignorant of actual test ban violations or that knowledgeable persons might be made immune to lie detection by hypnosis, drugs, or special training. The Defense Department subsequently sponsored a program of (inconclusive) research on countermeasures to defeat the lie detector but, in the meanwhile, the satellites began to fly and the urgency of this need dissipated.

Another proposal mooted at this IDA conference by a distinguished neurophysiologist[2] was vastly more ambitious. First, the standard field polygraph, a relatively primitive device reflecting 1930s technology, would be modernized, transistorized, and otherwise brought up to date. Then it would be rechristened; the Lie Detector would become the Truth Verifier. Finally, redesigned and renamed, the instrument would be employed at the highest levels of international diplomacy. We were asked to imagine then-President

Kennedy or Chairman Khrushchev addressing the General Assembly of the United Nations. The president or chairman, on the podium confronting all the world's representatives and TV cameras, would be connected to the Truth Verifier; the Verifier, in turn, would be connected to a huge meter positioned on the wall over the speaker's head. As long as each national leader confined himself to what he believed to be the truth, the meter-pointer would bounce along comfortably near zero. But, should he assert anything about his nation's actions or intentions that he knew to be misleading or deceptive, the pointer would then swing revealingly over into the lie zone.

One's first reaction to such a scenario is mocking incredulity; this is a science fiction pipedream. But, if there is a specific lie response, then we can surely design an instrument to measure it. And, if we had such a Truth Verifier, almost infallible (nothing in the real world is wholly infallible), why not use it as a specific antidote for the international suspicion and distrust that constitutes the most important single threat to world peace? Deception is so pervasive in human intercourse that it is difficult to imagine a world in which dissembling had become impossible. How far would Hitler have been able to pursue his plans, prior to the invasion of Poland, if all the world had known *for certain* what his true intentions were from the time he became chancellor? Surely France, Britain, and the Soviet Union would have mobilized in pace with Germany to meet the threat. The surprise attack on Pearl Harbor with its enormous military advantages for the Japanese could not have happened if diplomacy had been conducted with the help of a Truth Verifier. Moreover, it is unthinkable that American public opinion, however reluctant and inner-directed, would have failed to support military preparedness if shown unequivocal proof of Japanese intentions as early as 1938.

Diplomatic mendacity is not always an essential precursor to hostilities, of course. A stronger nation might openly decide to attack a weaker neighbor that had neither friends nor resources adequate to mount a serious resistance. In earlier times well-matched rivals frequently engaged each other for emotional reasons rather than for coldly calculated material advantage. Street fights sometimes occur precisely *because* the combatants know the truth about each other and not as any consequence of lying. But the current, postnuclear threat to world peace is thought to be of a different order. It is inconceivable that the Russians and the Americans would push the buttons of mutual annihilation because of injured pride or dreams of glory. It is generally agreed that neither side will strike if it is convinced that the opponent will retain the capacity for devastating retaliation. But both sides fear that the opponent may develop technology of offense or defense that will unbalance the deterrence—and therefore, both sides work and spend feverishly to accomplish just such an imbalance! But suppose both sides knew *for certain* not only the current intentions, but the other's military capabilities as well. Suppose further that all weapons research was, in effect, conducted publicly with its fruits immediately available to both sides. What would be the risk of nuclear holocaust then?

To accomplish such a happy reduction of mutual fears and suspicion, the Truth Verifier would have to be used carefully, and both sides would be required to permit free access to each other's military planners and technicians. Unaccustomed to operating in a context of openness and truth, both sides undoubtedly would at first shy at the thought of exchanging all their secrets, no matter how securely verified as to completeness and accuracy. But the benefits of such an exchange, on a continuing basis, would surely overwhelm these initial doubts. Not only would the danger of war be reduced, but also the great weight of military expenditure. Both parties to such an agreement would doubtless continue to study possible methods of defeating the Truth Verifier, for fear that if such a method did exist, the other side might discover it first, but each side's progress in this respect would be fully known to the other. Expensive and dangerous weapons research, on the other hand, might be expected to receive less and less priority. Why spend billions to perfect a laser deathray when your prospective enemy is all the while looking over your shoulder—and not spending anything? The stalemate of deterrence could presumably be maintained with a fraction of the nuclear weapons that are currently deployed. Substantial disarmament might finally be achieved once both sides could be given verified assurance of the other side's compliance.

Having accomplished disarmament and world peace, what other changes might the Truth Verifier work upon our cynical society? One thinks first of the law courts, most of whose time is presently devoted to the toilsome and often frustrated effort to determine the truth about what really happened and who did what to whom. While conflicting testimony does not always indicate that somebody is lying, our courts would be transformed beyond recognition if perjury were no longer possible. Juries would certainly become redundant in criminal courts and in most civil cases as well. To find out if the defendant is guilty, if he in fact did what the prosecution alleges he did, we would have only to ask him, with the Truth Verifier calibrating his reply. Such a radical change would no doubt be opposed at first. To require a defendant to plead to the charges while being monitored by the Truth Verifier would be said to be in violation of Fifth Amendment guarantees against self-incrimination. But no one is happy with the present system in which the guilty too often get off, especially if they can afford the best lawyers, while the innocent too often go to jail, especially if they are poor. If the Verifier could arrive at the truth in a few minutes while the present system, often after weeks of costly argument, goes frequently astray, who can doubt that the Fifth Amendment would eventually be interpreted so as to permit the use of the fairer and more efficient method? The respected legal scholar, Professor Wigmore, whose *Rules of Evidence* is known to every lawyer, once suggested having a lie detector in the courtroom in a position where the jury could see the readings as they were made—recorded electronically as the witness testified.[3] The Defense Department did not invent the Truth Verifier after all!

The Truth Verifier would deter crime not only by ensuring the conviction of apprehended criminals, but also by increasing the likelihood of their apprehension in the first instance. Who knows how many criminals each year are questioned by the police and then released for lack of probable cause? It is estimated that 95 percent of felonious crimes in the United States remain unsolved;[4] that shocking figure, itself in part responsible for our high crime rate, would certainly be lowered if every suspect were to be questioned under the scrutiny of a Truth Verifier. In any situation where one now may be required to swear or sign an affirmation of veracity, the use of the Verifier would be commonplace. Income tax evasion would dwindle to insignificant proportions; so would welfare fraud, forgery, contractual misprison, voting fraud, misrepresentation of identity, citizenship or other credentials, deception in employment applications. Ultimately, to the consternation of civil libertarians, the notion of periodic Verifier screening of all citizens would be bound to be suggested. Just the one question, "Since your last Verifier screening, have you committed one or more felonious crimes?"—those who ring the Verifier's bell to be interrogated further. An indignity, perhaps, and certainly a small nuisance, but what would it be worth to convince the would-be criminal that the probability of his being caught and punished for his crime was, say, 99% rather than the present sporting figure closer to 5%?

The political arena would be hardly recognizable in the Age of Truth. A Truth Verifier would certainly be kept in the White House auditorium where the presidential press conferences are held, this instrument to be calibrated and maintained by the National Bureau of Standards. It seems likely that all the leading news agencies and wire services, the major newspapers, and the broadcasting networks would equip their reporters with Mini-Verifiers for on-the-spot interviews. Congressional oversight committees could for the first time genuinely monitor the actions of the CIA and the other investigative agencies. Senior bureaucrats could be held strictly accountable for their departments since, because of the Verifier, they could no longer reasonably plead ignorance of the misfeasance, malfeasance, or nonfeasance of their subordinates. The Truth Verifier would be a cross that the seekers of elective office would have to learn to bear. A considerable adjustment would be required, not only of the politicians, but also on the part of the electorate, before we could all live comfortably under a system where everyone knew what the candidates really thought about the issues—and also which issues the candidates really knew nothing about.

It is but a short step from political campaigns to the world of marketing in general. Some of the earliest models of the Verifier would quickly appear in television commercials, the president of some company whose product really is better than the competition's, staring woodenly into the camera and declaring that "Gumgrip holds your dentures tighter!"—with the Verifier by his side to prove it. Do not imagine that we have descended into trivialities when we think about the advertising applications of the Verifier. Think of the impact on the producers of inferior products. In the Age of Truth, they could not advertise at all. As everybody knows, except the spokesmen for the Advertising Council, billions are spent each year to persuade us that inferior or overpriced products are not only desirable, but cheap at the price. Under the influence of the Verifier, those billions would have to be invested instead in research and development aimed either at producing a better or at least a cheaper product, so that the company could get back on the air again.

The impact of the Truth Verifier on everyday human relations is harder to forecast. If we are to accept Professor Sissela Bok's analysis,[5] to lie to someone, even with the best intentions, is to commit a form of bloodless violence upon them, ethically acceptable only in the same rare and special circumstances where physical violence might be justified (for example, concealing someone's whereabouts

from an evil pursuer) or where one can be certain that the harm done
by the truth will substantially outweigh the injury of deception. (I do
not give an example of this situation because I cannot think of one;
the classic example, in which the physician hides the grim truth from
his patient, is the one Bok's book was written to refute.) My own
personal view, for what it is worth, is that face-to-face lying, as distinguished from institutional deception (where either the liar or the
lied-to or both are institutions rather than individuals) is a lot less
frequent than we normally suppose, that most interpersonal falsehoods are committed in the heat of passion or in the murk of self-
deception and do not involve a clear intention to deceive. In any
case, since the Truth Verifier *is* science fictional after all, we may as
well decree that it will never be usable covertly, without attachments to the body of the person monitored, so that it will not become
a standard household gadget governing our everyday relationships
with family and friends.

Is There a Truth Verifier?

We have already noted that for there to be an instrument which
literally detects lying, there must be a specific lie response, a distinctive, involuntary, bodily reaction that everyone produces when lying
but never when telling the truth. There will never be a Truth Verifier (lie detector) until a specific lie response can be identified. Subjectively considered, it seems plausible that lying might involve a
characteristic physiological accompaniment; we all know a "guilty
feeling" when we experience it and most of us usually feel guilty
when we lie. Guilty feelings must involve different internal states
than do feelings of fear or anger or delight, since otherwise we could
not distinguish one from another. Could the specific lie response
consist of that involuntary psychophysiological reaction that accom-
panies the feeling of guilt?

The subjective experience of the various emotions is so vivid and
distinctive that it is natural to assume that each emotion is associated
with a unique pattern of autonomic response, to believe with Franz
Alexander[6] that "every emotional state has its own physiological
syndrome." But the evidence for this assumption is surprisingly
scanty. In a classic study done in 1953, Albert Ax employed a complex laboratory polygraph to monitor some dozen different physiological variables in his subjects while they were hoodwinked by

elaborate stagecraft designed to make them either angry (Group A) or frightened (Group F).[7] On the average, fear and anger produced different patterns of physiologic reactions. J. Schachter repeated Ax's study in 1957, adding a third group, who experienced the dull, aching pain of a "cold pressor" test (holding one's foot or arm submerged in ice water) instead of a specific emotion.[8] Again, the averaged response patterns for the fear, anger, and pain groups were significantly different from each other. But the response patterns of individual subjects were extremely variable. Guessing which subjects had been angry and which frightened based on their reaction patterns would have yielded a high proportion of mistakes even though fear and anger seem subjectively quite different and in spite of the very elaborate set of measurements that were obtained in these expensive laboratory investigations. This variability in autonomic response to the same stimulus has been extensively studied by psychophysiologists under the name *autonomic response-stereotypy*.[9] Jones may tend to show Pattern A both when he is angry and when he's afraid, Smith may show Pattern F in both cases, and Fisbee still a different pattern.

Nearly 100 years ago, William James suggested that emotion consists of the perception of bodily changes, that we are afraid because we tremble, rather than the other way around.[10] If the Jamesian theory were literally correct, then Ax and Schachter should have found distinctive fear and anger patterns in each of their subjects. Jones, Smith, and Fisbee could not have been experiencing the same emotions, no matter what they may have reported, since their bodily reactions were so different. But James' theory has been substantially refuted by Walter Cannon, among others.[11] One of Cannon's arguments cited the work of Marañon, who had studied the psychological effect of stimulating visceral reactions by direct injection of adrenaline.[12] Adrenaline produces the same physiological response pattern that Ax and Schachter found to be associated, on the average, with fear. But most of Marañon's subjects experienced only "as if " emotions, "I feel as if I ought to be afraid but I'm not." Clearly, the essence of emotional response occurs in the brain, not in the gut. On the other hand, normal emotional experience involves both an essential and, presumably, distinctive brain state together with the perception of peripheral autonomic arousal. A few of Marañon's subjects found that their initial "cold emotion" suddenly warmed up into a genuine feeling of fear or panic. Any stimulus commonly associated with fear is likely to become a conditioned stimulus for fear; the dry mouth, pounding heart, and trembling hands produced by the adrenalin injection is just such a stimulus and may have such a result. James was a superbly observant psychologist and his theory was accurate as a description of an interesting phenomenon, namely, that trembling—or any other fearful behavior—can actually precipitate a genuine emotion. That is why it is adaptive to simulate self-confidence or assertiveness when fear threatens. By avoiding the expressive behavior one normally shows when afraid, one can often stave off fear itself. Similarly, in a study of the effects of high spinal cord injuries on emotional reactions, Hohmann[13] found that these patients systematically reported a diminution in the frequency or intensity of feelings of both fear and anger. Sexual feelings were also attenuated but experiences of sentiment were increased. Presumably, for some emotions, the perception of peripheral arousal plays such an important role that, when visceral sensation is cut off by injury and the normal brain-gut-brain reverberations are thus prevented, that aspect of emotional experience is reduced. But even persons with high cervical injuries, deprived of all sensation lower than the neck, *can* experience fear and rage and the whole spectrum of emotions. Emotional feeling derives from the excitation of presently unspecifiable centers or networks in the brain; bodily reactions play an ancillary, facilitating role.

If we could identify these hypothetical emotion centers in the brain, and if we were able somehow to monitor the ebb and flow of their activity, then we might indeed be able to determine just how Fisbee is feeling, whether Fisbee wanted us to know or not. Brain centers which play important roles in the emotional apparatus have been identified, and neuropsychologists have been able to produce intense emotional reactions in experimental animals, or to inhibit normal emotional responses, by electrical stimulation in these areas. But the microscopic neural circuits involved in these mechanisms are a thousand times more complex than present techniques can manipulate or present understanding comprehend. The situation can be illustrated in the following way: Assemble the finest team of neuropsychologists in the best-equipped laboratory. Provide them a human subject willing to have his skullcap removed and any number of electrodes inserted directly in his brain. While the subject's attention is engrossed by an emotionally evocative film, let any number and variety of measurements be taken of the electrical and chemical activity of his brain, analyzed however extensively in the most powerful computer. Those scientists still will have no firm idea whether the film has made the subject sad or contented, frightened or angry, guilty or proud.

If we must leave the subject's skullcap on and measure only his peripheral bodily reactions, interpretation will be hopelessly uncertain. Probably there are distinctive processes in one's brain when one is angry or frightened or, perhaps, guilty; we simply do not know what these processes are or how to measure them. At the periphery, however, all the evidence indicates that different reactions may accompany the same emotion in different people or even in the same person on different occasions. The only aspect of the psychological state that we can measure with any confidence from bodily reactions is unspecified arousal. We may be able to say with some assurance from the polygraph record that this subject was more aroused by Stimulus A than he was by Stimulus B. But we cannot identify the *quality* of that arousal, whether Stimulus A made him angry or scared or filled with proud delight. Exotic new techniques like Positron Tomography may someday allow us to trace emotions in the brain without the need for implanting electrodes. But peripheral responses—of muscle tension and voice changes, of heart rate and vasoconstriction, of blood pressure and respiration, of pupil size and palmar sweating, responses which the polygraph can measure—will never provide a basis for emotion detection in this qualitative sense.

We have considered the feasibility of an emotion detector because we had speculated that the feeling of guilt might be the specific lie response, which, it appears, we must be able to identify if we are to develop an actual Truth Verifier, an instrument for detecting lying. It appears that a polygraphic guilt detector is not and will not be feasible. Moreover, it is easy to see that the feeling of guilt could not constitute a specific lie response, anyway. People can and do lie without feeling guilty, some people much of the time, most people some of the time. My wife would lie and lie, for instance, to keep her sons from being drafted to fight someone else's war and never feel the slightest twinge of guilt. And, many people have had the experience of feeling guilty even when they were telling the truth, expecting not to be believed for some reason or knowing that their (true) story sounds incredible. Like a blush, the feeling of guilt can invade a susceptible person for no other reason than that he fears that it might. Perhaps it is just as well that we cannot construct a lie detector based on guilt detection since such a device would be inevitably undependable.

Current Status of the Specific Lie Response

To say that there is no peripheral, measurable specific lie response implies, as we have seen, that the instrumental lie detector of popular mythology cannot exist. But this is not to say that lie detection is impossible, and later chapters will be devoted to discussing how this is attempted and how well it works. We shall talk about guilt detection as well, not the detection of the emotion or feeling of guilt, but rather the detection of *guilty knowledge:* does the respondent know about or recognize events or faces or objects of which he claims to be ignorant, knowledge which only the guilty suspect might be expected to have?

But the phantom of the old specific lie response still lurks about, confusing laymen and professionals alike, and we should try to bury it once and for all, a stake through its heart if we can manage it. The problem is complicated by inconsistencies, both logical and semantic, in the literature of polygraphy. The control question lie test was developed precisely because no specific lie response exists. An innocent but reactive subject might respond strongly to the relevant or "Did you do it?" questions, so most modern examiners ask control questions, unrelated to the issue under investigation, to provide an index of the subject's reactivity against which to compare his response to relevant questions. Yet the *inventor* of the control question technique, John Reid, in the most recent edition of his widely used textbook on polygraphy, devotes pages of text and illustration to what he calls "deception criteria" or "typical deception responses."[14] For example, shallow breathing, heavy breathing, a speeding up or a slowing down of respiration, a "sigh of relief" after a crucial question, are all represented as being "dependable" or "very reliable" criteria of deception. *There is no objective evidence to support such claims.*

The layman will find it hard to understand how honorable men, respected in their field, can persist in making claims, wholly unverified by systematic, controlled study, which almost certainly are false. I consider this phenomenon to be neither surprising nor scandalous. An experienced examiner like Reid accumulates years of unsystematic observations, a fertile source of hypothesis and speculation. But, in the vast majority of those thousands of polygraph examinations, he will have had no way of knowing independently and with certainty whether the respondent was lying or not. If "staircase respiration" is found to be associated with a known lie on one occasion and then is observed again with nine other subjects who might have been lying (but are never proved to be), the temptation seems almost irresistable to conclude that this response pattern is a "dependable criterion of deception." The history of polygraphy is littered with similar claims, forceably asserted and honestly believed by their proponents, claims that have since been proven to be wrong. Vittorio Benussi claimed to have demonstrated in 1914 that lying was reliably accompanied by a change in the ratio of expiration to inspiration but no one has taken Benussi's ratios seriously for years. Father W. G. Summers asserted in 1937 that if the "Did you do it?" question is repeated several times, the electrodermal response produced by each question will increase if the subject is lying but will decrease if he is being truthful. Summers reported 100% accuracy in detecting deception with this method on a series of criminal cases. Father Summers was chairman of the psychology department at Fordham University, not only a man of high integrity but a trained scientist. And yet few modern polygraphers have even heard of Summers' criterion or his Pathometer. W. M. Marston reported in 1915 that lying produces an increase in systolic blood pressure, and 23 years later he described experiments seeming to corroborate these claims with accuracies of 97% to 99%. Ominously, in one of these experiments, Marston also tested both Benussi's and Summers' claims and rejected them. Subsequent studies by others similarly have refuted all three claimants.

Marston himself remarked in 1938, that "some of the most amusing lies on record have been told in connection with the Lie Detector itself." I would substitute "untruths" for "lies." It seems most unlikely that all or any of these competing claims, including Marston's own, involved deliberate deception. They were the product instead of overenthusiasm, a lack of adequate criteria, and generally inadequate measurement techniques. Consider just one example. For more than 50 years polygraphers believed that they could assess blood pressure changes from the "cardio" tracing of the polygram, the tracing drawn by the pen connected to the arm cuff. Some workers in fact believed that the upper and lower margins of the tracing, respectively, changed with variations in systolic and diastolic blood pressure. In 1977, Geddes and Newberg demonstrated that the behavior of the "cardio" tracing depends entirely on whether the subject's mean blood pressure is higher or lower than the pressure to which the examiner happens to have pumped up the cuff.[15] Thus, the type of response that examiners have universally been interpreting as a blood pressure *increase* may actually be produced by a *decrease* in pressure and vice versa.

In addition to lack of independent criteria ("Was this subject really lying or not?") and inadequate measurement techniques ("Was this an increase in blood pressure or a decrease?"), mythology about alleged specific lie responses is encouraged by the sheer complexity of the polygraph recordings on which, to borrow Professor Younger's graphic phrase.[16] "the needles move as subtly as Raskolnikov's soul." Those four squiggly lines can change in so many ways that it is almost always possible to find some change or pattern which, on a particular chart or set of charts, seems to have some particular significance. In 1978, for example, Raskin and Hare reported results of a mock crime experiment in which it could be certainly established which answers were lies and which were truthful.[17] These authors were able to look for literally dozens of physiological changes which might have been associated with known lies. They do not report success with the Benussi or the Summers or the Marston stigmata but instead claim some new ones, changes involving "abdominal respiration baseline" and the amount of heart rate deceleration following the initial acceleration usually produced by a relevant question. Because of faulty statistical analysis, Raskin and Hare cannot even properly assert that their liars and truthtellers differed *on the average* with respect to these complex patterns. What their study really shows, like so many others, is that *no pattern of physiological response is unique to lying.*

I can only agree with the recent comment by R. J. Weir, Jr., a past-president of the American Polygraph Association and director of polygraph operations for "a federal agency" (a "spook" phrase that usually denotes the CIA) for many years:

I have even heard experienced examiners get mousetrapped into a discussion as to whether there is some mysterious difference between the reactions created by lies and those from strong emotions such as fear or anger. All I know is that I know of no way to make this distinction merely from the chart patterns.[18]

A polygraph examiner who asserts that a respondent "showed deception" or "gave a deception response" on a particular question is making either a misstatement or a false statement. He may be entitled to say, based on the charts, that the respondent made a larger response to this question than he did to that one, and he may proceed to draw some inference based on this difference. But the myth of the specific lie response should be laid at last, permanently, to rest.

Notes

1. Marston, W. M. *The Lie Detector Test*, New York: Richard R. Smith, 1938, pp. 32, 8.
2. Gerard, R. W. To prevent another world war: Truth detection. *Journal of Conflict Resolution*, 1961, *5*, 212–218.
3. Linehan, J. G. Lie detection pioneer profiles. *Polygraphy*, 1978, *7*, 95–100.
4. U.S. Department of Justice. *Sourcebook of Criminal Justice Statistics*, Washington, D.C.: Department of Justice, 1973.
5. Bok, S. *Lying: Moral Choice in Public and Private Life*, New York: Pantheon, 1978.
6. Alexander, F. *Psychosomatic Medicine*, New York: Norton, 1950.
7. Ax, A. F. The physiological differentiation between fear and anger in humans. *Psychosomatic Medicine*, 1953, *15*, 433–442.
8. Schachter, J. Pain, fear and anger in hypertensives and normotensives. *Psychosomatic Medicine*, 1957, *19*, 17–29.
9. Lacey, J. I. & Lacey, B. C. Verification and extension of the principle of autonomic response-stereotypy. *American Journal of Psychology*, 1958, *71*, 50–73.
10. James, W. What is emotion? *Mind*, 1884, *9*, 188–205.
11. Cannon, W. B. *Bodily Changes in Pain, Hunger, Fear and Rage*, 2nd Ed. New York: Appleton-Century-Crofts, 1929.
12. Marañon, G. Contribution à l'étude de l'action émotive de l'adréna-line. *Revue Français Endocrinologie*, 1924, *2*, 301–325.
13. Hohmann, G. W. Some effects of spinal cord lesions on experienced emotional feelings. *Psychophysiology*, 1966, *3*, 143–156.
14. Reid, J. E. & Inbau, F. E. *Truth and Deception*, 2nd Ed. Baltimore: Williams & Wilkins, 1977, pp. 61–68.
15. Geddes, L. A. & Newberg, D. C. Cuff pressure oscillations in the measurement of relative blood pressure. *Psychophysiology*, 1977, *14*, 198–202.
16. Younger, I. (Review of the first edition of Reid & Inbau's text) *Saturday Review*, December 31, 1966.
17. Raskin, D. C. & Hare, R. D. Psychopathy and detection of deception in a prison population. *Psychophysiology*, 1978, *15*, 126–136. See also my critique: Lykken, D. T. The psychopath and the lie detector. *Psychophysiology*, 1978, *15*, 137–142.
18. Weir, R. J., Jr. In defense of the relevant-irrelevant polygraph test. *Polygraph*, 1974, *3*, 119–166, p. 124.

CHAPTER

5

Evaluating The Evidence

There are three kinds of lies; lies, damn lies, and statistics.

—Disraeli

As psychologists we do not trust our memories, and have no recourse except to record our predictions at the time, allow them to accumulate, and ultimately tally them up. We do not do this because we have a scientific obsession, but simply because we know there is a difference between veridical knowledge and purported knowledge, between knowledge that brings its credentials with it and that which does not. After we tally our predictions, the question of success (hits) must be decided upon. If we remember that we are psychologists, this must be done, either by some objective criterion, or by some disinterested judge who is not aware of the predictions.

—Paul E. Meehl
Clinical and Actuarial Prediction,
1954

How dependable *is* the lie detector, then? Here is a straightforward question for which there is no simple answer. Since "dependable" is vague and the "lie detector" does not exist, I must start by rewording the question. There are several different types of polygraphic examination, each based on different assumptions; one cannot assume that all these types will have the same degree of accuracy. To provide some initial perspective, remember that the purpose of a polygraph examination is to diagnose the individual respondent as Deceptive or Truthful with greater accuracy than one could achieve without the examination. I can classify subjects as Truthful or Deceptive and be correct half the time by flipping a coin; the *chance accuracy* of this type of dichotomous classification is 50%—if 50% of the subjects are actually lying. If my subjects are all defendants who have been brought to trial on criminal charges, and if the statistics show that 80% of this group, on the average, are in fact guilty, then I could attain 80% accuracy just by classifying everyone as Deceptive. For a test to be useful, its accuracy must obviously be higher than one can achieve by chance and, usually, it should be higher than the base rate of the more frequent classification in the group tested.

Finally, we must ponder the deeper question of how accurate a lie test *ought to be* for particular applications. If one is hiring policemen or CIA operatives, then perhaps any additional clues, any improvement over chance at all might be worthwhile. These are sensitive positions in which the wrong person can do great mischief, and it may be in the public interest to use a screening procedure that reduces the number of undesirable candidates hired, even if this means excluding also a large number of perfectly acceptable people, wrongly called Deceptive by the test. But in the United Nations fantasy that we considered earlier, it would be disastrous to settle for even 90% accuracy in the Truth Verifier. If so much weight is placed on the test result that one makes less effort to seek other information or is lulled into a feeling of great confidence in the result, then one should make sure that the test result is very dependable indeed.

The Limitations of Expert Opinion

In the standard textbook of polygraphic interrogation, Reid and Inbau state, "Our actual case experiences over the years have involved the polygraph examination (either personally or under our direct supervision) of over 100,000 persons suspected or accused of criminal offenses or involved in personnel investigations initiated by their employers. On the basis of that experience, we are confident that the technique, when properly applied by a trained, competent examiner, is very accurate in its indications. The percentage of known errors with the technique used in the laboratories of John E. Reid and Associates is less than 1 percent."[1] Another highly regarded polygraphist of wide experience, R. O. Arther, similarly claims an accuracy of 99%.[2] Fifty years ago, the then-chairman of the psychology department at Fordham University, the Reverend Walter G. Summers, S.J., claimed 100% accuracy on more than 200 criminal cases.[3] Testifying before a committee of the Minnesota State Legislature in 1975, a polygraphist from Texas stated that he had given more than 20,000 lie tests in his career and had "never been shown to have made a mistake."

These are not selected examples; nearly every experienced polygraphic examiner who has recorded an opinion about the accuracy of tests he has himself administered has chosen an estimate in this range, where 95% is "conservative" and 99% is perhaps typical. And these are honorable men; it would be absurd to accuse all these people of venal misrepresentation. In many seemingly parallel situations, both in the courtroom and in everyday life, the opinions of such experts, based on their long experience, are taken very seriously. In an Iowa courtroom in 1967, an experienced polygrapher from the Reid firm testified that the defendant had been deceptive when he denied his guilt. This examiner then proceeded to explain to the jury that the methods he employed had been shown to be accurate more than 99% of the time and, moreover, that when a rare mistake was made, the error was in classifying a deceptive subject Truthful; almost never was a truthful subject erroneously diagnosed as Deceptive. It is no surprise, therefore, that the jury found this defendant to be guilty as charged of murder in the first degree.

One must realize, first, that someone who has devoted a career to lie detection, who has given thousands of tests the results of which have seriously affected for good or ill the lives of many people, must inevitably be strongly motivated to believe that these tests have been accurate. An experienced polygraphist would be less than human if he were not quicker to perceive positive than negative evidence of the value of his work. Secondly, the utility of polygraph testing does not depend solely on the accuracy of the lie test. The polygraph examination acts as a powerful inducer of admissions or confessions and, because of the mystique of the procedure, would do so even if the polygraph were just a stage prop. An examiner who frequently is able to elicit admissions of misconduct or, in criminal cases, admissions of guilt, may therefore feel that he controls a powerful technique—and "powerful" is easily transmuted into "valid." Moreover, like everyone else, the polygrapher is more inclined to remember the good cases than the bad ones, to have a clearer recollection of those instances where his efforts solved some mystery than the ones where he remained in doubt.

These considerations are especially important because, *in the vast majority of examinations, the polygrapher never knows if he was right or wrong.* In criminal cases, many crimes are never solved, most suspects never go to trial. Sometimes a suspect will confess in the course of examination, but these cases are useful in assessing test validity only when the confession is deferred until the test has been completed and scored. When a suspect confesses in the midst of testing, no real check on test accuracy is possible and yet who can doubt that such instances are stored in the examiner's mind as "hits" for the polygraph?

Moreover, if a number of suspects are to be tested in regard to the same matter, an examiner may withhold a final judgment on any of the tests until all have been completed or until one suspect has confessed. If the 20th test results in a confession, will not the first 19 be recorded as valid negatives? This is not to suggest any duplicity on the part of the examiner; if he were to go back over those 19 charts again, he might find compelling reasons for classifying all of them as Truthful. The question is what would another examiner conclude, reading those same charts without any prior knowledge or expectation as to how many, if any, were actually truthful? Years of research documenting the [biasing] effects on human judgment of prior [hopes or] expectations tells us clearly that we cannot trust *post hoc* analyses or retrospective scoring by someone who already knows which respondents have confessed or been cleared.

The great preponderance of polygraph tests are given privately for commercial or industrial clients for employee screening. In these applications it is doubtful if an examiner discovers if his diagnosis was right or wrong in as many as one case in 100. Here, even more frequently than in criminal cases, the respondent may offer admissions of wrongdoing or prior misrepresentation, either in the pretest interview or in the course of testing. When this occurs, an examiner may record that test as a positive, having brought out some significant truth. This is perfectly reasonable from the employer-client's point of view since he will normally trust an actual admission more than the examiner's judgment that the employee was deceptive. And yet an admission tells us nothing whatever about the accuracy of the associated lie test; indeed, we may suppose that most tests are never even scored, once damaging material has been admitted.

Considering the realities of the polygraph business, it is doubtful that any professional examiner is ever able objectively to evaluate the accuracy of more than a few percent of all the tests he administers. I would be very skeptical of any polygraphist who claimed to have established "ground truth" on more than 10 percent of tests given *and scored* before the criterion information was available. How then do we account for the claims of 95% and 100% accuracy? We must attribute them to the inevitable distortion—but distortion nonetheless—that results when a true believer attempts to evaluate the soundness of his own beliefs using "noisy" and inadequate data.[4] That examiner who testified before the Minnesota Legislature said that in 20,000 cases he had never been proved to be wrong; he did not reveal whether he had ever been proved to be right. One can only assume that until someone somehow proves him wrong he will continue honestly to think that he is an infallible lie detector. One might suspect further that if that one mistake were proved, he would continue to claim, honestly but incorrectly, that his batting average was (20,000/20,001) or much better than .999. The chief polygrapher for a federal agency, a past-president of the American Polygraph Association, recently wrote, "I have never seen an authenticated case of a 'false-positive' presented yet"—that is, a truthful subject erroneously diagnosed as Deceptive. Here is a breathtaking example of what the Church might call invincible ignorance; here are eyes that will not see.

The conclusion seems inescapable that the opinion of the professional examiner as to the accuracy of the polygraph test, based on his clinical experience, however extensive, is of negligible probative value. He is in the position of the astrologer who believes in what he is doing but almost never has a chance to actually test whether his predictions are correct or not. But, like astrological predictions—or psychological test results or medical diagnoses—the accuracy of polygraph diagnoses *can* be assessed by objective, controlled scientific study. A number of such studies have been reported, ranging in quality from reasonably good to plainly worthless. Surveys of this literature have tended to ignore these wide differences in the quality and relevance of this material. Abrams, for example, tabulates a dozen such studies spanning 56 years, some using the relevant/irrelevant test and others the Lie Control Test, studies based on as few as 11 cases or as many as 157, studies using clinical evaluation and others using independent chart evaluation—and then Abrams simply averages the percent correct claimed in each study.[5] I shall try to avoid such meaningless exercise.

Lykken's Law

C. Northcote Parkinson cannot have been the first person to notice that bureacratic activity expands to fill whatever time or space has been allocated to it. But he codified this principle, now known as Parkinson's Law.[6] L. J. Peter was not the first to realize that competent people keep getting promoted until they reach the level at which their abilities are overtaxed. When succinctly stated as the Peter Principle, however—"administrators rise to the level of their incompetency"—this insight became much more generally available.[7] Although Peter and Parkinson may not have been the first explorers in their respective areas, they made the first maps and thereby performed a public service.

The territory that I should like to map is one in which people try to make evaluations or predictions based on a mixture of evidence, no piece of which is conclusive by itself. A graduate school committee deciding which student applicants should be admitted, a jury evaluating the evidence against a defendant, an employer deciding whom to hire: in all these situations people are confronted with a collection of relevant information, some of it pointing in one direction and some in the other. The task is to attach weights to each bit of evidence—How important is it? How much do I trust it?—and then to combine them in arriving at a final decision. The graduate student's application, for example, will include letters of reference, the student's essay explaining why he wants to enter the program and what he thinks his strengths are, the list of the undergraduate courses he has taken, copies of papers he has written, his grade average, and his aptitude test score. Which of these pieces of evidence will have the most weight in the final decision? Almost invariably, the students admitted will turn out to have the highest test scores and the best grade averages.

Grades of A in Beginning Volleyball or Intermediate Basket Weaving may not tell us as much about a student's potential as do grades of A or even B in Calculus, Theoretical Physics, or Microbiology. Yet the student who elects tough courses and does well in them may have to yield his place to one who achieves straight A's by taking easier courses. A B+ average from Harvard may promise more than an A average from Chickesaw State. Yet, in the press of decision making, the committee's eyes are drawn to that unblemished record. For decades, my own university department has used a high-level aptitude test, the Miller Analogies Test, in selecting graduate students. I once did a study of the way in which more than 150 of our students actually performed in graduate school, in relation to their MAT scores. There was no discernible relationship. Those scoring above the 90th percentile on the MAT were just as likely to fail or drop out as they were to be rated "outstanding." But we still use the Miller. Grade averages and aptitude test scores are so simple and unambiguous. They make it possible to rank people objectively and without argument.

Uncertainty is painful to the decision maker. Complicated evidence can only be evaluated subjectively and subjectivity leads to doubt and disagreement. One longs for some straightforward, definitive datum that will resolve the conflict and impel a conclusion. This longing not infrequently leads one to invest any simple, quantitative, or otherwise specific bit of evidence with a greater weight than it deserves, with a predictive power that it does not really possess. In decision making, the objective dominates the subjective, the simple squeezes out the complicated, the quantitative gets more weight than the nonmetrical, dichotomous (yes/no, pass/fail) evidence supersedes the many-valued. This is Lykken's Law.

One reason why the lie detector has become so important in American decision making can be understood in terms of this principle. However subjective the process may be of arriving at a lie test diagnosis, the diagnosis itself is objective from the point of view of the employer or the jury; the job applicant or the defendant either passed or failed. Nothing could be simpler than that. This policeman may have a spotless record; he may have gone out of his way to return money that accidentally came into his possession and that he could have kept. But he flunked the lie detector test and so we conclude that he accepted a bribe to smuggle a weapon into the jail. This store manager is known in the community as a devout family man who lives modestly with no sign of affluence. But he failed the lie test so we believe that he has been stealing thousands from the store. This rape victim relates a harrowing account of being threatened, abused, and violated. But she could not pass the lie test, so we conclude the sex act was consensual and refuse to prosecute the man that she accuses. The results of a polygraph examination are almost always simple and specific. But we must not confuse simplicity with validity. The lie test diagnosis may be unambiguous; the important question is whether it is correct.

Reliability versus Validity

The layman is inclined to use the terms "validity" and "reliability" interchangeably when referring to the accuracy of a test. But there are two aspects to test accuracy which it is important to distinguish and for which it is useful to have separate labels. In standard psychometric parlance, the *reliability* of a test is the consistency with which the test measures whatever it is that it measures. The *validity* of a test, on the other hand, is the extent to which the test measures that which it is claimed to measure. A test can be highly reliable but have low validity; on the other hand, a test with low reliability cannot have high validity.

Reliability

Many psychological tests, IQ tests for example, are intended to measure the amount of some trait possessed by the respondent. Tests used in polygraphic interrogation, however, are usually designed to classify respondents into one of two categories, deceptive versus truthful, or guilty versus innocent. The reliability of a lie test—the consistency with which it classifies people—might be estimated by having the same group of respondents tested twice, by two different examiners. If the test were perfectly reliable, the two examiners' decisions should agree 100% of the time. If the reliability of the test were zero, then the percent of agreement will not be zero but, rather, about 50%. For example, suppose the "test" used by each of the examiners was just the flip of a coin; heads you're truthful, tails you're lying. Such a "test" would have no reliability at all; how you were classified the second time around would have no relationship to whether you passed or failed on the first testing. This situation is illustrated in Table 5-1. We would expect each examiner (each "testing") to classify half the people as Deceptive and half as Truthful. But only 50% of the people called Deceptive on the first test would be expected to be called Deceptive on the second test also. The total agreement expected between the two examiners is obtained by adding the upper-left and lower-right cells in the table, the number of persons called Deceptive by both tests, plus the number called Truthful by both. For this case of a wholly unreliable test, the expected rate of total agreement is 50%.

TABLE 5-1 A hypothetical reliability study using a wholly unreliable test, such as a coin flip, to classify people as Deceptive or Truthful. It is assumed that Examiner A "tests" the 100 subjects first, then Examiner B tests them again. The total agreement between the two "tests" will be 50% (on the average).

	EXAMINER B		
EXAMINER A	*Deceptive*	*Truthful*	*Total*
Deceptive	25	25	50
Truthful	25	25	50
Total	50	50	100

But this chance level of agreement may differ from 50% if the two examiners "fail" more or less than half the group. Suppose Examiner A thinks that about 90% of the suspects are probably guilty, so he simply passes every tenth person he tests and fails all the rest. And suppose Examiner B, slightly less cynical, passes every fifth person tested, thus failing 80% compared to 90% for A. If B tests the people in a different sequence than does A, then we can say again that these "tests" have a reliability of zero. Nevertheless, these two (wholly imaginary!) examiners, just by summarily flunking 80% or 90% of all people they test, choosing their victims arbitrarily, would nonetheless agree on *74%* of their scorings! This result is illustrated in Table 5-2, which assumes that 100 people are tested altogether, first by Examiner A who fails 90 of them at random, and then by B who fails 80, also at random. Then, of the 90 people failed by A, we would expect B to fail 80%, or 72 people. Of the 10 people called Truthful by A, B should call 8 Deceptive and 2 Truthful. Hence, A and B should agree on 72 + 2, or 74 of the 100 cases, just by chance alone.

TABLE 5-2. Expected results of a "reliability study" in which Examiner A randomly calls 90% of a group of 100 subjects Deceptive and Examiner B randomly calls 80% of the same group Deceptive also.

| | EXAMINER B | | |
EXAMINER A	Truthful	Deceptive	Total
Truthful	2	8	10
Deceptive	18	72	90
Total	20	80	100

What this all means is that *the total percent of agreement is a poor way of assessing the reliability of a polygraph test.* It is also a poor way of measuring the validity of this type of test, as we shall see later. The correct way to find the test reliability from data like those in Table 5-1 or 5-2 is as follows: (1) Find A's percent agreement with B on those cases B called Truthful; in Table 5-2 this would be 100(2/20), or 10%. (2) Find A's agreement with B on those cases called Deceptive by B; in Table 5-2, this would be 100(72/80), or 90%. (3) Average these two percentages; in Table 5-2, this would give (10 + 90)/2, or 50% agreement.

With this method, we shall always be able to say that 50% agreement represents chance expectation or zero reliability. Perfect reliability, of course, will always be indicated by 100% agreement. The reliability of actual tests will fall between 50% and 100%. The method works even in extreme cases like the one illustrated in Table 5-3. Here, two examiners both test 100 residents of a dormitory to discover which one is guilty of having stolen some money. Under such circumstances, each examiner will naturally expect to find only one culprit, and for the sake of this illustration, we shall assume that Examiner B identifies a different culprit than Examiner A chooses. Notice that in this case, even though the two examiners completely disagree about who the guilty party was, their total agreement, figured in the usual way, would be 98 + 0, or 98%! Calculated in the correct manner, however, their agreement (the test reliability) is 49.9%, close enough to 50% for our purposes.

The examples so far have been chosen to show what the data might look like with totally unreliable tests and should not be taken to suggest that real polygraph tests behave in this manner. To redress

TABLE 5-3. Examiners A and B each identify a different one of the 100 residents of a dormitory as the possible thief.

	EXAMINER B		
EXAMINER A	*Truthful*	*Deceptive*	*Total*
Truthful	98	1	99
Deceptive	1	0	1
Total	99	1	100

NOTE: Total agreement is 98%, but the corrected average agreement is obtained by averaging 98.99%, the agreement on the cases B called Truthful, with 0%, the agreement on the cases B called Deceptive, getting 49.99%, which indicates a reliability of zero. (Fictitious data.)

this balance, some actual lie test reliability data are given in Table 5-4 showing 85% agreement, very high reliability indeed.

TABLE 5-4. Actual lie test reliability data, calculated from data reported by Horvath on 112 criminal suspects whose charts were read independently by 10 examiners.[8]

	EXAMINER B		
EXAMINER A	*Truthful*	*Deceptive*	*Total*
Truthful	36	8	44
Deceptive	8	60	68
Total	44	68	112
Percent Agreement	82	88	85

NOTE: Data shown represent the average of all possible pairings of the 10 independent examiners.

Global Scoring versus Independent Chart Evaluation

If two examiners each test the same subjects and achieve a high degree of agreement (reliability), this might mean only that they agreed in their clinical impressions of the subjects, or in their judgments about the case facts, rather than in their scoring of the polygraph charts. Two bigoted examiners, for example, might achieve high reliability merely by agreeing in their tendency to classify one racial group as Deceptive and another as Truthful. If we want to assess the reliability of the polygraphic lie test by itself, uninfluenced by clinical impressions and the like, then we have to make sure that the test results are based solely on the polygraph charts. This in turn can be done only by having the charts scored independently by polygraphers who did not administer the tests in question and who are "blind" with respect to all knowledge of the subjects except for whatever information they can glean from the polygrams.

Therefore, the best way to assess the reliability (or the validity) of any form of lie test is to administer the test to each respondent only once and then to have a representative group of polygraphers independently score each set of charts. We would calculate the average reliability for the group by computing the agreement between each possible pair of polygraphers and then averaging all of these pairwise values.

Validity

While the reliability of a lie test is measured by the agreement between repeated tests, or between independent scorings of the same tests, the *validity* of a lie test is measured by the agreement between the results of the test, on the one hand, and "ground truth" —which respondents were in fact lying and which truthful—on the other hand. Therefore, to assess the validity of any form of polygraph test, it is necessary to obtain a *criterion measure* against which to compare the test results. The criterion is easily obtained in a laboratory experiment where one can decide in advance which subjects will lie and which will tell the truth on the test. In field situations, for obvious reasons, it is usually much harder to obtain dependable criterion measures and one may have to make do with a criterion that is less than perfect. In a series of criminal cases, for example, we might say that those subjects who are ultimately found guilty by a court must have been lying during the earlier polygraph test, while those who are exonerated by a "not guilty" verdict or by the conviction of another person might be said to have been truthful when earlier tested. But judicial decisions are wrong at least some of the time and, thus, must be regarded as an imperfect criterion. The strict rules of evidence observed by our courts sometimes allow a manifestly guilty defendant to escape conviction. Therefore, a possible improvement over using formal adjudication as a criterion is to use instead the consensus of a panel of legal experts who review the case facts and,

uninhibited by the limitations on admissibility which must constrain
the courts, decide whether a criminal suspect was probably innocent
or guilty or whether the facts are insufficient to permit a judgment
to be made.

A study published in 1969 by P. Bersh used this latter approach.[9]
Four experienced trial lawyers evaluated the completed case files on
323 suspects, all Army personnel who had earlier been given a Clinical Lie Test as part of the standard investigative procedure used by
the Army Criminal Investigation Division. (The Army C.I.D. has
since converted to the Backster type of Polygraphic Lie Test using
numerical scoring.) Told to disregard legal technicalities, the four
lawyers independently rated each suspect as Guilty, Innocent or,
when they felt the file data insufficient to support a confident decision, as Inconclusive. The opinion of a majority of this panel thus
provided a criterion against which the prior opinion of the polygrapher could be compared. We shall return to the Bersh study in
Chapter 6.

Finally, confessions can be used as a criterion. Suspects who have
been tested may subsequently confess their guilt, showing that they
had lied on the test, while others may subsequently be cleared by the
confession of another person. Although probably the best criterion
we have for field studies of polygraph validity, even confessions fall
short of the ideal. On rare occasions people do confess to crimes they
did not commit (see Chapter 17.) More importantly, perhaps, suspects who eventually confess are unlikely to be representative of
deceptive suspects in general. Some guilty persons confess because
the stress of continued denial is more than they can bear; such "bad
liars" may be especially easy to detect during the lie test. Moreover,
confessions are often precipitated by the polygraph examination itself (see Chapter 17.) A failed lie test stimulates more determined
interrogation and the knowledge that he has failed the test helps
persuade the guilty suspect to abandon further efforts to deceive.
This means that studies using confession as the criterion are less
likely to include that type of guilty suspect who produces a false-
negative lie test—having "beaten" the lie test, such suspects are less
likely ultimately to confess. Such studies, therefore, will tend to be
biased in the direction of showing inflated validities for the criterion-
guilty group.

In spite of these difficulties, a reasonably trustworthy criterion
must be obtained if we are to estimate the validity of any form of
polygraph test; and it is essential that the accuracy of so important

a decision-making procedure be established empirically. For many years, the validity of the lie test has been largely assumed: "If he is so disturbed by the question, then he must be lying." More recently, common-sense arguments have been vigorously advanced against the lie detector: "You would be disturbed by these accusatory questions, too, if you were the innocent accused." Implausible assumptions do sometimes turn out to be correct, while plausible arguments are sometimes wrong. The final answer must be empirical. In a properly conducted validity study, using an acceptable criterion of "ground truth," in what proportion of cases does the given form of polygraph test agree with the criterion?

Percentage agreement with the criterion is not an adequate measure of test validity, however, since even a totally invalid test might agree with the criterion in a high proportion of cases. This important point is illustrated in Table 5-5, which is based on the following imaginary circumstances: Suppose that International Mass Merchandising Corp. employs the firm of Diogenes, Inc. to administer polygraph tests to all of IMMC's employees. However, IMMC plans to check the accuracy of the polygraph screening before signing a long-term contract. Toward this end, it arranges that the first 100 persons tested shall be trusted employees, of whom 90 are instructed to be truthful while 10 are told to lie during the test. Diogenes, we shall pretend, is a new firm, its examiners have not been properly trained, and its only polygraph is second-hand and defective. Being incapable of conducting valid lie tests, Mr. Diogenes instructs his examiners as follows: "Just go through the motions of giving a real test and flunk every tenth employee. We can assume that 90% of IMMC's people are honest, so if we flunk 10% we should be about right." (Needless to say, no such firm as Diogenes, Inc. exists, so far as I know, and no self-respecting polygraph examiner would countenance any such behavior.) As shown in Table 5-5, under the peculiar circumstances hypothesized, the dishonest and wholly invalid "tests" given by Diogenes, Inc. would none the less agree with the criterion 82% of the time! By passing 90% of the respondents at random, Diogenes would be likely to pass 81 of the 90 truthful employees. By failing 10% at random, 1 of the 10 planted liars would be expected to be "identified."

The problem illustrated by this example is similar to the one we considered in searching for a method of expressing lie test reliability. The solution is similar also. Instead of using total agreement between test and criterion, which may be influenced by factors unrelated to

TABLE 5-5. Hypothetical example illustrating how a wholly invalid test might produce as high as $(81 + 1) = 82\%$ agreement with the criterion in a validity study.

	CRITERION		
RANDOM "LIE TEST"	*Truthful*	*Deceptive*	*Total*
Truthful	81	9	90
Deceptive	9	1	10
Total	90	10	100

test accuracy, we simply compute the test's performance with the criterion-truthful and the criterion-deceptive subjects separately and then average these two percentages. For the fictitious data in Table 5-5, the random "lie test" achieved an apparent accuracy of 90% on the criterion-truthful subjects but was correct on only 10% of the criterion-deceptive respondents; these two numbers yield a mean accuracy of 50%, which, as the example illustrates, is the accuracy expected on the basis of chance alone.

For a more realistic example, let us consider data from a validity study by Drs. G. Barland and D. Raskin, reported in 1977 to the Law Enforcement Assistance Administration. These data are shown in Table 5-6.[10] (The Barland and Raskin study is an important one and will be considered more fully later in this book.) For convenience, the data have been expressed as percentages to facilitate comparison with Table 5-5. Notice that the total agreement between lie test and criterion is equal to $(76 + 10)$, or 86%, but this does not tell us the validity of the lie test used. It happened in this set of data that most (78%) of the persons tested (by Barland) were criterion-guilty. It also happened that Raskin scored most (88%) of the polygraph charts as indicating deception. Therefore, the test would have classified 71% of the subjects correctly by random allocation of the 88 "fails" and 12 "passes." To get a realistic assessment of the test validity, we must consider its accuracy on the Guilty and Innocent subjects separately. On the criterion-guilties, the lie test accomplished 97% correct classification; on the criterion-innocents, it was correct only 45% of the time; the true validity, therefore, is $(97 + 45)/2$, or 71%, where an agreement of 50% would indicate chance accuracy.

TABLE 5-6. Validity data from Barland and Raskin. Cases have been omitted for which either the lie test or the criterion judgment was inconclusive. The actual number of cases (grand total) was 51; the figures above have been converted to percentages for easier comparison with Table 5-5.

		CRITERION	
DIAGNOSIS LIE TEST	*Guilty*	*Innocent*	*Total*
Deceptive	76	12	88
Truthful	2	10	12
Total	78	22	100
Percent Agreement	97	45	71

The Single-Culprit Paradigm. A fairly common application of the polygraph is the situation in which a crime has been committed and numerous individuals are potential suspects, of whom only one is plausibly guilty. In such instances, the examiner will be most reluctant to classify more than one subject as Deceptive. Thus, for example, investigating a theft in a dormitory with 81 residents, psychologists Bitterman and Marcuse found in 1947 that 7 residents produced apparently Deceptive records on the first testing using the relevant-irrelevant format.[11] After from one to five retests, all 7 gave apparently Truthful records, so these investigators were led to conclude that none of the 81 residents were guilty of theft. If only 1 of the 81 persons tested had produced a Deceptive result on the first testing, one supposes that there would have been less insistence on repeated retesting.

These single-culprit situations, while not without interest, are especially susceptible to misinterpretation. One real-life example is illustrated in Table 5-7. In 1975, a supermarket in a South Carolina town experienced extensive losses. The parent company sent a team of two commercial polygraphers to test each of the store's 52 employees. As a result of this testing, the assistant store manager was identified as being responsible for the losses and he was discharged. The company subsequently published an apology, acknowledging the lack of any evidence of this man's misconduct, so we can reasonably assume that the lie test that identified him as Deceptive was inaccurate. Assuming that the cited losses were real, it is reasonable to suppose that some other employee was responsible; if so, we might conclude that one of the other lie tests, which classified the true culprit as Truthful, was also in error. This result is illustrated in Table 5-7, where we can see that even though the lie test wrongly stigmatized an innocent person *and* failed to identify the actual thief, the total accuracy of the procedure could nonetheless be evaluated as 48/50, or 96%! Correctly evaluated, however, as the average of 98% accuracy on the Innocent respondents and 0% accuracy on the Guilty, we obtain a chance accuracy figure of 49%. This same example illustrates one weakness of the method advocated for computing average accuracies as estimates of true validity. If we assume that all 52 of these employees were in fact innocent of wrong-doing, then there would have been no criterion-deceptive cases on which to base an average accuracy. As is generally true of statistical procedures, no rule is foolproof.

TABLE 5-7. Fifty-two supermarket employees are interrogated, one wrongly diagnosed as Deceptive. It is assumed that another employee, classified as Truthful, was actually guilty. Although total agreement equals 96%, the mean accuracy on Truthful and Deceptive subjects considered separately equals (98 + 0)/2 or 49%.

	CRITERION*		
DIAGNOSIS LIE TEST	*Truthful*	*Deceptive*	*Total*
Truthful	50	1	51
Deceptive	1	0	1
Total	51	1	52
Percent Agreement	98	0	49

*The inclusion of one false-negative is merely an assumption; none—or several—of the persons classified as truthful may have been deceptive.

Relation of Validity to Reliability. Since a test's reliability is the consistency with which it measures, then the extent to which a test measures what it *claims* to measure—its validity—must be limited by the test's reliability. Specifically, for dichotomous classification tests like the polygraph lie test, the maximum possible validity—average agreement with the criterion—is equal to the square-root of the reliability, measured as the average agreement between retests or between scorers. This relationship is illustrated for various reliabilities in Table 5-8.

TABLE 5-8. Unreliability limits the possible validity of a polygraph test.

Interscorer Reliability*	50	60	70	80	90	100
Range of Possible Validity†	50–71	50–77	50–84	50–89	50–95	50–100

*Expressed as percent agreement between independent scorers.
†Expressed as percent agreement between test result and "ground truth."
NOTE: For each reliability value from the chance level (50) to perfect consistency between examiners (100), the validity of the test might range from chance expectancy (50) to the maximum value indicated in the table.

The Burden of Proof

It is widely agreed that the best objective psychological test for differentiating among psychiatric disorders is the Minnesota Multiphasic Personality Inventory or MMPI. One of the most serious psychiatric disorders is schizophrenia. In the acute form of this illness, an untreated patient may closely resemble the layman's stereotype of someone who is deranged or crazy. If we administer the MMPI to 100 schizophrenic patients and to 100 random citizens off the street, then ask an expert psychologist to tell us which MMPI profiles had been produced by the patients and which by the healthy people, he will be correct about 80% of the time. If I now announce to my scientific colleagues that I have invented a new test that can identify schizophrenia with 90% or 95% accuracy, my colleagues will be interested—but skeptical. I would be expected to support my assertions with experimental evidence and that evidence would be very critically examined. Even if my proofs withstood such scrutiny, many would reserve judgment until an independent investigator had confirmed my findings. All this skepticism about a claim that my new test can distinguish "crazy people" from normal ones! The tools of the psychologist are not precision instruments; really high accuracy is seldom achieved. Skepticism is appropriate.

Nevertheless, when the polygrapher announces that his psychological test can separate liars from the truthful with a validity of 90%, or 95%, or even 99%, the typical reaction is a kind of marveling acceptance. The critic who questions these claims is greeted with surprise and skepticism. Nearly every American has heard of the lie detector; without really knowing what is involved, many assume that it is nearly infallible. So deeply ingrained is this mystique that, gradually over the past 50 years, the burden of proof has somehow shifted to the critic. No doubt it is assumed that the validity of the lie detector must have been proved long ago and that any critic should be prepared to dismantle a sturdy edifice of evidence. As we shall see, however, the first study of lie test accuracy worthy of serious scientific attention did not appear until 1969. The two investigations I consider to be the most informative were not yet in print in 1975. During the first 50 years of its history, proponents of the lie test never acknowledged the burden of proof. This dereliction is hardly unique, of course. During that same period, drug manufacturers were touting nostrums of all kinds without offering scientifically adequate evidence that these medicines were effective or safe.

But times have changed. The age of the consumer is at hand. The individual consumer cannot reasonably be expected to evaluate for himself all of the complicated products and services in the marketplace. Through agencies of government, we are beginning to enforce honesty in advertising, to require manufacturers to accept responsibility for proving that their claims should be believed. The individual citizen, be he criminal suspect, job applicant, juror, or employer, cannot be expected to personally evaluate claims made about the lie detector test. The use of the lie test now is so widespread and its ramifications so important that the burden of assaying the validity of these tests is a heavy one. As we shall see, the existing evidence is scant; some of it is worthless; none of it is conclusive. If there were no evidence at all, how then should we proceed? Should we continue to decide increasing numbers of important matters on the basis of the lie test until some critic has undertaken to demonstrate that the claims of very high validity are wrong? I would argue instead that the burden of proof belongs on the shoulders of the lie detector industry.

Do not ask, then, whether I can prove that the lie detector has only modest accuracy, or that it is especially undependable in detecting truthful responding. Ask rather whether the polygraphers have provided convincing evidence that the lie detector is correct at least 90 times for every 100 people tested.

Notes

1.   Reid, J. E. & Inbau, F. E. *Truth and Deception,* 2nd Ed. Baltimore: Williams & Wilkins, 1977, p. 304.

2.   Arther, R. O. *The Scientific Investigator,* Springfield, Ill.: Charles C. Thomas, 1965.

3.   Summers, W. G. Science can get the confession. *Fordham Law Review,* 1939, *8,* 334–354.

4.   If an experienced examiner had verified, say, 10% of his cases, and if these 10% were strictly representative of all his cases, then the accuracy obtained on this sample might reasonably be generalized to all his cases. But the verified sample is never a random or representative subset of the total, and this is not the way in which these high estimates are arrived at. In Inbau and Reid's first text on lie detection, for example (*Lie Detection and Criminal Interrogation,* 1953), the error rate was computed by dividing the number of known errors by the entire number of tests administered (not just the verified ones), yielding the astonishing claim of only .07% errors (actually reported as .0007% due to a failure to convert from decimals to percentages). The more recent text does not show how the calculation was done and gives only the results.

5.   Abrams, S. *A Polygraph Handbook for Attorneys,* Lexington, Mass.: Lexington Books, 1977.

6.   Parkinson, C. N. *Parkinson's Law and Other Studies in Administration,* Boston: Houghton Mifflin, 1957.

7.   Peter, L. J. *The Peter Principle.* N.Y.: W. Morrow, 1969.

8.   Horvath, F. S. The effect of selected variables on interpretation of polygraph records. *Journal of Applied Psychology,* 1977, *62,* 127–136.

9.   Bersh, P. J. A validation study of polygraph examiner judgements. *Journal of Applied Psychology,* 1969, *53,* 399–403.

10. Barland, G. & Raskin, D. *Validity and reliability of polygraph examinations of criminal suspects.* (Report No. 76–1, Contract 75–NI–99–0001, U. S. Department of Justice, 1976.)

11. Bitterman, M. E. & Marcuse, F. L. Cardiovascular responses of innocent persons to criminal investigations. *American Journal of Psychology,* 1947, *60,* 407–412.

LIE DETECTION: THE METHODS

What we, the American people, are witnessing is the beginning of the end of mankind's search for an honest witness. For the first time in the history of civilization, mankind has the opportunity to prove beyond any reasonable doubt the veracity of his testimony through a generally accepted and scientific (*sic*) valid examination of his own psyche. God gave us the polygraph.

—Michael B. Lynch, in *Polygraph,*
The Journal of the American
Polygraph Association, 1975

These eight chapters are devoted to a critical evaluation of the various methods that are commonly used for purposes of lie detection. Many polygraphers believe that the examiner is the real "lie detector" and that polygraphers can be trained to be expert practical psychologists able to spot the "symptoms" of deception more skillfully and accurately than the rest of us can. Polygraphers of this persuasion use the polygraph recordings in reaching their diagnosis, but only as an adjunct. They think of themselves rather like experienced medical diagnosticians who rely heavily on the look and feel and history of the actual patient in reaching their conclusions. Chapter 6 considers the logic of this approach and the evidence concerning how well it seems to work.

Some of the more recently trained polygraphers, in contrast, try to focus on the polygraph recordings exclusively. They do not pretend to be especially perceptive in evaluating people nor do they claim that the polygraph itself can detect lying. They contend instead that the polygraph charts provide evidence from which an expert can reliably infer whether the subject was being truthful or deceptive. However, the polygraph recordings will be informative only if the subject has been asked the right questions in the right sequence and after he has been psychologically prepared in the right way. Polygraphers use at least six different question formats in lie detection; which one is used with a particular subject will depend on the examiner's training and on the problem at hand. Each of these six types of polygraphic lie test has a chapter of its own in Part II; these chapters are all short, except for Chapter 8, which discusses the only lie test for which adequate validity data are available.

Whichever question format is employed, we are dealing with a *polygraphic lie test* only if the results of the examination are determined entirely by the polygraph recordings, so that a second polygrapher, seeing only the charts, would arrive at the same conclusion. If other information is allowed to influence the results, if the examiner is the "lie detector" (Chapter 6), then we are dealing with a *clinical lie test,* no matter which of the six question formats has been used. When the examination is evaluated subjectively in this manner, we cannot tell what role the actual polygraph results played in the outcome; we cannot then speak of the validity of the polygraph test but rather only of the validity of that particular examiner.

The current vogue in lie detection circles is for a relatively new technique that is said to be able to assess "stress"—and from these assessments, to infer deception—in the *voice* of the subject. These

"voice stress analyzers" can be used in place of—or together with—
the conventional polygraph in any of the various interrogation
modes. The curious and, I think, scandalous story of the voice stress
analyzers is told in Chapter 13.

6

The Clinical Lie Test: The Examiner As "Lie Detector"

When the eyes say one thing, and the tongue another, a practical man relies on the language of the first.

—Emerson

I do not distinguish by the eye but by the mind, which is the proper judge of man.

—Seneca

"Sure, a lie's a lie," said Mr. Hennessy. "I always know whin I'm lyin'."
"So do I," said Mr. Dooley.

—F. P. Dunne

Mary St. Claire was killed during a drunken party in the woods, a party shared with Mary's stepdaughter, Charlene, and with John Fontaine. Death was caused by the blow of an axe which nearly severed the head from the body. John was arrested the next day and for weeks he stood mute, refusing to explain what had happened. At last he instructed his attorney to enter a plea of guilty to second-degree murder, although the account he then gave of the incident specified that Charlene had struck the fatal blow. "Charlene has a family and a job and I don't, so it is better if I take the blame." His attorney was reluctant to plead his client guilty if he was truly innocent and so he came to me for help. Would I give John a lie detector test to establish who, in fact, had chopped off Mary's head?

I was careful to explain that not even the elaborate apparatus in my laboratory could actually detect lying. But I knew from the published research that untrained persons can distinguish liars from the truthful with about 70% accuracy. Since I am a clinical psychologist with considerable experience, I assumed that I could do at least that well. Moreover, I could use all the tricks of the polygraph examiner: the special interviewing tactics, the scientific stage props. If John was guilty, I might be able to get him to confess and remove the ambiguity. If he did not confess, in spite of all my efforts, then perhaps we could be more confident that his story was the truth.

The night John was brought to my laboratory by the sheriff's deputies, thousand of dollars' worth of electronic equipment was whirring and humming. I unerringly determined, seemingly from the polygraph, which card it was that John had selected from my (fixed) deck. I spent more than an hour in the pretest interview, preparing the ground. After the first charts had been run, I tightened the psychological thumbscrews:

John, I'm getting reactions here that show you aren't telling the whole truth about what happened that night. Can you think of any reason why you might be giving these reactions?

John looked bewildered and made no effort to modify his story or to explain these alleged "reactions." We ran another chart.

John, I realize that you were drunk, that you had every reason to get mad at Mary, the way she was behaving. And I know how hard it is, when you're sober, to look back at the things you did when you were drunk. But the polygraph says that you haven't told me the whole truth about this. If you want your lawyer to let you plead guilty, at least do him the favor of letting him know what really happened.

John stuck with his previous account; Mary and Charlene were fighting and he tried to break it up. Mary fell and Charlene seized the firewood axe and struck her where she lay.

I told the lawyer what I had done, that I had not managed to shake

John's story, that my clinical opinion was that he was telling me the truth. Two weeks later, back in jail, John told his attorney that he had swung the axe himself. I still do not know "ground truth" with any certainty. Had John's stoicism fooled me or was this new confession merely John's way of implementing his decision to take the blame? We are all of us "human lie detectors"; I had thought I was more skillful than most. I could still insist that my original opinion was correct, but nearly 30 years' experience as a psychologist has taught me a little humility. People are complicated; it is dangerous to be too sure of what you think you know about them.

Subjective Scoring and "Behavior Symptoms"

What I did with John Fontaine is an example of a clinical polygraph examination. I, the examiner, was the lie detector. Traditional polygraphers, like John Reid or Richard Arther, speak of the results of such an interrogation as a "diagnosis." This is an appropriate term, because the examiner is acting rather like a physician does in examining a patient, taking all sources of information into account, including clinical impressions based on his experience; he combines them according to some subjective formula and arrives at his best guess as to what is going on. I thought hard about John's story of what happened on the fatal night, about whether his account seemed consistent and plausible. I studied his behavior for more than two hours, my clinical "radar" turned full on, looking for signs that he was covering up or inventing as he went along. I applied pressure to see if he would modify his story in order to make it more convincing or to explain away the indications of deception that I pretended to see in the polygraph. I did not put much weight on the actual polygraph tracings because I did not think that they contained much useful information. A clinical polygrapher would pay more attention to the charts than I did, but even he cannot know, either in general or in a particular case, how strongly he is being influenced by the actual polygraph data, because he arrives at his diagnosis subjectively; he exposes himself to all the available information and the diagnosis simply emerges from the mysterious computer of his mind. Clinical judgments, by definition, do not employ specific rules for combining the available information. The process is partly deductive and partly oracular.

It is therefore difficult to discuss the theory underlying the subjective scoring methods of Keeler or Reid or Arther. If the principles according to which the different types of evidence are supposed to be combined had ever been clearly specified, then an "expert" would not be required. The results of an examination could be determined by a clerk following a rule book, just as a Backster-trained polygrapher can score the charts from a polygraphic lie test administered by a colleague. Perhaps we can infer the essentials of the theory from a closer study of the way a Reid-type examination is conducted. The examiner does everything he can to impress the subject with the impartiality, professionalism, and the scientific basis of the procedure. The waiting room may be hung with the examiner's diplomas and furnished with reading material attesting to the respectability and validity of polygraph methods. The examiner will behave toward the subject in a polite and professional way. The examining room is carpeted and quiet and dominated by the impressive aspect of the polygraph itself.

The subject will not be connected to this apparatus until a lengthy pretest interview has been conducted. During this interview and the polygraph test itself, the examiner will be studying his subject, observing his demeanor, his actions and appearance, his "behavior symptoms." If a secretary is available in the waiting room, she may be instructed to note how the subject comported himself while awaiting the polygrapher. A well-equipped examining room will contain a one-way mirror, disguised as a picture or (in at least one room I have visited) as a tropical fish tank set into the wall. The examination may then be interrupted at some point and the subject left to stew alone while the examiner observes him from the adjacent room.

In 1953, Reid and Arther reported the results of a five-year tabulation of "behavior symptoms," which they said discriminated between lying and truthful subjects during a polygraph examination.[1] In the last edition of the Reid and Inbau textbook, a section entitled "Symptoms of Lying" explains that the deceptive subject is reluctant to take the test and may postpone or be late for his appointment.[2] Appearing nervous, resentful, aggressive, "appearing to be in a shocked condition," exhibiting "mental blocks," having a dry mouth or a gurgling stomach, refusing eye contact, moving restlessly, appearing "overly friendly or polite," describing himself as religious, complaining of pain from the blood pressure cuff, being eager to finish the examination and leaving promptly—all these are behavior symptoms of the liar. Under "Symptoms of Truthfulness," Reid and Inbau list an eagerness to take the examination, a feeling of confidence in the test, an attitude of sincerity and straightforwardness, an appearance of composure, and behaving in a cooperative manner. To emphasize that these are diagnostic symptoms and not merely tendencies or trends, Reid and Inbau include a third list of behaviors said to be "Common to both Liars and Truthtellers" and which therefore lack the diagnostic specificity of the other two tabulations. Other examiners develop their own lists of behaviors that they think are revealing (Arther has been especially creative in this regard) and any examiner will diagnose as Deceptive a subject who he thinks is attempting to control his polygraphic reactions by moving, breathing erratically or breathing too regularly, or twitching the muscles in the arm carrying the blood pressure cuff.

Most polygraphers of the Keeler-Reid-Arther pursuasion consider the *posttest interrogation* to be an essential component of the examination. If the examiner's impressions up to that point have led him to believe that the subject is being truthful, and if this view seems to be confirmed by a lack of strong physiological reaction to the relevant questions, then the interrogation may be dispensed with. But when the polygrapher thinks that the subject is lying or may possibly be lying, then he will remove the polygraph attachments, seat himself facing the subject, knee to knee, and begin: "The polygraph shows that you are not telling the truth." Or, as in the Peter Reilly case, "Pete, I think you got a problem, I really do. . . . These charts say you hurt your mother last night." (We shall have more to say about this notorious case in Chapter 17.)

The interrogation obviously is calculated to elicit a host of additional "behavior symptoms." It is also calculated to elicit a confession. Most old-school examiners of the type we are concerned with here, "human lie detectors," are primarily interrogators and their real goal, the prize that most clearly demonstrates their skill and the potency of their technique, is a confession. And the polygraph examination from first to last is a powerful inducement to confession.

If the subject does not confess, however, then the examiner must render his decision. He considers the polygraph charts, the behavior symptoms he has noted, the case facts as he understands them, and the subject's explanations or alibi as elicited during the pretest interview and the posttest interrogation. There may be other relevant information available as well. If this is just a routine screening of a bank employee, then there will be less prior expectation of deception than if this subject was the only person known to have had access to the vault from which a sum of money has been stolen. If 20 employees had access to that vault and 19 remain to be tested, the examiner may be less inclined to render a Deceptive diagnosis than if this man appears to be the only suspect. If the case involves one person's word against another's and the other person has already been diagnosed as Truthful, then it will be harder for the examiner to classify the present subject as Truthful. Finally, of course, there are the irrelevant and even unconscious sources of bias which the examiner will strive to ignore: his own attitude toward the subject, the subject's age, sex, appearance, race, ethnic or cultural background. There are no rules for selecting, weighting, or combining these various pieces of evidence. Reid and Inbau assert in their textbook that one should not place "sole or even major reliance" on behavior symptoms, yet, testifying in a courtroom in Toronto in 1976, John Reid said that the identification of behavior symptoms "is a big part of our course, much more than running charts, they don't mean anything almost. You can put a small boy in to do that. This is unimportant.[3] Most old-school examiners would probably agree that this central question—how to weigh and combine the available information to produce a final diagnosis—is decided according to each individual polygrapher's experience and intuition.

Assumptions of the Clinical Polygraph Examination

Polygraphers have not provided an agreed-upon name for the kind of examination taught by the Keeler, Reid, and Arther schools, in which the examiner himself serves as lie detector and the polygraphic information is combined with impressions of behavior and other data in arriving at a diagnosis. But we need to distinguish this approach from the Backster method, which attempts to let objective scoring of the charts alone determine the result. Both are psychological procedures aimed at arriving at a judgment about the subject's psychological state. The Backster technique is arguably a psychological test, but the Keeler-Reid-Arther procedure is clearly not a test at all, although it is commonly referred to in this way. A psychiatrist's interview, a physician's physical examination, a jury's evaluation of a witness, a subjectively scored polygraph examination, these all can be described as clinical assessments rather than as tests. Although the theory of the *clinical polygraph examination* has never been spelled out in the literature of the field, let us examine the assumptions on which the procedure seems to rest.

ASSUMPTION 1. *The examiner will be able to convince every subject that the results of his polygraph examination are virtually certain to be accurate.*

Unless a truthful subject has real faith in the "test," he is likely to show some of the behavior symptoms attributed to lying and also to show strong polygraphic responses to the relevant questions. The procedure clearly assumes that the deceptive subject will feel stress and that the truthful subject will not; this is plausible only if all subjects genuinely believe that the "test" will reveal the truth.

Can polygraphers persuade all their subjects that the polygraph method is nearly infallible? In the United States, the examiner has 50 years of mythology working for him. I was once consulted by a young man who had failed a lie test relating to a theft: his faith was so strong that he believed the polygraph results rather than his own memory. He hurried home from the examination to search his apartment for the missing $400, thinking that he must have taken it during a "blackout" since he had no recollection of it. He came to me fearing that he was losing his mind. I have talked with another man who knew he had not stolen the money in question but who concluded that the polygraph must have detected some deeper stain on his character, that he would not have failed the test unless he was in fact "bad" in some way. The transcripts quoted in Barthel's *A Death in Canaan* dramatically illustrate how 18-year-old Peter Reilly's faith in the machine (and in fatherly Sergeant Kelly, the polygrapher) led him to believe against the evidence of his senses that he had murdered and mutilated his own mother.

The "Stim Test"

To augment this kind of faith, standard polygraph procedure involves using a stimulation procedure, or "stim test," in which the examiner pretends to be able to determine from the polygraph charts which card the respondent has chosen from a deck. Reid and Inbau explain:

The cards are arranged and shown to the subject in such a way that the examiner will immediately know which card has been picked by the subject. The reasons for this are (1) the card test record itself may not actually disclose the card "lie"; (2) the primary purpose of the card test is the "stimulation" effect that results . . . by reason of the subject's belief that his card test "lie" was detected, and obviously, unless his chosen card is correctly identified after the card test, the stimulation effect is lost completely.[4]

Oftentimes the subject's largest polygraphic response will follow the question referring to the card he actually chose, so that the examiner's guess, based on the polygraph, would be correct. A number of studies confirm this.[5] In a study using charts obtained during polygraphic interrogation of actual criminal suspects, one group of investigators were able to identify the correct card 55% of the time. Laboratory studies have reported success rates from about 30% to 73%. As Reid and Inbau point out, however, since the object of the "stim test" is to convince the subject that the polygraph can determine when he is or is not lying, being correct only half or two-thirds of the time is not good enough. Therefore, one must resort to a stacked deck.

Some polygraphers use a different procedure that they believe to be less deceptive. The subject is asked to pick a number, say, from 1 to 7. That number is then recorded on a card or paper so that both the subject and examiner can see it. As in the card test, the subject is told to reply to "No" to each question of the form, "Did you choose number X?" The subject is also told that the purpose of this procedure is to calibrate the polygraph, "so that I can determine what your polygraph responses look like when you are lying and when you are telling the truth." The ability of the procedure to inspire confidence in the subject depends upon this latter statement, which, of course, is untrue and misleading. Since there seems to be as much charlatanry in this method as in Keeler's or Reid's, it does not seem to be a real improvement. If one is going to deceive the subject, why not use the deception that is most effective?

Against those who object to these "stim tests" on ethical grounds, it can be argued that the truthful subject will be safer (more likely to "pass" the test) if he can be deceived in this way and that the deceptive subject has no inherent right to be treated truthfully by others. A more serious objection, perhaps, is that it is risky to base a widely used procedure on a kind of trick or fraud which, inevitably, some people will learn about, perhaps especially those people tuned in to the underworld grapevine over which such information is disseminated. Someone who has read this book, for example, will be less likely to be impressed by the card test and also less likely to take the control questions as seriously as the relevant questions, having learned that his or her fate may depend on *not* giving large responses to the latter. As an eminent Canadian jurist wrote after hearing testimony from both Reid and Arther on the methods they espouse,

Convincing a subject that the machine is infallible which is certainly not true and using a rigged card test for this purpose is a formula no competent scientist would accept.[6]

ASSUMPTION 2. *If all subjects have faith in the procedure, then there are certain behavior symptoms that will be shown only by truthful subjects and other, different symptoms that only deceptive subjects will manifest.*

This is the sort of claim that makes a psychologist's hair stand on end. Does it really require years of postgraduate study to realize that every "symptom" some people show when they lie, other people will sometimes display when they are being truthful? Just a few hours alertly spent at a poker table will reveal that whatever Smith does when he's bluffing, Jones may only do when he is holding a strong hand. Reid and Arther claim to have demonstrated the validity of their symptom lists in a five-year study published in 1953. Frank Horvath, one of Reid's colleagues, published a somewhat less impressionistic study in 1973 that seemed to confirm these claims, at least in part; deceptive subjects more often showed "typical liar" symptoms than did truthful subjects and *vice versa*.[7] But Horvath's data consisted of notations made by Reid examiners in the course of routine polygraph tests. Horvath acknowledges that these observations were inevitably contaminated in such a way as to tend to produce the expected findings. To take just one example, the "liar" symptom of "poor eye contact" was noted for half of the deceptive subjects but for none of the truthful ones. Classifying eye contact as "good" or "poor" involves some subjectivity. An examiner trained to regard poor eye contact as symptomatic of lying will be unlikely to classify a subject's eye contact as "poor" if he believes on other grounds that that subject is being truthful. And the examiner has many other grounds for forming such an opinion during the interview: the strength of the evidence against the subject, the subject's own story, his demeanor and other behavior. To obtain truly objective and independent estimates of how consistently "lying symptoms" indicate a deceptive subject, or what proportion of truth-tellers have good eye contact, a cooperative attitude, and are "genuinely" but not "overly" friendly, would require an elaborate and expensive experiment. One would want to videotape interviews and examinations and have different judges independently rate the various symptoms under circumstances designed to minimize the tendency for judges to see what they think are the symptoms of lying in anyone whom they have already classified as a liar. Thus, for example, quality of eye contact would be rated by judges who are shown the videotapes with the sound turned off to minimize extraneous cues. Since one would require thousands of such taped interviews to yield a sufficient number of cases subsequently confirmed, say, by confession, it is unlikely that any trained investigator would undertake such an expensive project merely to demonstrate that Reid and Arther's claims are simplistic and greatly overstated. Thus, the cited studies stand alone in the field and the only antidote available is common sense—which, it appears, is too weak a potion.

Law professor E. A. Jones, an experienced labor arbitrator, offers a more sophisticated view of the dependability of "behavior symptoms."

Anyone driven by the necessity of adjudging credibility who has listened over a number of years to sworn testimony, knows that as much truth has been uttered by shifty-eyed, perspiring, lip-licking, nail-biting, guilty-looking, ill-at-ease fidgety witnesses as have lies issued from calm, collected, imperturbable, urbane, straight-in-the-eye perjurers.[8]

Similarly, after hearing extended testimony from both Reid and Arther, the leading exponents of the clinical lie test, consider the reaction of Mr. Justice Morand:

I was amazed at the naive and dogmatic pronouncements by polygraphers concerning interpretations of behavior, many of which were founded on the assumption that a reluctant subject or an opponent of the polygraph is probably a liar. Little or no account was taken of the variations in psychological reactions which require great flexibility in assessment of individuals.[9]

I have not disproved Assumption 2; that would be an expensive and thankless undertaking. But I have tried to show that this assumption is so "naive and dogmatic" that a considerable burden of proof lies on those who would have us believe that certain behavior symptoms almost always reveal whether someone is truthful or lying. Neither the Reid and Arther study nor the later report by Horvath was properly designed so as to provide the proof required.

This is not to say that a perceptive observer cannot frequently separate the truthful sheep from the deceptive goats just be observing them during an interrogation. In a laboratory study using a mock crime situation, Kubis found that his experienced examiners could correctly classify 65% of their subjects, one-third of whom were "guilty," one-third "accomplices," and one-third "innocent," just by observing their interrogations. On a small sample of criminal suspects, Barland made diagnoses based on interview behavior that were correct 69% of the time.[10] It seems safe to assume that a perceptive observer, an experienced police detective for example, could interrogate 100 criminal suspects, half of whom are truthful, and then classify them as truthful or deceptive with about 70% accuracy. There is no evidence that a study of Reid and Inbau's lists of behavior symptoms would improve on this level of accuracy. My guess is that the opposite would happen; that what now one sees "as through a glass, darkly," one might then not see at all.

ASSUMPTION 3. *When a behavior symptom cannot be directly observed but must be inferred by the examiner (e.g., "subject is nervous" or "subject is sincere"), all examiners will be skillful enough to make correct inferences in dealing with all varieties of subjects.*

Assumption 3 requires that examiners will be able to make correct inferences about each subject's attitudes and feelings, gauging nervousness, identifying sincerity, measuring the subject's confidence, after a six-week course and a six-month apprenticeship. These are judgments that we all make frequently in ordinary life, but evidence shows that we are not nearly so accurate as we think. Studies of stage fright, for example, show that ratings by the audience of a speaker's nervousness or confidence have only the roughest sort of relationship to how the speaker really feels, as measured either by his subsequent report or by polygraph recordings made while he is speaking. Experienced psychotherapists may spend dozens of hours in intimate conversation with a patient before they can read with confidence those feelings that the patient tries to hide. If their perception sharpens after all those hours, it is because they learn the idiosyncratic meaning of the "behavior symptoms" shown by that individual patient. Assumption 3 also has to be rejected, not so much because the typical polygrapher has negligible psychological training, but because not even a psychologist could make these subtle judgments with high accuracy on the brief acquaintance provided by a polygraph examination.

ASSUMPTION 4. *Given that the subject believes that the polygraph "works," then all deceptive subjects will be more aroused by the relevant questions than by irrelevant or control questions and all truthful subjects will be equally or less aroused by the relevant or "Did you do it?" questions than by the other questions asked of them.*

Assumption 4 concerns the polygraph portion of the examination, how strongly truthful and deceptive subjects can be expected to react, physiologically, to the various types of questions asked. The plausibility of this assumption will depend upon which type of question—which test format—is to be used, and we shall consider this assumption in relation to these various formats later on. But the first three assumptions of the clinical polygraph examination are each so implausible that—at the very least—one should require strong experimental evidence before accepting claims that diagnoses based on these assumptions are 90% to 99% accurate.

Validity of the Clinical Lie Test

In view of the millions of clinical lie tests that have been administered to date, it is surprising that only one serious investigation of the validity of this method has been published, Bersh's 1969 Army study.[11] Bersh wanted to assess the average accuracy of typical Army polygraphers who routinely administered clinically evaluated lie "tests" to military personnel suspected of criminal acts. He obtained a representative sample of 323 such cases on which the original examiner had rendered a global diagnosis of Truthful or Deceptive. The completed case files were then given to a panel of experienced Army attorneys who were asked to study them unhindered by technical rules of evidence and to decide which of the suspects they believed had been guilty and which innocent. The four judges discarded 80 cases in which they felt there was insufficient evidence to permit a confident decision. On the remaining 243 cases, the panel reached unanimous agreement on 157, split three to one on another 59, and were deadlocked two to two on 27 cases. Using the panel's judgment as his criterion of "ground truth," Bersh then compared the prior judgments of the polygraphers against this criterion. When the panel was unanimous, the polygraphers' diagnosis agreed with the panel's verdict on 92% of the cases. When the panel was split three to two, the agreement fell to 75%. On the 107 cases where the panel had divided two to two or had withheld judgment, no criterion was of course available.

Bersh himself pointed out that we cannot tell what role if any the actual polygraph results played in producing this level of agreement. In another part of that same Defense Department study, polygraphers like those Bersh investigated were required to "blindly" re-score one another's polygraph charts in order to estimate polygraph reliability. The agreement was better than chance but very low. As these Army examiners then operated (they have since converted to the polygraphic lie test, which is more reliable), chart scoring was conducted so unreliably that we can be sure that Bersh's examiners *could not* have obtained much of their accuracy from the polygraphs: validity is limited by unreliability. But, although these findings are a poor advertisement for the polygraph itself, can they at least indicate the average accuracy of a trained examiner in judging the credibility of a respondent in the relatively standardized setting of a polygraph examination?

Bersh's examiners based their diagnoses in part on clinical impressions or behavior symptoms, which, we know from the evidence mentioned above, should have permitted an accuracy of about 70%. But they also had available to them at the time of testing whatever information was then present in that suspect's case file: the evidence then known against him, his own alibi, his past disciplinary record, and so on. In other words, the polygraphers based their diagnoses in part on some portion of the same case facts that the four panel judges used in reaching their criterion decision. This contamination is the chief difficulty with the Bersh study. When his judges were in unanimous agreement, it was presumably because the evidence was especially persuasive, an "open-and-shut case." It may be that much of that same convincing evidence was also available to the polygraphers, helping them to attain that 92% agreement. When the evidence was less clear-cut and the panel disagreed three-to-one among themselves, the evidence may also have been similarly less persuasive when the lie tests were administered—and so the polygrapher's agreement with the panel majority dropped to 75%. An extreme example of this contamination involves the fact that an unspecified number of the guilty suspects confessed at the time of the examination. Because the exams were clinically evaluated, we can be sure that every test which led to a confession was scored as Deceptive. Since confessions were reported to the panel, we can be sure also that the criterion judgment was always Guilty in these same cases. Thus, every lie test that produced a confession was inevitably counted as an accurate test although, of course, such cases do not predict at all whether the polygrapher would have been correct absent the confession. That the polygraph test frequently produces a confession is its most valuable characteristic to the criminal investigator but the occurrence of a confession tells us nothing about the accuracy of the test itself.

Thus, the one available study of the accuracy of the clinical lie test is seriously compromised. Because of the contamination discussed above, the agreement achieved when the criterion panel was unanimous is clearly an overestimate of how accurate such examiners could be in the typical run of cases. When the panel split three to one, then at least we know that there was no confession during the lie test or some other conclusive evidence available to both the panel and the examiner. The agreement achieved on this subgroup was 75%, not far from the previous estimates based on clinical observation alone, and as we have seen, Bersh's examiners could not have improved much on their clinical and evidentiary judgments by referring to their unreliable polygraphs.

Verdict

Although firm statistics are not available, it is safe to say that most of the million or more lie tests administered annually in the U.S. will be clinical polygraph tests. Whatever the question format may be, whether the test is for general screening purposes or deals with a particular crime or other specific issue, most lie tests are scored according to the examiner's subjective appraisal of the subject's truthfulness. In criminal cases, this appraisal will be influenced by the examiner's knowledge of the case facts; this knowledge will usually depend in part on rumor or hearsay, it will often be incomplete, and it will sometimes be inaccurate. In all cases, the examiner's appraisal will be influenced by his clinical impressions of the subject and whatever behavior symptoms he thinks he has observed; most of us can assess credibility with some accuracy in this way, but there is no reason to suppose that polygraphers, as a group, are especially skillful. In all cases, the examiner's appraisal *may* be influenced by extraneous factors: the subject's race, age, sex, or social class; whether the subject or someone else is paying for the test; by the examiner's personal stake, if any, in the outcome.

Referring to clinical lie tests of this type, Justice Morand concluded that they involve

only an assessment of credibility based on observations that jurists have been making for years, by persons who are untrained in conducting psychological examinations and who apparently accept naive and simplistic criteria of what is deceptive behavior and what is not.[12]

We may agree that some people are more gullible than others, but we should not concede that anyone, any group of self-styled professional *Menschenkenner* or polygraphers, is so especially discerning and perspicacious that we would be willing to surrender the important responsibility of credibility assessment primarily to them. Unless the result of a polygraph examination is based solely on the charts—the polygraph recordings—then the result will be influenced to an unknowable extent by the examiner's clinical impressions, evidentiary judgments, personal attitudes, and expectations. The clinical judgment of a polygraph examiner is no more valid than that of any other observer, just as subject to bias and prejudice, and probably wrong 25% of the time.

Notes

1. Reid, J. E. & Arther, R. O. Behavior symptoms of lie detector subjects. *Journal of Criminal Law and Criminology,* 1953, *44,* 104–108.
2. Reid, J. E. & Inbau, F. E. *Truth and Deception,* 2nd Ed. Baltimore: Williams & Wilkins, 1977, pp. 293–295.
3. Quoted in the report of the *Royal Commission into Metropolitan Toronto Police Practices,* 1976, Hon. Mr. Justice Donald R. Morand, Commissioner, p. 247.
4. Reid, J. E. & Inbau, F. E. *op.cit.,* p. 42, note 49.
5. Van Buskirk, D. & Marcuse, F. The nature of errors in experimental lie detection. *Journal of Experimental Psychology,* 1954, *47,* 187–190; Gustafson, L. A. & Orne, M. T. Effects of heightened motivation on the detection of deception. *Journal of Applied Psychology,* 1963, *47,* 408–411; Kugelmas, S. *et al.,* Experimental evaluation of galvanic skin response and blood pressure change indices during criminal interrogation. *Journal of Criminal Law, Criminology and Police Science,* 1968, *59,* 632–635.
6. Justice D. R. Morand, in *Royal Commission into Metropolitan Toronto Police Practices,* 1976, p. 244.
7. Horvath, F. S. Verbal and nonverbal clues to truth and deception during polygraph examinations. *Journal of Police Science and Administration,* 1973, *1,* 138–152.
8. Jones, E. A., Jr. Evidentiary concepts in labor arbitration: Some modern variations on ancient legal themes. *U.C.L.A. Law Review,* 1966, *13,* p. 1286.

9. Justice D. R. Morand, *op.cit.*, p. 245.
10. Kubis, J. *Comparison of voice analysis and polygraph as lie detection procedures.* Contract DAAD05–72–C–0217, U.S. Army Land Warfare Laboratory, Aberdeen Proving Ground, Maryland, 1973. Barland, G. *Detection of Deception in Criminal Suspects.* Doctoral dissertation, University of Utah, 1975.
11. Bersh, P. M. A validation study of polygraph examiner judgements. *Journal of Applied Psychology,* 1969, *53,* 399–403.
12. Justice D. R. Morand, *op.cit.*, p. 261.

7

The Relevant/Irrelevant (R/I) Test

When we lie, our blood pressure goes up, our heart beats faster, we breathe more quickly (and our breathing slows once the lie has been told), and changes take place in our skin moisture. A polygraph charts these reactions with pens on a moving strip of graph paper. . . . The result is jagged lines that don't convey a lot to you. But . . . an examiner can tell from those mechanical scribbles whether or not you've spoken the truth.

—Chris Gugas, polygrapher. *The Silent Witness,* 1979

The widespread and growing use of polygraphic interrogation methods is not based on public acceptance of the idea that polygraphers are better Human Lie Detectors than are judges or juries or personnel interviewers or, indeed, than people in general. Suppose that, in a criminal trial, the prosecution called to the stand Mr. Reid or Dr. Larson or Father Summers and sought to have any one of them accredited as an expert witness without benefit of the polygraph:

Your honor, Mr. Reid has many years of experience in interrogating criminal suspects. He has spent two hours interviewing this defendant. He has reviewed the case facts, heard the defendant's alibi, asked him various searching questions and closely observed his demeanor and behavior. As an expert in the diagnosis of deception, Mr. Reid is prepared to testify that, in his expert opinion, this defendant is lying when he denies his guilt in the present matter.

One does not have to be learned in the law to predict how 99 judges out of 100 would rule on this motion. Yet, there is currently a trend for trial judges in some U. S. jurisdictions to qualify polygraph examiners as expert witnesses under special circumstances. Clearly the difference has to do with the polygraph itself, this mysterious machine that draws those mystic markings on the chart paper, and with the aura of scientism and expertise that surrounds the person who can operate the machine and read the markings.

Therefore, it is necessary to consider separately the validity that can be achieved in detecting deception strictly on the basis of the polygraph charts. In the next six chapters we shall examine six of the *polygraphic lie tests* in common use, the assumptions on which they are based, and the evidence, if any, of their validity. The only way to assess the validity of a polygraphic lie test, independent of clinical impressions, is to have the polygraph charts scored by a second polygrapher who did not observe the subject and is unfamiliar with the case facts. Since polygraph charts are seldom scored this way in practice, however, it should be remembered that most lie detector "tests" are really clinical examinations, subject to the problems and limitations discussed in the previous chapter.

In addition to this requirement of "blind" scoring, validity studies must be conducted in the field, in real-life testing situations. Volunteer subjects in laboratory experiments are not under the same emotional pressure that affects criminal suspects or persons being screened for employment purposes. Deceptive subjects may be less reactive in the laboratory than when lying about real crimes at the police station. Truthful subjects will almost certainly be more reactive in the field situation and, for this reason, more likely to be misclassified by the polygraphic lie test.

Assumptions of the R/I Test

In the parlance of polygraphy, a Relevant Question is the "Did you do it?" question: Did you kill Fisbee?, Did you fire the bullet that killed Fisbee?, and so on. An Irrelevant Question, sometimes called a "norm," will be both unrelated to the matter under investigation and also nonstressful: Is today Tuesday?, Are you in Chicago now? All polygraphic lie tests also employ "control questions," but these are less easily defined. Confusingly, the Relevant/Irrelevant or R/I test, Larson's original invention and the forerunner of them all, uses "control" questions that are entirely different in function than those used in the various "control question tests" to be discussed later. In the R/I test, the control question is irrelevant but provocative: "Have you been drunk at any time during the past year?" or "Do you remember my name?" The sole purpose of these questions is to produce some sort of polygraphic response and thus prove that the subject is capable of responding under the present conditions. If the subject has responded to some of the previous questions on that same chart, the control question may be omitted.

A typical relevant/irrelevant test will consist of three relevant questions, each preceded and followed by irrelevant questions, with an evocative control question at the end of the list. The American Polygraph Association advocates the name General Series Test for this venerable technique, a label that has the disadvantage of being devoid of meaning. "Relevant/irrelevant" is a more straightforward name that served well enough for 50 years and will serve well enough here. If the subject shows a strong polygraphic reaction to some or all of the relevant questions, but not to the irrelevant questions, then his answers to the relevant questions are classified as Deceptive. Most psychologists will find it hard to credit that so simple-minded a procedure has been in constant, serious use since the 1920s. But since the R/I method is still being taught and is widely used, we must consider it seriously. The assumptions on which the R/I test is based are these:

ASSUMPTION 1. *A guilty subject whose relevant answers are lies will be more aroused by the relevant than by the irrelevant questions and this difference will be revealed by his responses on the polygraph.*

The first assumption is certainly plausible but it is important to see that it cannot be taken as certain in all cases. Some individuals may be so fearless that they are not worried about the consequences of the test or so lacking in conscience that they are not aroused by references to their crime or by the act of lying. A guilty subject may become habituated to such references as a result of prior questioning or may possess unusual emotional control with which to steel himself against reacting. One would expect most guilty suspects to show greater arousal to the relevant questions, but no psychophysiologist would expect this to happen without fail.

ASSUMPTION 2. *An innocent subject who is answering truthfully will not be disturbed by the relevant questions and will show no more reaction to them than to the irrelevant questions.*

The second assumption is wildly implausible. One has only to imagine oneself on trial, testifying in one's own defense, and the moment arrives when counsel asks the critical, "relevant" question: "Did you commit the grave crime of which you now stand indicted?" and one must face the jury, eye to eye, and answer, "No!" How would you be feeling at that moment? What would the polygraph pens be saying about your heartbeat, your breathing, and the sweating of your palms? But suppose you *are* innocent, telling the truth? Would that fact armor you with confidence so that you could reply to, "Are you guilty?" as calmly as you had previously stated your name and address? How could two generations of polygraphers have been unable to see that the relevant question is a stimulus as threatening and arousing for the innocent as for the guilty, that the truthful denial can be as emotional as a false one?

Adherents of the R/I technique will reject this witness-box analogy as inappropriate and misleading. In the privacy of the polygraph room, using "stim tests" and other methods, the examiner will be able to inspire the subject with such respect for the power and accuracy of the procedure that the truthful subject, having nothing to fear, will be unmoved by the relevant questions. We have seen this assumption before in the discussion of the clinical polygraph test in the previous chapter. Most examiners who use the R/I format also use clinical assessment. But polygraphers *cannot* convince all subjects that the polygraph is infallible. Moreover, "Are you guilty?" will continue to be a significant, arousing stimulus for some people even when they feel certain that their innocent denial is about to be confirmed by the magic machine.

Validity of the R/I Test

So much for theory and common sense; what is the evidence? It is astonishing to discover that, in 50 years of use, the *only** published study assessing R/I test accuracy using "blind" evaluations of charts obtained from criminal suspects was apparently the one described briefly by Larson in 1938.[2] Nine judges read the charts of 62 suspects. Only one of the 62 suspects had actually lied and yet the number scored as Deceptive by the 9 judges ranged from 5 to 30. This amount of disagreement among the nine judges indicates poor reliability. The average judge scored about one-third of the innocent suspects as Deceptive, which means that two-thirds of these innocents failed to give large reactions to the relevant questions and were scored as truthful, just as Assumption 2 demands. One might have thought that Assumption 2 would nearly always be wrong and that most subjects would fail the R/I test whether innocent or guilty. Apparently, however, many people do not find the relevant questions as threatening as might have been expected, possibly because they have been persuaded to have great faith in the procedure. But the important finding is that about one-third of the innocent subjects *were* erroneously classified as Deceptive. Since this study of Larson's is the only one we have of the R/I test administered in a criminal context and scored "blindly" from the charts alone, we should not put too much faith in the exact percentage of errors found. But we can say that, just as common sense would predict, a high proportion of innocent subjects *will* "fail" the R/I test.

Verdict

The relevant/irrelevant form of lie test is based on a flagrantly implausible assumption. Common sense indicates that the R/I test will be strongly biased against the truthful subject and the single

---

*A number of studies have been reported in which a large group of suspects were tested by the R/I method in relation to the same crime. In every instance except for the cited study by Larson, the persons who scored the charts were aware that not more than one person could reasonably be guilty and therefore the scorers could have achieved very high "accuracy" just by calling everyone Truthful. Thus, Bitterman and Marcuse[1] tested 81 residents of a college dormitory where $100 had been stolen from a student's room. Finding that 7 of 81 students "failed" the R/I test the first time around, Bitterman and Marcuse retested those 7 and finally concluded that all of them were innocent. The only useful evidence of lie test accuracy is obtained when the chart evaluator reads each chart independently with no outside reason for expecting either a Truthful or a Deceptive result.

available piece of evidence, from the inventor of the R/I procedure himself, supports this assessment.

Notes

1. Bitterman, M. E. & Marcuse, F. L. Cardiovascular responses of innocent persons to criminal investigation. *American Journal of Psychology*, 1947, *60*, 407–412.
2. Larson, J. A. The lie detector polygraph: Its history and development. *Journal of the Michigan State Medical Society*, 1938, *37*, 893–897.

CHAPTER

8

The Lie Control Test (LCT)

Can you nominate in order now the degrees of a lie?

—Shakespeare, *As You Like It*

It is manifest that man is . . . subject to much variability.

—Darwin, *The Descent of Man*

The polygraphic lie test most commonly used in criminal investigation is the method developed by John Reid and known in the trade as the control question test. Several other types of lie test also use control or comparison questions, however, so it will be convenient to employ a more specific name for the Reid method. Since Reid's control questions are intended to elicit deceptive answers from the respondent, I shall refer to this standard technique as the Lie Control Test or LCT. Backster's Zone of Comparison method is a popular variant of the LCT that differs slightly from Reid's in the arrangement of questions and the methods of scoring.

The format of the Lie Control Test is illustrated in Table 8–1. The first question is the familiar irrelevant type. Question 2 is relevant in substance but is not used in scoring the charts; it is called a "sacrifice relevant." Question 3 is an "outside issue" question designed for the situation in which the subject might be afraid that the interrogation will stray into an area about which he has real concern. If he seems disturbed by this question, testing will be postponed until he can be convinced that the only questions asked will be those previously reviewed with him. The three relevant questions, Numbers 5, 7, and 10, all refer to a certain fatal stabbing for which this subject has been indicted. Question 8 is another irrelevant, interpolated mainly to provide a rest stop between the more arousing questions that precede and follow it.

TABLE 8–1. Example of a Lie Control Test administered by D. Raskin to a defendant accused of homicide by stabbing.[1]

1. Were you born in Hong Kong?	—YES	(IRRELEVANT)
2. Regarding the stabbing of Ken Chiu, do you intend to answer truthfully every question about that?	—YES	(SACRIFICE RELEVANT)
3. Do you understand that I will ask only questions we have discussed?	—YES	(OUTSIDE ISSUE)
4. During the first 18 years of your life, did you ever hurt someone?	—NO	(LIE CONTROL)
5. Did you cut anyone with a knife on Dumfries St. on January 23, 1976?	—NO	(RELEVANT)
6. Before 1974 did you ever try to seriously hurt someone?	—NO	(LIE CONTROL)
7. Did you stab Ken Chiu on January 23, 1976?	—NO	(RELEVANT)
8. Is your first name William?	—YES	(IRRELEVANT)
9. Before age 19, did you ever lie to get out of trouble?	—NO	(LIE CONTROL)
10. Did you actually see Ken Chiu get stabbed?	—NO	(RELEVANT)

Let us now consider Questions 4, 6, and 9, the control questions. These are based on the idea proposed by Reid in 1947 and, in Backster's phrase, are intended to "capture the psychological set" of the innocent subject. Although they do not refer to the specific issue of the stabbing, they do refer to related activities in the past, to hurting someone and to lying to get out of trouble. During the pretest interview, the examiner should have rationalized these questions to the subject, suggesting that if the subject is the kind of person who has gone around hurting people and lying in the past, then it will be harder to believe in his innocence in the present instance. Such preparation will make these questions seem more important and may predispose the subject to deny them. If, as in this case, the subject says that he can answer "No" to a control question, the examiner privately assumes that this answer is a lie. Reid and Inbau's textbook explains that the examiner should select as controls only questions to which the subject shows "behavior symptoms of deception" (hesitation, breaking eye contact, squirming, etc.). Other examiners simply assume that everyone has done the sorts of things referred to in these questions and that a "No" answer *must* be deceptive.

If the subject wishes to answer "Yes" to a control question, the examiner should pretend to be surprised and concerned. He will ask, "When did you lie to get out of trouble?" and proceed to take notes of the reply. He will say, "Except for that incident, have you ever lied to get out of trouble?" and make it clear by his manner that he now expects a denial. Should the subject think of a second instance, the examiner redoubles his appearance of shocked concern, writes down that second instance, and tries again. His aim is to induce the subject to answer "No" at a point where he is at least in doubt whether this answer is strictly true. Whether the respondent is innocent or guilty of the specific offense referred to in the relevant questions, it is assumed that his answers to the control questions are actually deceptive, or at least that the subject is doubtful about whether he has answered truthfully. Therefore, this most widely used type of control question is (somewhat optimistically) referred to as a "known lie" control.

The scoring of the Lie Control Test is straightforward. If the polygraph responses to the relevant questions are systematically larger than those elicited by the "known lie" controls, the subject is considered to have been deceptive in his answers to the relevant questions. If his responses to the controls are the larger, then he is classified as truthful. The test is declared to be inconclusive if there is minimal difference in size between the two sets of responses. In the Zone of Comparison version of the LCT, advocated by Backster and illustrated by the question list shown in Table 8–1, each relevant response is compared only to the controls that are adjacent to it.

A Genuine Known-Lie Control Test. The theory of the Lie Control Test is obscure and confusing, so it may be helpful to begin by indicating what the LCT clearly is *not*. Suppose that the stabbing suspect referred to earlier had committed a previous murder and that, unknown to him, we have in our possession incontrovertible evidence of his guilt. Let us call the present crime, in which he is only a suspect, Crime X and the previous one, for which he thinks that he is equally only a suspect, Crime Y. Under these unusual circumstances, the relevant question, "Did you commit Crime X?" will be psychologically equivalent to the control question, "Did you commit Crime Y?" *if the subject is also guilty of Crime X.* He should see himself in equal jeopardy in both cases and his "No" answers to both questions will be lies. In this imaginary situation, we would have produced a control question which truly functions as a control in the usual scientific meaning of that term. Specifically, the response to the control question provides us with a prediction of how this subject *ought to respond* to the relevant question if his denial of that question also is a lie. We are not required to assume, against common sense, that all lies are the same size or importance. We have created a situation in which we can be sure not only that the control reply is deceptive, but also that the subject, if he is guilty of both crimes, will construe both questions as about equally threatening, equally arousing. If he in fact shows much *less* physiological arousal after the relevant question, as compared to the control, then we can probably be fairly certain that he is innocent of Crime X.

What if he shows as much or more response to the relevant question? Can we then be certain he is guilty of Crime X? That is, are we justified in assuming that someone will always be more aroused by a true accusation than he will by a false charge in an equally serious matter? I find that somewhat harder to accept. The false charge might seem unfair, harder to deal with. Since the polygraph measures only relative arousal, not lying or guilt, the suspect's uncertainty and indignation about the Crime X accusation (of which he is innocent) *might* produce as much polygraphic activity as he shows to the question about Crime Y, which charge he has accepted in his mind and is prepared to "tough out."

The Lie Control Test that is actually used by polygraphic examiners differs fundamentally from this genuine known-lie example. The subject's answers to the LCT's control questions are *not* "known" lies but are only assumed to be lies. Moreover, there is no attempt to match the control "lie" to the relevant lie in magnitude or importance to the subject, no attempt to predict from the control response what this person's response to the relevant question ought to be if he is lying. Therefore, the lie control question is no "control" at all in the scientific sense. It is merely a kind of comparison stimulus, just as Reid originally called it, intended to be more provocative than an irrelevant question but, for a guilty subject, *less* provocative than the relevant question. With a genuine known-lie control, a suspect who is guilty of both crimes ought to give about equal responses to the relevant and control questions—provided we have fooled him with our pretense that our evidence of his involvement in Y is no better than our evidence about X, and provided that *he* considers both crimes to be equally important or emotional (and provided that he does not bite his tongue or otherwise self-stimulate to augment his response when we ask him the control question: see Chapter 19).

Assumptions of the Lie Control Test

The theory and assumptions of the LCT have never been clearly set forth by any of its proponents. Therefore, we must infer theory from practice, deduce how the test is supposed to work from the way it is administered and scored. And we must be careful not to infer unnecessary assumptions or to set up a straw-man theory that is easy to topple but unfair to polygraphers who have faith in this method. Let us, therefore, proceed cautiously.

ASSUMPTION 1. *A given subject will respond more strongly to a relevant question if he answers it deceptively than if his denial is truthful. That is, if his response would be R_I if he is innocent and R_G if he is guilty, then R_G will be larger than R_I ($R_G > R_I$).*

This clearly is an assumption of *any* form of lie test and it seems generally plausible. But in an area where the tradition has been to ignore individual differences, to take a simplistic view of human nature as if all people came off the same assembly line, it is important to emphasize that "plausible" does not imply "inevitable." For example, Mary K. reports that Walter, whom she met last night in a bar, drove her out into the country and forcibly raped her. The county attorney is reluctant to prosecute Walter unless Mary's allegations are confirmed on the polygraph. On Mary's LCT, she is asked the relevant question, "Did you voluntarily agree to have intercourse with Walter?" and she answers in the negative. If Mary is lying and has accused Walter out of spite or to mollify her parents or her husband, this question and her deceptive answer ought to constitute an arousing stimulus. But what if Mary is telling the truth? Instead of a consensual sex act, what if Mary's memory of this experience with Walter are memories of fear and pain and brutal violation? How "arousing" will this same relevant question be to her then? In Yakima County, Washington, where all women who report rape are required to take lie detector tests, 60% "fail" the tests due to strong reactions to the relevant questions.[2]

This first assumption of the Lie Control Test may be true for most subjects in most situations—but not for all subjects nor in all situations.

ASSUMPTION 2. *A skillful polygraph examiner formulates "known-lie" control questions and presents them to the subject during the pretest interview in such a way that, on the polygraph test itself, the subject will either answer these questions untruthfully or at least he will be uncertain and concerned about his answers.*

Many polygraphers literally believe that the answers to their control questions can be assumed to be lies, for all subjects and situations. While this is absurd, it would be unfair to state Assumption 2 in this uncompromising way. Such an assumption would be patently implausible and is not a necessary or even useful component of the theory of the LCT. If all control questions *did* elicit "known lies," this would not guarantee that innocent subjects would therefore react more strongly to the control than to the relevant questions. The polygraph response is a reaction to the stimulus package that includes the question and the subject's answer. For most people, a moderately threatening control question may be more arousing if answered deceptively rather than truthfully. But this plainly does not mean that the control response will be larger than that produced by a *very* threatening relevant question answered truthfully. For example, if I falsely deny ever having stolen anything (the control question), I would expect to be less aroused than when I truthfully deny some serious criminal charge that may send me to prison. It is not true that all lies are psychologically equal or that any question answered deceptively will yield more polygraphic activity than any other question, no matter how relevant or threatening or emotional, that is answered truthfully. All that one can reasonably say about the known-lie control is that, properly set up and presented, it should generate more concern, stress, and arousal than an irrelevant question—and that it *may* elicit answers that the subject knows or suspects to be untrue.

This assumption begins to tax the psychological sensitivity and dramaturgical skills of the examiner because he must be able to condition (that is, deceive) the subject in specific ways. He must make the subject think that it will be detrimental to his interests to admit the sorts of misdeeds referred to in the control questions; the subject must not be allowed to catalog every lie he has ever told or every dime or pencil he has ever "stolen." And the polygrapher must make the subject think that, if the polygraph somehow shows that his answer to a control question is deceptive, then he will "fail" the test. Both of these ideas are untrue and yet the subject must be led to *think* that they are true if the control question is to produce real stress or concern.

This second assumption of the Lie Control Test, like the first, may plausibly be true for many subjects—but it will not be true if the examiner is inept in enacting his role; or if the subject in knowledgeable about the test and not easily deceived; or if the subject can actually answer "No" to the control questions truthfully and without concern.

ASSUMPTION 3. *A subject's arousal response elicited by the control question* (R_C) *will be smaller than his response would be to the relevant question if he is guilty* (R_G) *but larger than his response would be if he is innocent* (R_I); *that is* $R_G > R_C > R_I$ *for all subjects.*

Here is the real nub of the theory of the LCT. There can be no argument about whether Assumption 3 is required because it is directly on this basis that the charts are scored. Notice that this third assumption includes Assumption 1; namely, that R_G will be larger than R_I. It also includes Assumption 2; namely, that R_C will be a substantial response, large enough at least to be greater than R_I. But Assumption 3 goes further, making the amazing claim that R_C will tuck neatly between R_G and R_I. The examiner has no way of knowing how strongly this particular subject will react to the relevant question if he is guilty or if he is innocent. That is, he cannot know how large this subject's R_G or his R_I would be (if he did know either of these values, he would not need a control question, but could score the chart merely by comparing the actual response with the known value of R_G or R_I). Instead, he assumes that R_G would be larger than R_I and he *also* assumes that the stimulus package of his control question, plus the subject's reply, will be *just arousing enough for this particular subject* so that it will elicit a R_C that is larger than this subject's R_I would be, while at the same time smaller than this subject's R_G would be. This truly is behavioral engineering of a precision hitherto undreamed of!

Wayne K. was fired from his responsible position at the bank because he failed a LCT based and scored on these assumptions. James Galloway is in an Iowa prison, convicted of murder after the jury had been told that he failed a LCT and that these tests were accurate more than 99% of the time. Although eyewitness and physical evidence fully supported his plea of self-defense, James Ray Mendoza was convicted of first degree murder by a Wisconsin jury after hearing testimony that he had failed a LCT; he was sentenced to life in the penitentiary. This is not academic hair-splitting we are engaged in. What the LCT assumes and whether these assumptions are credible are important social questions. In the Galloway case, a typical relevant question was, "Did you shoot Harry Shannon?" and I would estimate that Galloway's average response on three presentations of this question was about 6 units on an arbitrary scale of 0 to 20. The adjacent control question was, "Did you ever threaten anyone with a gun?" and I would estimate his average response to this question was about 5 units. The polygrapher believed that Galloway's relevant answer was deceptive because his relevant response was (slightly) larger than his control response. But this reasoning necessarily assumes that, if Galloway was innocent and had been in Missouri at the time of the robbery as he insisted, then his relevant response would have been smaller (say, 4 units) *or* his control response would have been larger (say, 7 units): this is the concrete, real-life (and arbitrary) meaning of Assumption 3.

This brings us to an idea promulgated by Backster in 1974 under the forbidding title, "The anticlimax dampening concept." Backster's notion was that "a person's fear, anxieties and apprehensions are channeled toward the situation which holds greatest immediate threat to his self-preservation or general well-being," and that there is, "an ability within us to tune in that which may indicate trouble or danger by having our sense organs and attention set for a particular stimulus and oriented in a manner that will dampen any stimulus of lesser importance."[3] As applied to the LCT, this hypothesis can be used to argue that the control response of a guilty subject will be "dampened," i.e., made smaller than it otherwise would be, by the presence in the question list of the relevant questions, which pose a greater immediate threat to the guilty suspect's well-being. Similarly, if the subject is innocent *and if he can be made to believe that the control question poses a greater threat than the relevant question,* then his response to the control question should be larger and his relevant response should be "dampened." But Backster's hypothesis, even if it were true, would not salvage the LCT from the pits of implausibility where last we left it. Analyzing the theory of the LCT from this vantage point, we might set aside the three assumptions already discussed and substitute two others in their stead:

ASSUMPTION 1-B. *All guilty subjects will regard the relevant questions as more threatening than the control questions and therefore R_G will be larger than R_C.*

ASSUMPTION 2-B. *All innocent subjects will regard the relevant questions as less threatening than the control questions and therefore R_C will be larger than R_G.*

Again, we cannot help but be impressed by the simplistic, robot-like conception of human nature, the blithe disregard of the subtleties and idiosyncracies of real human minds. Infallibly, the relevant question is "most threatening" to the guilty subject; therefore, we simply deny the possibility that some guilty persons might become inured to or defended against such references to their crime; we deny that any other question might be more arousing to them; we ignore the possibility that the guilty subject might covertly augment his physiological response to the control question. Universally, we are told, the relevant question is *not* "most threatening" to the innocent subject because the polygrapher will always make him believe that the control questions pose a greater threat. Therefore, the truthful rape victim will respond more strongly to the control question, "Have you ever thought of having sex with someone in the woods?" than she will to the relevant question, "Did you voluntarily agree to have sex with George Wilson last Saturday?"—even though Wilson hurt and terrified and degraded her last Saturday and she still trembles at the mention of his name. Although James Galloway has been arrested for a robbery-murder in Davenport, Iowa, he will regard the control question, "Have you ever threatened anyone with a gun?" as more threatening to his well-being than the relevant question, "Did you shoot grocer Harry Shannon?", if he is actually innocent as he claims to be.

Some Real-Life Examples. A psychologist must contemplate the theory of the Lie Control Test with a kind of awe. The great difficulty in explaining the lie test to lawyers and laymen is that they find it hard to accept that the mythological lie detector actually teeters on such implausible premises. It seems plain that any sensible subject, whether guilty or innocent, should tend to be most aroused—and therefore to give the strongest polygraphic response—to the relevant or "Did you do it?" questions. For the LCT to work as advertised, each subject must be made to believe that the test is nearly infallible (not true) and that giving strong control responses will jeopardize him (the opposite is true). It is implausible to suppose that all polygraphers will be able to convince all subjects of these two false propositions. Based on my analysis, one would expect that most—but not all—guilty subjects would fail the LCT—and that many innocent subjects would fail it also.

How is it possible that thousands of polygraphers have managed to believe such implausible ideas? I think part of the answer lies in the fact that the theory and basic assumptions of the LCT have never before been spelled out in bold relief. Another reason, however, is the fact that many truthful subjects actually do behave as Reid and Backster would predict! I have seen polygraph charts on which persons accused of serious crimes responded to relatively innocuous control questions with physiological reactions that were clearly stronger than the ones elicited by the relevant questions. A father accused of incest by his 14-year-old daughter, referred for testing by a California juvenile court, was diagnosed as truthful on the basis of a LCT. The daughter subsequently recanted, admitting that she was jealous of her father's multiple marriages and had wanted to punish him. A young man in New Hampshire was accused of forcible rape by his own sister, convicted and sentenced to the state prison for 7 to 10 years. Months later, after the man had been severely beaten by his fellow inmates—convicts tend to be punitive with alleged sex criminals—he was given a lie test by Deputy Sheriff G. E. Tetreault of Exeter, N.H. Observing weaker responses to questions like, "Regarding your sister _____, did you ever have sexual intercourse with her?", than were elicited by the control questions, Deputy Tetreault concluded that the brother was innocent and initiated a further investigation. The sister and alleged victim was persuaded to submit to a polygraph test, failed it, and then confessed that she had made the false charge because she was pregnant by her boyfriend and had decided to sacrifice her brother in order to protect her lover. Additional corroboration was provided by the fact that both baby and boyfriend displayed a heritable physical anomaly not present in the mother's pedigree. The murder defendant who was asked the questions shown in Table 8–1 was diagnosed as Truthful on the basis of that LCT. We cannot be sure that this diagnosis was correct; the jury brought in a verdict of Guilty in spite of the lie test evidence. But it is impressive that this defendant could have been more aroused by those innocuous-seeming control questions than he was by the relevant questions concerned with the actual stabbing. Based on our examination of the theory, one might expect that most suspects would fail the LCT whether innocent or guilty, yet it is clear that at least some persons are surprisingly unreactive to what appear to be provocative and stressful relevant questions, that some innocent suspects are able to clear their names and escape prosecution by passing the test—and perhaps a few guilty ones as well.

Our common-sense expectations are vindicated, however, by the illuminating case of Sam K.[4] Sam was on business in Phoenix in 1975 and became acquainted one evening in the bar of his motel with a young woman, Mary V. According to Sam's account, the couple repaired to Mary's motel room when the bar closed, had intercourse there, smoked and talked for a time, had intercourse again, and then Sam returned to his own room and to bed. Before he left, Mary wrote out for him her name and home address in pledge of future meetings and he had that scrap of paper in his wallet when he was awakened several hours later by the police, summoned to arrest him on the charge of rape. After a long and unexplained delay, Mary had called the police to make this complaint. She had also called the newspapers, the first of many actions by Mary that are uncharacteristic of most rape victims and which led the state's attorney to doubt whether he could successfully prosecute Sam K., a respectable young man with an unblemished record, on Mary's word alone. As the months went by, Mary's behavior grew increasingly eccentric. Finally, the prosecutor approached Sam's attorney with the following proposal:

Let us give your man a polygraph test. We will agree in advance to drop all charges against him if he passes. But you must similarly stipulate that we can use the test results as evidence in court if your client flunks the lie test.

Arizona is one of some 20 states that permit the introduction as evidence in court of the results of lie tests administered after such prior stipulation by both parties. In my experience, these stipulated lie test propositions are only offered by prosecutors who have a weak case. If the defendant passes, there is nothing lost anyway. But if he fails, then the weak case becomes suddenly much stronger.

Sam's attorney accepted the proposal. Sam was administered an LCT of the Zone of Comparison type—and he flunked it badly. His polygraphic reactions to the three relevant questions were strong and unequivocal, much stronger than his control responses. Now Sam was in real trouble and his attorney appealed for help. He explained to me his reason for accepting the prosecution's offer this way:

You know, I do mostly criminal defense work and most of my clients are guilty as hell, but I really thought this guy was innocent. In fact, I had even had him polygraphed privately just to satisfy myself that he was telling me the truth. He passed that first test with no difficulty. That crazy woman kept calling the newspapers and Sam's family was upset and his employers were talking about letting him go. So when the State came to me with their deal, I thought it was an easy way to put an end to all the hassle. He was innocent, he'd already passed one lie test, all he had to do was pass another one and that would be the end of it.

Interestingly, that first private polygrapher used the old-fashioned R/I format, which one would expect to be especially hard for a reactive subject like Sam to pass. But less was at stake during that test because the results were to be confidential, for his lawyer's eyes only. And perhaps Sam regarded this first examiner, hired by his own attorney, to be friendly and sympathetic to his interests. But here we were in court, now, with the prosecution confident of a conviction. In 1975, the two good studies of the actual validity of the LCT had not yet appeared in print and all I could offer as a witness for the defense was an explanation to the jury of the implausibility of the LCT and my opinion that it would be not at all surprising for an innocent man to respond as Sam had on such a test under these circumstances. What really saved Sam K. was a little mixup of communication between the prosecutor and his polygrapher. The three relevant questions that this examiner employed were as follows:

(1) Did you force your way into Mary V.'s motel room on the night of May 14th?
(2) Did you threaten to choke Mary V. in her room on May 14th?
(3) Did you rape Mary V. in her motel room on the night of May 14th?

Sam answered "No" to each of these questions and the polygraph pens gyrated wildly as he did so; there was no possibility here that another polygrapher might have scored this result as Truthful or even Inconclusive. But the mixup was that Mary V.'s own account of what had happened began with her admission that she had invited Sam into her room that night after the bar closed. She said he had needed a toilet and, her room being closer, she had invited him to use her bathroom. Sam was not accused of "forcing" his way into Mary's room that night; we know, therefore, that his answer to the first relevant question was truthful. Yet he reacted just as strongly to that question as to the other two.

"Can you explain, Doctor," Sam's lawyer asked me during his direct examination, "why the defendant gave such a strong reaction to that first question even though, as we know, his answer was truthful?"

"I would assume he responded as he did because this question referred to the serious crime he had been charged with, it named the woman who had brought this charge against him, and it referred to the time and place of the incident that led to his being arrested. Compared to the so-called control questions, all three relevant questions were obviously important; all three were strong, stressful stimuli for the defendant under the circumstances and they produced strong reactions."

"Well, Doctor, given that we know the defendant's answer to the first of the three questions was truthful, have you formed an opinion as to the truthfulness of his answers to the other two questions, where his polygraph reaction was just as strong as the one he gave when we know he answered truthfully?"

"I have. I believe the only reasonable inference to be that the other two answers were as truthful as the first."

The jury agreed and there now hangs on my wall a handsome Navaho rug, a gift from that relieved and innocent defendant after his close call. That second polygrapher had inadvertently created a

Truth Control Test by his mistake, a test format that, as we shall see later, makes considerably more psychological sense than the Lie Control Test and that was what actually saved the day for Sam K.

Validity of the Lie Control Test

The Lie Control Test is regarded by most examiners as the optimum technique for specific-issue situations like those of criminal investigation, and these examples are useful for illustrating how it works—and fails to work—in real life. My common-sense analysis suggested that nearly everyone might be expected to fail the LCT, but I have listed striking instances to disprove that expectation. Polygraph examiners, on the other hand, claim that the LCT almost always returns a correct diagnosis, that its assumptions, however implausible they might seem, turn out to be true 90-plus percent of the time. Examples like the case of Sam K., which corroborate my psychological analysis, at the very least cast doubt on these claims of high validity. But the real answer must come from controlled empirical studies of LCT validity in real-life applications. For 50 years the lie detector technique gathered adherents and grew in acceptance almost entirely without benefit of such evidence. Then, in the early 1970s, there appeared several validity studies from the Reid organization that seemed to show that the LCT did indeed have surprisingly high validity. As we shall see, however, these four Reid studies actually tell us nothing about validity, but only that Reid-trained examiners, asked to read the same charts, will tend to score them the same way. But, at last, two good studies of the validity of the LCT have appeared, different enough in their design so that their remarkable agreement in outcome entitles us to place considerable credence in their findings.

In these six studies of the LCT in real-life situations, the polygraph charts of criminal suspects were scored blindly by a different polygrapher than the one who gave the test. These diagnoses were then compared with some independent criterion specifying which suspects had been lying and which truthful. Four of the studies were conducted by employees of John Reid Associates. At the time of their publication, the scientific credentials of the senior authors consisted of master's degrees awarded by the Reid College of the Detection of Deception. All four studies made use of cases from the files of the Reid organization, cases that had been "independently verified" as to the guilt or innocence of the person tested. In the study by Horvath and Reid, these verifications were based on confessions of the person tested or of someone else, clearing the person tested. In the other studies, the nature and quality of verification is less clear. Horvath and Reid began with 75 verified cases, but eliminated 35 from further consideration because these charts were either "obvious" or "uninterpretable." This maneuver alone invalidated the experiment; one must use all the cases available or at least a strictly random sample of all cases. I do not mean to suggest that Horvath and Reid handpicked that half of their original sample that would yield favorable results. I do suggest that no one knows precisely how these cases were selected; therefore, no other researcher could repeat and verify this experiment.

Horvath and Reid's[5] 40 charts were independently scored by 10 polygraph examiners employed by the Reid firm. Hunter and Ash[6] used charts from 10 Innocent and 10 Guilty suspects and had them read by seven Reid polygraphers. Wicklander & Hunter[7] also used 10 Innocent and 10 Guilty charts and had them scored by six of Reid's polygraphers. Slowick & Buckley[8] reported findings based on 15 Innocent and 15 Guilty suspects whose charts were scored by seven polygraphers. The fatal defect shared by all four of these in-house studies is this: Instead of being estimates of lie test *validity,* they are merely demonstrations that Reid's examiners score charts in a similar way.

As we have seen, the lie test method taught by Reid is based on the assumption that deceptive subjects will give larger polygraphic responses to the relevant questions than they do to the control questions asked of them; truthful subjects are expected to show the reverse pattern. In *all* of the cases selected for independent rescoring in the four studies mentioned, the original examiner had found the charts to show these expected Truthful patterns for the verified Innocent subjects, or the expected Deceptive patterns for the verified Guilty suspects. Therefore, when the other Reid-trained examiners subsequently rescored these particular charts, the extent to which they agreed with the criterion was really just a measure of their agreement with the original examiner's scoring, a measure of the test's *reliability* rather than of its *validity.*

Here is how one might "prove" the validity of astrological theory by the same technique. First, we shall have one astrologer predict the sun sign (Leo, Gemini, Scorpio, and so on) of a large number of celebrities, based on their popularly known personalities and characteristics. Even if there is nothing in astrology at all, this first set of guesses will be correct some of the time just by chance. Suppose that this first astrologer makes his guesses for 1,200 celebrities and historical figures and, as chance would predict, that he is correct for 100 of them. Now let us take *just these 100 cases* and have a second astrologer predict their sun signs; suppose he is correct 80% of the time. Have we proved the validity of astrology? No, we have shown merely that the two astrologers entertain the same set of beliefs as to which personality traits go with which sun signs. We would have proved nothing at all about whether this consensus had any actual validity.

It is not clear whether useful data about the validity of the lie test *could be* obtained from the files of the Reid organization. We do not know whether all tests and all subsequent verifications are systematically recorded in those files without selection or bias. But the only way that blind rescoring studies can possibly contribute to our understanding of the real-life accuracy of any polygraphic test procedure is when they are based on a representative sample of cases chosen consecutively or strictly randomly, without regard to whether the charts produced by those subjects did or did not conform to the theory on which the test is based.

A fifth study, also by Horvath,[9] used cases from the files of a state police agency, charts obtained from criminal suspects, half of whom later confessed while the other half were cleared by the confession of someone else. These charts were read "blindly" and independently by 10 polygraphers and scored as Truthful or Deceptive. Like the previous four studies, all of the charts used by Horvath also had been scored by the original examiner in the direction which later proved to be correct. But these state police examiners did not base their diagnoses entirely on the polygraph charts, but used case facts and other evidence. We know this because Horvath's 10 examiners who rescored the charts agreed with each other about 89% of the time (just as did the polygraphers in the Reid studies), but they agreed with the original examiners—and with "ground truth"—only 63% of the time. In this study, his doctoral dissertation at Michigan State University, Horvath did not select for rescoring only those charts which looked like Truthful or Deceptive charts are supposed to look according to polygraph doctrine. Therefore, even though he did use only charts on which the original examiner had been correct, the positive bias resulting from this was not enough to make this just another study of interscorer reliability.

Half of Horvath's 56 criminal suspects were in fact innocent and half were guilty. His 10 polygraphers scored 63% of the charts as Deceptive; as common sense would predict, the data show a bias against the innocent subject, a tendency for most of the charts to be read as Deceptive. Therefore, most of the actually guilty subjects— 77% of them—were correctly diagnosed. But only 51% of the innocent subjects were correctly classified as Truthful; *half* (49%) of the actually truthful subjects were erroneously classified as Deceptive on the basis of their LCT polygraph charts.

The last of the six Lie Control Test studies was also conducted by professional polygraphers who, like Horvath, had scientific training. In Salt Lake City, Dr. Gordon Barland administered LCT examinations to 102 criminal suspects.[10] Then the evidentiary files on each of these cases were reviewed by a panel of five experts in criminal law. These prosecutors or defense attorneys were asked to ignore legal technicalities and to judge, on the basis of the case facts (which included evidence of confessions, guilty pleas, and the like), whether the suspects were innocent or guilty. As often happens in the courtroom, the evidence in many of these cases was insufficient to permit the panel of judges to reach a clear verdict; a majority of the judges agreed on only 64 cases. Another polygrapher, Dr. David Raskin, scored these 64 charts blindly—without knowledge of how the subjects had behaved or of the case facts. Raskin classified 13 of the 64 charts as Inconclusive, leaving 51 cases where there was both an LCT diagnosis of Deceptive or Truthful and also a subsequent criterion judgment of which subjects had actually been Guilty and which Innocent. Most of these 51 suspects, 40 or 78% of them, were Guilty. Raskin scored most of the charts as Deceptive—45 or 88% of them. Not surprisingly, therefore, he diagnosed most of the Guilty subjects as Deceptive; 39 or 98% of them. But he did this at the expense of calling more than half—6 out of 11—of the Innocent subjects Deceptive also. Averaging his accuracy on the Guilty and the Innocent subjects figured separately, we get an average validity of 72%, which we can compare with the average of 63% achieved by Horvath's polygraphers. Remembering that 50% is the accuracy that one would expect to obtain just by flipping a coin, Horvath's typical polygraphers achieved 63% with the LCT, while two of the most highly trained polygraphers in the world, both Ph.D.'s, obtained 72%. Since Raskin called more of his subjects Deceptive than Horvath's examiners did, he managed to correctly classify more of the Guilty subjects, 98% compared to 77% for Horvath. But he also misclassified more of the Innocent subjects, calling 55% Deceptive as compared with 49% for Horvath.

Verdict

The Lie Control Test, widely regarded among polygraphers as their most refined technique, is the only lie detection method to have been seriously studied with respect to its validity. As we have seen, some of these studies are defective or irrelevant; none of them are definitive. The burden of proof, however, is on the proponents of the method. Can they substantiate their claims? After listening to a week of testimony from critics of polygraphy and from such leading polygraphers as John Reid and Richard Arther, Justice Morand concluded:

The polygraph examiners had many opportunities to answer the problems and criticisms suggested by psychologists and physiologists. Unfortunately, their response was invariably that the criticisms were not valid because, in their experience, the test worked. I have come to the conclusion that I must accept the evidence of the psychologists and physiologists, which is consistent with both my common sense and my personal experience, that all individuals do not react in identical ways in a given situation, and that programming human responses is at best imperfect. In my opinion there is a real possibility that many innocent persons accused of crime would be unconcerned with what has been suggested to me are good control questions in comparison with the actual accusation. I have no doubt that some people do react as polygraph operators insist they must, but I am not convinced that this latter group of people would be an overwhelming proportion of our population.[11]

Notes

1. *Proceedings at trial, Queen v. William Wong.* Supreme Court of British Columbia, No. CC760628, Vancouver, Canada, October 1976.
2. Lie Test for Rape Victims. *Mother Jones,* July 1979, p. 10. This practice is widespread in the U.S. Jan Leventer, codirector of the Women's Justice Center in Detroit, determined in 1978 that rape victims were being subjected to polygraph tests in at least 17 states. The WJC brought suit to stop the practice in Detroit and, in January of 1979, the Detroit Police Department agreed to these demands. In Maryland, one of the "relevant" questions routinely asked during lie tests of rape victims was, "Did you have an orgasm?"

3.   Backster, C. Anticlimax dampening concept. *Polygraph*, 1974, *3*, 28–50.

4.   *Arizona v. Pete* Superior Court of Arizona, No. CR–77905, October 1974.

5.   Horvath, F. & Reid, J. The reliability of polygraph examiner diagnosis of truth and deception. *Journal of Criminal Law, Criminology, and Police Science*, 1971, *62*, 276–281.

6.   Hunter, F. & Ash, P. The accuracy and consistency of polygraph examiner's diagnosis. *Journal of Police Science and Administration*, 1973, *1*, 370–375.

7.   Wicklander, D. & Hunger, F. The influence of auxiliary sources of information in polygraph diagnosis. *Journal of Police Science and Administration*, 1975, *3*, 405, 409.

8.   Slowick, S. & Buckley, J. Relative accuracy of polygraph examiner diagnosis of respiration, blood pressure, and GSR recordings. *Journal of Police Science and Administration*, 1975, *3*, 305–309.

9.   Horvath, F. The effect of selected variables on interpretation of polygraph records. *Journal of Applied Psychology*, 1977, *62*, 127–136.

10. Barland, G. & Raskin, D. *Validity and reliability of polygraph examinations of criminal suspects.* (Report No.76–1, Contract 75–NI–99–0001, U.S. Department of Justice, 1976.)

11. Justice D. R. Morand, in *Royal Commission into Metropolitan Toronto Police Practices*, 1976, p. 225.

CHAPTER 9

The Truth Control
Test (TCT)

There is no worse lie than the truth misunderstood.

—William James

Reids's 1947 proposal for the use of a guilt complex comparison question never really caught on among polygraphers. Although the name "guilt complex" is unfortunate, with its unnecessary psychiatric connotations, Reid explained the principle with admirable clarity.

The "guilt complex" question is based upon an entirely fictitious crime of the same type as the actual crime under investigation, but one which is made to appear very realistic to the subject. . . . The purpose of the "guilt complex" or fictitious crime question is to determine if the subject, although innocent, is unduly apprehensive because of the fact that he is suspected and interrogated about the crime under investigation. A reaction to the fictitious crime question which is greater than or about the same as that to the actual crime question would be indicative of truthtelling and innocence respecting the real offense. On the other hand, however, a response to the actual crime questions, coupled with the absence of a response to the fictitious crime question, or by one considerably less than that to the actual crime questions, would be strongly indicative of lying regarding the offense under investigation.[1]

For example, when James Galloway was interrogated about that robbery-murder in Davenport, Iowa, he might also have been questioned about another holdup in Des Moines in which the victim also died. "This happened just the day before the Davenport killing, Galloway, and we have witnesses who identified your picture in both cases." But, unknown to the suspect, there was no such killing in Des Moines on the date in question so we know that his denial of that crime is truthful. Here we have the obverse of the "genuine known-lie" situation discussed earlier; Crime X of which our subject is a suspect, and Crime Y, of which we know he is innocent because Crime Y never happened. If our man is also innocent of X, then it might not be too difficult to make him think that he is in equal jeopardy with respect to both crimes; they are equally serious, the evidence implicating him is similar in both cases, and in both cases he knows that he was somewhere else. This fictitious crime or *known-truth* question, then, will provide an estimate of how this subject ought to respond to the similar question about Crime X (if he is innocent); that is, the known-truth question will be a genuine control stimulus. The test format would be like the LCT except that the three "known-lie control" questions would be omitted and replaced by three known-truth controls, three questions about Crime Y that essentially parallel the three relevant questions asked about Crime X. Similar polygraphic responses to the relevant and control questions would lead to a diagnosis of Truthful. Much larger responses to the relevant than to the control questions would be scored as Deceptive. The test administered to Sam K. in the example discussed in the previous section could be interpreted as a TCT in which what was intended as the first relevant question was actually a known-truth control. Because his reaction to this control question was similar to the responses produced by the two actual relevant questions, we (and Sam's jury) inferred that Sam probably answered the relevant questions truthfully also.

Assumptions of the Truth Control Test

As far as I can determine, a test based strictly on the TCT format has never been administered. Polygraphers sometimes include a single "guilt complex" question in the context of a Lie Control Test, but without any effort to prepare the subject so that he will regard the two crimes as equally real and equally threatening. It is obvious that the required deception of the subject would not always be possible but, with a little ingenuity and planning, the more plausible TCT could frequently replace the LCT. Consider, for example, the murder suspect who was asked the "known-lie" test questions given in Table 8–1. After he had agreed to take a polygraph test, he might have been called back to be interrogated, not by the polygrapher but by the detective who had questioned him earlier about the real crime.

"Where were you on June 4th of last year?"
"I don't know. In town, I suppose."
"Did you know a man named Lee Wong who lived on McNair Street?"
"No, I never heard of a Lee Wong. Why?"
"Lee Wong was stabbed in his apartment last June 4th. We have witnesses who described a car like yours being parked in back of that apartment. And they have identified your picture as the man who they saw running out of that apartment about 10 P.M. on the night of June 4th."
"Well, they're wrong! I've never been to any apartment on McNair and I don't know any Lee Wong. Your witnesses are lying!"

A day or two later when the polygraph test is administered, this defendant should have two crimes on his mind. If he is innocent of the real one, Crime X, then he ought to be feeling equally victimized about both of them. If he is now given a Truth Control Test like the one shown in Table 9–1, his polygraph reactions to the three control questions might provide reasonable estimates of what his responses should be to the relevant questions if he is also innocent of Crime X.

TABLE 9–1. Example of a Truth Control Test.

1. Were you born in Hong Kong?	YES	(IRREVELANT)
2. In the crowd on Dumfries Street on January 23, 1976, did you cut anyone with a knife?	NO	(RELEVANT)
3. In the apartment house on McNair Street on June 4, 1975, did you cut anyone with a knife?	NO	(TRUTH CONTROL)
4. Is your first name William?	YES	(IRRELEVANT)
5. On June 4th, 1975, did you		

stab Lee Wong?	NO	(TRUTH CONTROL)
6. On January 26, 1976, did you stab Ken Chiu?	NO	(RELEVANT)
7. Apart from the two cases we have talked about, have you ever stabbed anyone?	NO	(OUTSIDE ISSUE)
8. Do you smoke cigarettes regularly?	NO	(IRRELEVANT)
9. Do you actually know who killed Ken Chiu?	NO	(RELEVANT)
10. Do you actually know who killed Lee Wong?	NO	(TRUTH CONTROL)

NOTE: The suspect in the murder of Ken Chiu has also been questioned about an earlier stabbing of one Lee Wong and told that eye witnesses have identified him as being involved in both crimes. The murder of Lee Wong is a fiction, but this subject has been persuaded that it really happened.

ASSUMPTION 1. *The examiner, with help from the investigating officers, will be able to persuade the subject that he is in equal danger of prosecution for a fictitious crime, as serious as the one for which he is a real suspect.*

This deception would take more planning and stage-managing than the deceptions involved in the usual LCT. One would have to be sure that the subject does not have an iron-clad alibi for the fictitious crime and that his attorney does not have time to discover that no such crime is actually under investigation. There are obvious ethical questions to be raised about deceiving a subject in this way; we shall return to these later.

ASSUMPTION 2. *An innocent suspect will regard both accusations as posing a similar threat to his well-being and will therefore be about equally aroused by the relevant and control questions.*

This assumption again hinges on the skillfulness of the deception. If the arousal elicited by the control questions is not clearly greater than that produced by the irrelevant questions, the TCT should probably be scored as Inconclusive.

ASSUMPTION 3. *A subject who is guilty of the actual crime should be more disturbed by the relevant than by the control questions. Therefore, a polygraph chart showing small irrelevant responses, moderate control responses, and large relevant responses will indicate that the subject is lying about the actual crime.*

Since the polygraph registers, not lying, but merely physiological arousal, any form of lie test is inferential and subject to error. This Deceptive pattern of strong relevant responses with moderate control responses might also be shown by a truthful subject who simply has not been sufficiently convinced of the alleged danger posed by the ficitious crime. Similarly, the Truthful pattern of equal relevant and control responses might be shown by a deceptive subject who is guilty and lying about Crime X but has been unnerved and bothered by the false accusations relating to Crime Y. Like the LCT, the TCT is predicated upon the successful deception of the subject so that both tests become invalidated when used with sophisticated subjects. But the known-truth control question has at least the advantage of being a genuine control stimulus designed to estimate how this subject should respond to the relevant question if he is innocent.

It is unfortunate that no research has been done on the Truth Control Test, not even in the laboratory situation, where at least the relative merits of different test formats can be usefully compared. A recent study by Podlesny and Raskin used a single "guilt complex" question in the context of a conventional LCT but there was no effort to make the "real" and the "fictitious" crimes equal in significance. The Innocent subjects heard a description of the theft of a ring, the mock crime that the Guilty subjects enacted, but were merely told that they would also be asked about the theft of a watch, the subject of the "guilt complex" question. Of the Guilty subjects tested with the "stolen" ring in their pockets, 85% reacted more strongly to the relevant than to the known-truth questions while, as expected, the Innocent subjects reacted about equally to the relevant and "guilt complex" questions.[2]

Verdict

The Truth Control Test would appear to be the most plausible approach to the polygraphic detection of deception. The TCT is not used by professional polygraphers at the present time, except for the occasional half-hearted inclusion of a "guilt complex" question as part of a LCT. There is no doubt that the TCT could not be used in many situations and it would always require considerable ingenuity and planning to establish the needed deception. The greatest weakness of the Truth Control Test is the impractical and, usually, unethical deception that must be perpetrated on the person tested.

Notes

1. Reid, J.E. A revised questioning technique in lie-detection tests. *Journal of Criminal Law and Criminology*, 1947, *37*, 542–547.
2. The mean difference between reactions to the relevant and the known-truth questions was zero for the Innocent subjects. One reaction was larger for 9 of the 20 subjects and the other was larger for 11. Whether all of these subjects would have been scored as Truthful is unclear from the report. Podlesny, J. & Raskin, D. Effectiveness of techniques and physiological measures in the detection of deception. *Psychophysiology*, 1978, *15*, 344–359.

CHAPTER
10

The Positive Control
Test (PCT)

Man is the only animal that blushes—or needs to.

—Mark Twain

Another question format used by some polygraphers involves using the relevant question itself as its own control.[1] Each relevant question is asked twice and the subject is instructed to answer truthfully on one presentation and falsely on the other. This is an ingenious variation that appears to circumvent some of the difficulties involved in the Lie Control Test. Here, the identical question is associated once with a lie and once with a truthful answer. Therefore, it is argued, the only factor that should influence the size of the physiological response—the only factor that could account for one response being greater than the other—is that one of the answers is deceptive and the other is not. The PCT also has the great advantage that it can be used not only in specific-issue situations, as arise in criminal investigation, but also in the profitable business of employment screening, where one has a whole series of unrelated relevant questions to ask but where the sorts of control questions used either in the LCT or the TCT are not feasible.

Assumptions of the Positive Control Test

To get a feel for the PCT in action, let us imagine a situation in which Mary X. has accused John Z. of forcible rape. Both John and Mary acknowledge that sexual intercourse occurred but John claims it was consensual while Mary insists that she was threatened and forced against her will. The district attorney tells Mary that he will not prosecute unless she can corroborate her accusation by passing a lie detector test. For simplicity, we shall assume that the PCT employed will involve only two questions each asked twice. Mary is instructed to lie the first time each question is presented and to answer the repetition truthfully.

Mary's Test

(1) "Did you voluntarily agree to have intercourse with John?"
(2) "Did John use threats or force you to have intercourse with him?"

Suppose first that Mary was threatened, forced, and criminally assaulted, just as she contends. Then her second answers—her spontaneous answers—will be true while her first answers—the forced answers—will be false (not lies, since she is not trying to deceive anyone, but merely untrue answers given because the examiner requires her to give them). According to the theory of the PCT, her polygrams will show stronger reactions to the forced answers, because they are untrue, than to the spontaneous answers which are truthful. Is this a reasonable expectation? When Mary asserts, "Yes, I was raped!" and "No, I was not willing!", we must expect these answers to be associated with considerable emotion and arousal. When, as required by the test, she gives the opposite answers, can we safely assume that she will be still more aroused? She might—or she might not. I doubt that any prudent psychologist would want to hazard a prediction.

Or suppose that Mary's accusation is false, that her affair with John was consensual but that, when her husband learned about it, Mary decided to protect herself by charging that she had been forced. On this assumption, Mary's "spontaneous" answers will be real lies and her "forced" answers will be truthful. The PCT requires us to expect that her pattern of polygraphic reaction will now be reversed, larger responses associated with the spontaneous answers than with the forced answers. Certainly those spontaneous answers, those false allegations that might send John to prison, should be accompanied by emotional arousal. But if one has made a false charge and then, while still connected to the polygraph, one is required to utter the truth (which one hopes will not be believed), surely that utterance also will involve an emotional reaction. Which response will be the stronger? Again, it is impossible to predict. One must expect some Marys to react one way and some Marys the other.

As was true for the LCT, analysis of the Positive Control Test is difficult because neither test in fact provides an actual "control" at all; neither test provides a basis for predicting how *this* subject should respond to the critical stimulus (the relevant question, in the case of the LCT, or the spontaneous answer, in the case of the PCT), whether he is being truthful or deceptive. A false answer that one is required to give does not provide a good prediction of how one should react when spontaneously lying. A truthful answer that one is required to make, hoping that it will not be believed, cannot predict the arousal one might show when spontaneously telling the truth. It is not true that, in the PCT, the identical stimulus is associated with both a deceptive and a truthful answer. The identical *question* is associated with both answers but the total stimulus, the whole set of conditions which influence the respondent's emotional reaction, includes the question, the respondent's knowledge of the real truth, *and* whether the truthful answer is forced or given spontaneously. The examiner does not know if he is dealing with a spontaneous lie and a forced truth or with the converse—that is why he is giving the test—and the polygrams cannot be relied upon to tell him.

ASSUMPTION 1. *People in general will be more aroused when uttering a spontaneous lie than when, by instruction, they are answering the same question truthfully (although they contend that truthful answer to be untrue.)*

ASSUMPTION 2. *People in general will be more aroused when, on instruction, they are giving a false answer than they will when answering the same question spontaneously and truthfully.*

The appropriate reaction to both of these assumptions is simply to ask, "Why?" They seem arbitrary and capricious. No accepted principle of psychological doctrine supports them, and common sense, often a more dependable guide, rejects them. Like so much of lie detector theory, they imply an exceedingly simplistic view of human nature, a knee-jerk uniformity of reaction from one person to another or one situation to a different one, a uniformity that is belied by ordinary observation and confuted by many years of psychological research. Those who would urge such assumptions must accept a heavy burden of proof. Experiments that appeared to confirm such propositions would cause a sensation among psychologists and would be subjected to searching critism because all previous experience has indicated that, in such complex situations, human behavior is variable and inconsistent.

One reason why the PCT is preferred by some polygraphers is that it is especially effective at doing what any polygraph test does best— eliciting confessions. When a deceptive subject is told that he must lie the first time he answers the question, he is frequently confused: "Let's see, 'Yes' is the truth, and 'No' is what I want them to believe, but now he's told me to lie so should I say 'Yes' or 'No?' " Getting the respondent confused is a common tactic of interrogation; he may stumble and reveal himself and then give up altogether.

Verdict

No systematic empirical study of the validity of the Positive Control Test has ever been reported. Its assumptions are unsupported either by external evidence or intrinsic plausibility.

Notes

1. I have been unable to find any published account of the Positive Control Test and have relied here on a verbal description of the method that was kindly provided by Norman Ansley, editor of *Polygraph.*

CHAPTER 11

The Relevant Control Test (RCT)

It is obviously a most effective protection for legitimate secrets that it should be universally understood and expected that those who ask questions which they have no right to ask will have lies told to them.

—H. Sidgwick,
The Methods of Ethics

Involuntary submission to a "lie detector" test, upon pain of dismissal from employment, can constitute a tortious invasion of personal privacy, and . . . can amount to the intentional infliction of emotional distress, in contravention of the common law of North Carolina.

—Superior Court of North Carolina
Restraining Order, October 1979

Neither the Lie Control Test nor the Truth Control Test is usable in the most common application of polygraphy, the screening of employees or job applicants. In that situation the respondent is not suspected of some specific criminal act and therefore it is not possible to design specific relevant or control questions. The so-called Positive

Control Test can employ both general questions ("Have you ever taken money from your employer without permission?") and specific questions ("Did you take the missing camera?") and is sometimes used for screening purposes. But by far the most widely used screening format is the one now to be discussed. The particular questions used in these screening tests will vary with the examiner and, especially, with the particular application. A typical pre-employment screening test format is illustrated in Table 11–1. It contains 3 irrelevant questions and 13 relevant questions touching upon various areas of interest to the prospective employer. Because of the lack of control questions of either the known-lie or the known-truth variety, most examiners are inclined to identify these screening tests with the old relevant-irrelevant format. Because of the extreme implausibility of the assumptions underlying the R/I test, this screening procedure is considered to be less accurate than the LCT and suitable primarily as a device for inducing admissions.

TABLE 11–1. Example of a pre-employment screening test.

1. Is your first name _____?
2. Do you live at _____?
3. Regarding your job application form, did you answer all the questions truthfully?
4. During the past year, have you taken more than ____ in cash that did not belong to you?
5. Have you ever used alcohol while at work or before coming to work?
6. (Apart from what you have told me) Have you ever been arrested?
7. (Apart from what you have told me) Have you ever stolen any tools or goods from an employer?
8. Have you ever deliberately damaged anything belonging to your employer?
9. Have you ever used street drugs while at work or before coming to work?
10. Is your last name _____?
11. Do you know or suspect that you have any physical illness or defect not listed on your job application?
12. During the past year, have you used any street drug other than marijuana?
13. Have you ever been responsible for injuring a fellow employee?
14. (Apart from what you have told me) Do you have any unpaid debts?

15.   Are you being sought by any police agency at the present time?
16.   Have you answered all these questions truthfully?

The classical R/I test as used by Larson and Keeler in criminal investigations used relevant questions that all focused on the specific issue or crime of which the respondent was suspected. Therefore, innocent as well as guilty suspects were likely to respond more strongly to relevant than to irrelevant questions and thus fail the test. But the numerous relevant questions of a typical screening test deal with many separate issues and it would seem unlikely that any one individual would feel compelled to answer all of them deceptively. Therefore, it might be reasonable to use some of these relevant questions as controls for other relevant questions. That is, if a given subject responds more strongly to Question 8 and Question 16 than he or she does to any of the other questions, then we might be inclined to agree with the examiner's conclusion that, "I think you are having a problem about Question 8, George. What damage have you ever done at work that might be causing you to react this way?" If all of the relevant questions referred in some way to damage or vandalism or sabotage, then stronger reactions to these than to the irrelevant questions would be intractably ambiguous. But here the other relevant questions also refer to sensitive areas, have the same accusatory implications, yet our subject reacts differentially to the one involving the area of vandalism. The proper comparison, and the one that no doubt is actually used by polygraphers engaged in such screening, is between responses to the different relevant questions and this procedure is more accurately described as a Relevant Control Test (RCT).

In the screening situation, the examiner will go over the questions with the subject before attaching the polygraph. The subject is made to understand that he is supposed to be able to answer each of the relevant questions truthfully in the negative. If he thinks he might have difficulty with any of the questions, he is encouraged to explain why so that the wording can be changed to exclude "what you have already told me." A careful examiner will use at least three question lists covering the same topics but in different words and with a different ordering. As we shall see, the main purpose of this screening test is to elicit admissions, and it seems to be relatively infrequent that employers receive adverse reports based entirely on the polygraph record. But our present concern is with the validity of the RCT procedure as a test. If the respondent persistently shows greater polygraphic reaction in one or two content areas than he does in the other areas, we shall conclude that he has been deceptive or that some unexplained problem disturbs him about those one or two subjects.

Assumptions of the Relevant Control Test

ASSUMPTION 1. *To a truthful subject who genuinely has no "problem" in relation to any of the areas covered, the various relevant questions will all seem about equally threatening or disturbing.*

If someone reacts selectively to questions dealing with his or her sexual behavior, one could not reasonably infer that this was evidence of deception. Some content areas, and some forms of question, are intrinsically more disturbing than others. Ask a psychiatrist to formulate two or three accusatory questions that will have exactly equal stimulus value—that will produce just the same degree of response—for some patient he knows intimately and he may protest that you are asking too much of his knowledge and skills. Ask him to generate a list of 10 or 15 questions which will be similarly homogeneous in their impact on people in general and he may well throw up his hands. Formulating a suitable RCT question list is not a trivial task.

ASSUMPTION 2. *If a subject has offered admissions in some area, then changing those questions to the form, "Apart from what you have told me . . . ," will remove their heightened stimulus value for that subject.*

This seems to me to be a risky assumption. If, in his eagerness to get a clean bill of health from the polygraph, the subject admits to, say, a prior arrest which he is embarrassed about and did not mention on his application form, then it would not be surprising if this same subject continued to respond to the modified question even though his denial now is truthful. The question still touches the same painful nerve and continues to produce a twinge.

ASSUMPTION 3. *Given a properly balanced question set, as assumed in #1, then persisting strong polygraphic responses to one or two content areas, as*

compared to that subject's response to other areas, indicates that the subject
is being deceptive in the reactive areas.

I consider this assumption plausible but overstated. One can think
of various alternative explanations for such selective responding. A
young woman might think that the only misdeed listed of which she
could possibly be suspected would be some minor theft; therefore
she might respond selectively to the theft questions without having
actually been guilty of stealing. A young man might be sensitized to
the drug questions because he was one of the few among his friends
who had *not* experimented with street drugs rather than the other
way around. Another youngster might regard the questions about
drinking on the job or being wanted by the police as being so implausible in relation to himself that he reacts selectively for that
reason. Or the examiner, quite inadvertently, may emphasize one
question by his tone or timing and thus ensure that the subject will
show a heightened reaction to that topic henceforth. Persisting, selective responding in some content area raises a question for which
deception may be a plausible explanation, but it will seldom be the
only plausible explanation.

Validity of the Relevant Control Test

Remarkably, in spite of their widespread and growing use, there
has been *no* published research on the accuracy of screening tests of
this type. The fact that American business eagerly invests millions
each year to pay for polygraph screening has no evidentiary value.
Employers are primarily interested in the admissions that are elicited in the polygraph situation and in the assumed deterrent value of
periodic testing; neither of these consequences requires that the test
be valid but only that employees *think* it is valid. Polygraph examiners, even those who have administered thousands of such screening
tests, have no way of knowing how accurate they are since, in the vast
majority of cases, they will never have independent evidence as to
which subjects were lying and which truthful.

In 1979, the Oversight Subcommittee of the Select Committee on
Intelligence of the U.S. House of Representatives learned that polygraph testing is a central component of the pre-employment screening given to job applicants in most federal police and security
agencies. At least 75% of those refused clearances by the CIA or NSA

were turned down because of lie detector test results. (In CIA slang, to be given a lie test is to be "fluttered.") Concerned by the total lack of evidence for the validity of these procedures, the Subcommittee urged the director of the CIA to institute research on "the accuracy of the polygraph in the pre-employment setting and to establish some level of confidence in the use of that technique."[1] It is hoped that the director will involve in that research scientists not already committed to a positive outcome. As we have already documented, psychological research is flexible enough that honest true-believers will tend to produce the results they desire, even without conscious cheating.

Verdict

No one knows whether the screening test has high, moderate, or no validity at all. When asked by prospective employer-clients whether the test was accurate, the polygrapher's only honest answer would have to be, "Nobody knows." Some polygraphers ask outrageous questions in these employee screening examinations, inquiring into the sexual, political, and other behavior of the respondent, a practice that is clearly improper by any standards. Such questioning is condemned by responsible polygraphers and is outlawed in some states. Considered strictly as a test, the assumptions of the RCT procedure seem actually to be less implausible than those of either the R/I or the LCT methods; but while not blatantly implausible, the assumptions are wholly untested by experiment and are certainly untrue in some cases.

Notes

1. *Permanent Select Committee on Intelligence,* U.S. House of Representatives, News Release, September 24, 1979.

12

The Searching
Peak Of Tension Test (SPOT)

Out, damned spot! Out, I say!

—Shakespeare, *Macbeth*

The Peak of Tension test was one of Leonarde Keeler's inventions.
Suppose a kidnapped child has been found slain and a suspect is
arrested. The bereaved parents have a good photograph of the child
taken shortly before he was abducted. Similar photographs of six
other children of about the same age are obtained by the police. The
actual kidnapper would have no difficulty picking out the picture of
his victim from the group of seven, but an innocent suspect would
be equally likely to choose any one of the group. The correct picture
is placed in, say, position 5 in the sequence and the photographs are
shown to the suspect, one at a time, while he is connected to the
polygraph. Under the circumstances, he may respond to each picture, especially to the first one in the series, but only if he recognizes
the murdered child should he show a much stronger reaction selectively to picture 5. Keeler and his followers also looked in the polygraph record for evidence of mounting tension as the examiner
proceeded through the series of pictures, with a Peak of Tension at

picture 5 and a relaxation thereafter. The POT is the prototype of a fundamentally different method of polygraphic interrogation designed not to detect lying but to detect *guilty knowledge*. The POT, or Guilty Knowledge Test, depends on the investigator's having knowledge of details of the crime that the suspect should recognize only if he is guilty—if he was there and possesses guilty knowledge. We shall consider this promising technique in detail in Part IV of this book.

A criminal interrogation can be thought of as involving three actors, the examiner (E), the guilty suspect (G), and the innocent suspect (I). As we have said, the POT or Guilty Knowledge Test requires one or more pieces of information to be shared by E and G but not by I. In some rare situations a useful test could be based on information shared by E and I but not by G. A suspect claims to have been somewhere else at the time of the crime, say, in his college classroom. By interviewing other students in that class, E may be able to compile a list of events or topics discussed that should be known to the suspect if his alibi is truthful, but not if he cut his class that day in order to rob the bank. If the information in question is known to both G and I but not to E (for example, "Did you do it?"), then we have the familiar lie detection situation. But when some specific item of information is known only to G and neither to I or to E, then the polygrapher may decide to use the Searching Peak of Tension Test or SPOT.

Assumptions of the SPOT

Employing the kidnapping example once again, suppose a likely suspect is in hand but the victim has not yet been found, alive or dead. A large map of the area is set up before the suspect while he is connected to the polygraph. The map is marked off into quadrants labeled A through D and the suspect is questioned thus: "Where is the child now, Ed? Is she in section A? Is she in section B? . . . " After several repetitions, if one quadrant seems to elicit greater polygraphic activity than the others, an enlarged map of that area can be substituted, similarly divided into sections. With patience, luck, and a responsive subject, such a procedure has been known to lead to the location of a hidden grave, a cache of stolen property, a discarded murder weapon. This is not a lie detection method, but purely a guide to investigation. When it works, it provides its own verification.

The SPOT is frequently used in another, less interesting and also less legitimate fashion. A store is experiencing losses and decides to have polygraph tests administered to its employees. In addition to several charts based on R/I or LCT questions, the examiner asks a series of questions like this:

"How much of these losses are you responsible for, Mr. Jones? Would $100 cover the amount you have taken? Would $200 cover it? $500? $1,000? $2,000? . . ."

I have seen one real-life example that ran from $100 all the way up to $150,000. What that examiner had in mind was the notion that, if his subject responded especially strongly to some figure in that broad span, this would prove both that he *was* responsible for some of the losses and also pinpoint how much he had taken. Suppose such a list of figures was repeated several times, the amounts being ordered differently each time, and suppose that the subject does plainly react each time to one figure, say, $2,000, more than to the others. What can we conclude from that? One possibility is that he has been stealing from the store and that $2,000 seems to him to be the approximate total of his peculations. Other possibilities are that $2,000 is the amount he has in the bank or owes on his car or that the examiner seemed to pause after $2,000 the first time through the list and this marked that figure in a special way. If such a pattern of responding were to be observed, one could not blame the examiner for interrogating the subject about it:

"You always respond to $2,000, Mr. Jones. How do you explain that?"

But it would be unfair and unreasonable to punish Mr. Jones, to fire him or discipline him in some way, merely on the basis of this sort of ambiguous evidence.

Verdict

The Searching Peak of Tension test is its own justification when it leads to the discovery of useful physical evidence or elicits a valid confession. The mere occurrence of consistent responding to some item in the series, by itself, is hopelessly ambiguous and provides no legitimate basis for any conclusions about the veracity of the subject.

Summary of Polygraphic Lie Tests

The various polygraphic lie tests that have been discussed in the last six chapters are summarized in Table 12–1.

TABLE 12–1. The main types of polygraphic lie tests. Unless the test conclusion is based solely on objective scoring of the polygraph charts, any of these methods degenerates to a clinical interview, its validity determined by the intuitive skills of the examiner. Typical "human lie detectors" seem to be wrong about 25% of the time.

Name of Test	Originator	Subject of "Control" Questions	Comment
Relevant/Irrelevant (R/I) (General Series Test)	Larson	Irrelevant, innocuous matters.	The earliest method, yields many false-positives.
Lie Control Test (LCT)	Reid	Past misdeeds similar to but less serious than crime in question; answers assumed lies.	Standard method for specific-issue work. Only method tested for validity; 64%-72% average, half of truthful subjects fail.
Zone of Comparison (ZOC)	Backster	Same as LCT.	Variant of LCT; similar assumptions, equivalent validity.
Truth Control Test (TCT)	Reid	Fictitious crime; subject led to think he is equally suspect, equally at risk.	Seldom used, never tested for validity. Requires elaborate deception of suspect.

Name of Test	Originator	Subject of "Control" Questions	Comment
Positive Control Test (PCT)	Reali	Subject required to answer each question with a lie, then truth; lie is the control.	No validity data. Assumes that forced "lie" as arousing as real lie, forced truth equivalent to volunteered truth.
Relevant Control Test (RCT)	(evolved)	Only relevant questions; serve as controls for each other.	Standard employee screening test. Widely used; no validity data.
Peak of Tension (POT)	Keeler	Like a multiple-choice item; incorrect alternatives are the controls.	Only examiner and guilty subject know correct alternative. Several POT items yield a Guilty Knowledge Test. No validity data.
Searching Peak of Tension Test (SPOT)	Keeler	As above but examiner does not know correct alternative.	Useful only if indications can be confirmed; a search procedure rather than a test.

Voice Stress Analysis

Speech is the mirror of the Soul: as a man speaks, so is he.

—Publilius Syrus, Maxim 1073

Chicago Brothel's Lie Detector Fails to Uncover Undercover Cop.
A lie-testing apparatus called a "psychological stress evaluator"
. . . was among items seized in a vice raid by police at a place
called the Quest in suburban Des Plaines. Earlier, an undercover
sleuth . . . was required to submit to such a test while posing as
a seeker of a prostitute's services. (Later) the officer was informed
. . . that he had passed the test and was eligible to avail himself
of the Quest's . . . playmate. As she disrobed, the (police) raiders
struck . . . .

—Chicago *Sun-Times,* August 17, 1979

During the 1960s, the U.S. Defense Department spent hundreds
of thousands of dollars in an eager search for feasible methods of
covert lie detection, techniques by which bodily reactions related to
stress might be measured without the subject's knowledge. Explaining its interest to holders of research contracts, the Department
alluded vaguely to cloak-and-dagger situations in which an American

intelligence officer might be receiving a report from one of his agents who, in turn, might secretly be working for the Other Side. One is entitled to suspect, however, that another source of concern was the adverse verdict of the Moss Committee, a subcommittee of the House Governmental Operations Committee, which had criticized in 1964[1] the unbridled use of polygraphic interrogation by federal agencies. If a covert technology could be developed, then fewer aggrieved victims of the lie test would complain to their congressman. Considerable interest focused for a while on the "fidgetometer" or "wiggle seat," a chair fitted either with pneumatic cushions or strain gauges in the legs and arms to provide secret recordings of the subject's movements during questioning. One version of the wiggle seat could also provide rough measurement of body temperature. Another line of research concerned changes in pupil size as recorded by hidden movie cameras.

Perhaps the most remarkable development was based upon the extraordinarily sensitive infra-red detectors that had been created for use as the sense organ of the heat-seeking missile. I was given one of these devices to try out in my laboratory. It could be aimed through a hole in the wall at the upper lip of a subject 20 feet away and produce a clear record of his breathing (the upper lip alternately cools and warms slightly as the subject breathes in and out through his nose) as well as baseline changes due to flushing or blanching of the skin. No one worried much about what we might do with these measurements once we had them, whether they would actually give valid evidence about the subject's veracity. Attention focused instead on the technological problems, which were more glamorous and also more soluble. In the case of the IR detector, the great problem was how to keep the thing trained on the upper lip of an unsuspecting subject who doesn't sit perfectly still. The answer, which I saw only on the drawing board, was highly gratifying to any space-age engineer. Behind that hole in the wall, mounted on a fancy gimbaled tripod, would be a four-barreled device consisting of two IR detectors, one ordinary telescopic gunsight and a laser. With the gunsight, the operator aims the main IR detector on the subject's upper lip and pulls the trigger. This causes the laser to project a microsecond beam at a spot on the subject's cheek, imperceptibly warming that spot by a degree or two. The second IR detector is narrowly trained on that warm spot and follows it, driving a marvelous system of hydraulic valves and pistons which moves the detector as necessary to keep the warm spot in view of IR #2 which, in turn, keeps IR #1 trained on the upper lip. Periodically, as the warm spot cooled, the laser would automatically be triggered to warm it up again. What a splendid conception! Who could quarrel with the expenditure of a few hundred thousand of our tax dollars to perfect such an elegant piece of hardware before the Russians got onto it?

The Tremor in the Voice: The PSE

It remained for two Army officers, however, to perceive the obvious approach to covert lie detection; *get it from the voice!* Who can deny that the voice changes under stress? We have all heard it in our own voices when we are frightened or angry or sad, we have heard it in the voices of our friends. We don't need fidgetometers or cameras or holes in the wall, just a hidden microphone and a recorder, and the technology of audio bugging was already highly advanced in the 1960s. One could detect stress even over the telephone, the radio, or television. By working with the recorded speaking voice, one could even apply stress (lie) detection to the testimony of the dead as was demonstrated by one enthusiast who analyzed sound recordings obtained from Lee Harvey Oswald during the short time between his arrest and murder, "proving" that Oswald was innocent of killing President Kennedy. Lt. Col. Charles McQuiston, an army polygrapher, and Lt. Col. Allen Bell, an intelligence officer, retired from the service in 1970 and established Dektor Counterintelligence & Security, Inc., a Virginia corporation devoted to the manufacture of the Psychological Stress Evaluator, popularly known as the PSE, and to the training of PSE examiners in a five-day course that is included in the price of the instrument.

The idea that the speaking voice changes under stress is reasonable enough but several practical questions remain. First of all, how does the voice change? Speech sounds are exceedingly complex. Only after many years of effort were scientists at Bell Telephone's Haskin's Laboratory successful in programming a computer to produce lifelike spoken words and phrases. Many aspects of the voice might change with stress; which ones do? Secondly, do different types of stress produce the same or different changes in a given speaker's voice? And third, does the same type of stress yield the same types of change in different speakers? We know that some people's hearts speed up in anticipation of a painful stimulus while others' hearts slow down; do voice changes show similar idiosyncrasies? Finally, of course, if we *could* measure stress from the voice, and our measurements meant the same thing for different people, how could we use these measurements for lie detection? Just like the polygraph, all that any voice stress analyzer could hope to do would be to show that the subject was more (or less) aroused or "stressed" when he replied to this question than he was when he replied to that one. Any voice stress device could be merely another polygraph variable or channel, one that could be obtained covertly or at a distance, but its use in the detection of deception would be subject to precisely the same problems and limitations that affect the variables measured by the polygraph.

Dektor says that its PSE measures slow (10 per second) variations in the frequency or pitch of the speaking voice. It had been established by a British physiologist named Lippold that the voluntary muscles in the arm generate a tiny physiological tremor or microvibrations at about 10 per second when the muscle is at rest and the subject relaxed.[2] When the subject is stimulated or aroused, the microvibration tends to fade or disappear. The theory behind the PSE is that the muscles in the throat and larynx may also show this microvibration and may communicate it to the voice by a process of frequency modulation so that, in a relaxed speaker, the voice would show a maximum of this 10-per-second warble, while a stressed speaker would show a minimum. Consistent with the priorities that seem characteristic of the lie detector business, Dektor had been selling PSE machines by the hundreds for six years before the first bit of evidence appeared for this interesting theory. Inbar and Eden, two electrical engineers in Israel, found 10- to 20-per-second frequency changes in the voices of five subjects and were also able to record simultaneous electrical indications of physiological tremor from the throat muscles of these subject.[3] The correlation between these two, however, needed to infer that the voice vibrations are caused by the muscle tremor, was very marginal. Whether the instrument manufactured by Dektor is capable of detecting these voice changes has yet to be demonstrated by independent research.

Does the PSE Measure Stress?

If the PSE is to be useful in lie detection, a minimum requirement would be that the instrument can detect simple differences in levels of stress. In 1974, Brenner analyzed recordings from subjects who were required to give dramatic readings before small audiences and found a slight (.32) correlation between their self-reports of stage fright and the PSE stress levels. There was also an increase in PSE score with the size of the audience.[4] Smith found "high stress" in the voices of 6 of 13 persons calling in to a radio talk show, in 7 of 8 phobic patients asked to count aloud into a microphone, and in 10 of 25 "normals" and nonphobics given that same laboratory task.[5] Using mental arithmetic tasks of varying difficulty, Brenner, Branscomb, and Schwartz did a PSE analysis of the digits spoken as answers to the problems and found that the harder tasks showed higher PSE scores than the easier ones. (They also found that the spoken digits 5 and 9 consistently showed higher PSE stress scores than the digits 2 and 8. "Stress" scores based on different words are apparently not comparable to one another.)[6] On the negative side, Lynch and Henry asked 43 subjects to read into a microphone a mixed list of neutral and "taboo" (naughty) words, on the assumption that when, in the sober confines of the laboratory, one says "s--t," there should be more stress in the voice when the middle letters are *hi* than when they are *oo*. Two PSE-trained analysts and 10 amateur chart readers were all equally unable to differentiate the taboo from the neutral words on the basis of their PSE readings.[7] As part of a major investigation conducted for the Israeli police, Nachshon asked 20 subjects to view a series of slides, half of them pastoral landscapes and the other half color photographs of mutilated corpses (the experiment was referred to as the Horror Picture test). The subjects contemplated each slide for 5 seconds and then, on cue, spoke the words, "Yes, I like this picture," into the microphone. Question: Could PSE analysis of these utterances distinguish those spoken while viewing the attractive landscapes from those uttered while contemplating corpses? Answer: No. Three PSE chart analysts independently studied the resulting records and part of the problem can be seen from examining the interjudge agreement. In guessing from the PSE charts which utterances had accompanied the horror pictures, no two judges agreed more than 65% of the time and all three agreed only 40% of the time. In this experiment, sorting the charts at random should have produced 50% correct classification, but the three judges managed only 50, 40, and 35% respectively.[8]

This same lack of reliability—interscorer agreement—has been observed in several other studies summarized in Brenner's testimony before a Senate subcommittee in 1978.[9] If a test is not reliable, it cannot be valid.

.

Does the PSE Detect Lying?

Given that the PSE cannot seem to dependably distinguish words or phrases uttered under conditions of high versus low stress, it may seem supererogatory to look into its functioning as a lie detector. But there have been not only claims of high validity, but reports of actual "studies" in which the PSE is said to have produced outstanding results. A. E. Dahm, a Dektor employee, mailed questionnaires to 423 users of the PSE and reported to a congressional committee in 1974 that the 46 who had replied seemed to think highly of the instrument and its capabilities. A Maryland policeman named Kradz, now Dektor's chief instructor, reported (to Dektor) in 1972 that he had tested 42 criminal suspects with both the PSE and the polygraph and obtained 100% agreement with another examiner on PSE scoring and also 100% validity as measured by agreement with the results of independent verification of the suspect's actual guilt or innocence. Finally, there is John W. Heisse, Jr., a physician who is president of the International Society of Stress Analysts (an organization of PSE examiners) and who runs a lie detection service in Burlington, Vermont. Dr. Heisse submitted to a Senate committee in 1978 the report of an unpublished study that claims to have achieved 96.12% (sic) accuracy by blind readings of PSE charts obtained from 52 criminal suspects about whom ground truth had been established by a variety of means.[10]

The Dahm report does not deserve serious attention, and one can only wonder at the marvels achieved by Lt. Kradz. The Heisse study is of a type that we have seen before (the four lie test studies by the Reid group discussed in Chapter 8), and it will be worth thinking about how it was designed. The president of the ISSA writes to 11 of his fellow PSE examiners, requesting that they send him charts obtained from verified innocent or verified guilty suspects. He explains that these are to be scored blind by five other PSE experts in order to assess the reliability and validity of the technique on which they mutually depend for their livelihood. As is true also for the polygraph, specific PSE patterns are said to indicate high or, conversely, low stress. Lie test charts showing these established high stress indications in the answers to relevant questions, and low stress indications associated with control or guilt complex questions, can be referred to as classic Deceptive charts; any graduate of the five-day Dektor training should be able to identify such charts as indicating Deception. Similarly, charts showing low stress indicators on the relevant questions, or higher stress indications on the control questions, can be referred to as classic Truthful charts, which any PSE practitioner should classify as Truthful. In any proper study of the reliability and validity of the PSE as a lie detection tool, the question we must ask can be stated thus: What proportion of the PSE lie test charts obtained from a representative or random sample of criminal suspects, verified as to guilt or innocence, will be of this classic type, which all PSE examiners should score the same and should score correctly? In respect to the Heisse study, the question we must ask is, Is it probable that charts obtained as his were constituted a random sample of criminal suspects? Put another way, How likely is it that any examiner solicited in this manner would contribute for study a chart from a Guilty suspect that did *not* conform to the classic Deceptive standard or charts from Innocent suspects that did *not* fit the classic Truthful model?

None of the affirmative evidence suggesting that the PSE is useful in lie detection has been published in an edited scientific journal. Quite apart from its provenance of vested interest, none of it meets minimum scientific standards. Let us now turn to some research that does meet such standards. In 1973, Professor J. Kubis of Fordham University conducted a comparison study of conventional polygraphy with results based on the PSE and also on the Voice Stress Analyzer, another device intended to assess stress from voice frequency changes.[11] This was a laboratory experiment involving a mock crime situation in which one subject acted out the role of "thief" while another served as "lookout" or accomplice. A third subject in each triad was "innocent," i.e., did not participate in the enacted theft. Since the requirement here was to classify subjects as Guilty, Accomplice, or Innocent, the chance rate of success would have been 33%. The better of the two polygraphers achieved 61% correct classification and, as is usual, did better at detecting the guilty (85%) than the innocent (54%). When allowed to compare the charts of the three members of a triad (so that he did not have to ask whether an individual chart appeared Deceptive or Truthful, but rather which of three given charts looked *most* "deceptive" or *most* "truthful"), the polygrapher, of course, did better, with an average of 76% success on 45 such triads. The immediate global impression of the examiner who administered the tests was correct 65% of the time and the clinical impressions of judges who merely listened to the tape recordings of the interviews were correct 55% of the time overall. The PSE, on the other hand, achieved only 32% accuracy in classifying 85 subjects (some recordings were not good enough for PSE analysis) and only 38% when the voice tapes were considered in triads. The Voice Stress Analyzer similarly managed only 35% hits in the triad analysis. Both of the voice analyzers, therefore, performed about as well as one might do by using random numbers.

Nachshon, in 1977, examined the ability of the PSE to identify the card chosen by a subject in the typical card test.[12] (Subject picks one of six cards, each bearing a different number, answers "No" to questions of the form, "Did you pick card Number X?") Using 20 college students as subjects, the average interjudge agreement on the number chosen, based on the PSE charts, was again very low, not over 30%. Similar findings were obtained on card tests administered to 19 criminal suspects as part of regular polygraph examinations. Horvath recently used the card design with 60 volunteer subjects, comparing the ability of trained examiners to identify the chosen card from PSE charts versus EDR records obtained with a standard polygraph.[13] Since there were five cards to choose from, chance "detection" rate was 20%. Using the EDR, two evaluators averaged 56% correct calls, but got only 23% using the PSE, no better than chance. Brenner, Branscomb, and Schwartz tried out the PSE in a guilty knowledge test design similar to one in which I had previously been able to "detect" 20 out of 20 subjects on the basis of EDR records.[14] The PSE, however, again did no better than chance.[15]

How does the PSE perform in the serious business of real-life interrogation of criminal suspects? Barland, in 1975, made simultaneous PSE and polygraph recordings in LCT lie test examinations of 66 criminal suspects.[16] The PSE decision as to Truthful or Deceptive agreed with the polygraph outcome 53% of the time and with independent judicial outcome 47% of the time, where 50% was chance expectancy in both cases. (An earlier report by Barland in 1973, based on a subset of these cases, had suggested positive findings, but this conclusion turned out to have resulted from a statistical error.) Tobin, using an Israeli modification of the PSE by Inbar and Eden, examined 32 criminal suspects with only chance results.[17]

Nachshon made audio recordings of 41 polygraph examinations being routinely conducted by the Israeli police on criminal suspects.[18] Three judges independently evaluated the PSE charts. The average agreement in scoring between pairs of judges was 51% (i.e., chance) and the average agreement between the PSE scoring and the conventional polygrapher's evaluation was also 51% or chance. The one apparently nonchance finding in this study was that, while the polygrapher classified about two-thirds of the suspects as Truthful, the PSE evaluators classified two-thirds of them as deceptive. Nachshon concludes that

the PSE is neither reliable nor valid for detecting emotional arousal [and] the findings of the field study further imply that PSE employment in real life situations is not only useless, but also dangerous [because] the judges, when making an incorrect evaluation, tended to incriminate the innocent rather than to clear the criminal![19]

At last report, a complete Psychological Stress Evaluator costs about $4,400 f.o.b. Dektor Counterintelligence & Security Inc. As we have exhaustively determined, using the PSE to differentiate levels of stress or to detect deception produces results that typically conform to what might more easily be achieved by flipping a coin. If one were to use a "silver" dollar coin, the net saving would be $4,399. It must be remembered that *hundreds* of these machines have been purchased and are in daily operation in the United States, separating the "liars" from the "truthful," deciding who will be hired and who fired. And most of these PSE examinations are being paid for by American businessmen, apparently the same hard-headed, clear-eyed managers who helped Richard H. Bennett, Jr., to become a millionaire.

Bennett was the president of Hagoth Corporation, manufacturer of a $1,500 device widely advertised in airline magazines with which, it is claimed, the businessman can determine truth from falsehood in office or telephone negotiations. The great thing about the Hagoth, apart from the sensational advertising campaign, is that it leaves no written record; the only output is an evanescent display of winking lights, some green (for "low stress") and some red ("high stress"). Therefore, when the businessman discovers that he has made an enemy through unwarranted suspicion or been swindled through Hagoth-induced credulity, he has nothing but a hazy memory of reds and greens to blame it on. Asked for evidence that the Hagoth works, Mr. Bennett breezily replied, "I'll show you my bank balance."

Verdict

There is no scientifically credible evidence that the PSE or the Hagoth or any other currently available device can reliably measure differences in "stress" as reflected in the human voice. There is considerable evidence that the PSE, used in connection with standard lie detection test interrogations, discriminates the deceptive from the truthful at about chance levels of accuracy; that is, the PSE lie test has roughly zero validity. In this free enterprise system of ours, no burden of proof is placed upon the manufacturers of machines that are claimed to measure "stress" but that apparently do not; *caveat emptor* appears to be the ruling principle, sell the things as long as people buy them. And what have we learned about the wisdom and discrimination of American businessmen, those key pieces on Adam Smith's chessboard whose moves, guided by the Invisible Hand of enlightened self-interest, are supposed to ensure our economic progress? Why have they, in their hundreds, been buying these machines or the services of the operators of these machines, without any believable evidence that the things work? What is good for General Motors may be good for the country; I will not try to argue that question here. But does General Motors know what it is doing, any more than the business clients of the voice stress analyzers have known what they were buying with their (ultimately, our) money? And what about those thousands of citizens who have been labeled Deceptive by these arbitrary oracles? They, in the end, have paid the biggest price.

Notes

1. Use of Polygraphs as "Lie Detectors" by Federal Agencies. *Hearings Before a Subcommittee of the Committee on Government Operations,* U.S. House of Representatives, 88th Congress, 1964–65.
2. Lippold, O. Physiological tremor. *Scientific American,* 1971, *224,* 65–73.
3. Inbar, G. & Eden, G. Psychological Stress Evaluators: EMG correlation with voice tremor. *Biological Cybernetics,* 1976, *24,* 165–167.
4. Brenner, M. Stagefright and Steven's Law. Presentation to the Eastern Psychological Association, April 1974.
5. Smith, G. Voice analysis for the measurement of anxiety. *British Journal of Medical Psychology,* 1977, *50,* 367–373.
6. Brenner, M., Branscomb, H. & Schwartz, G. Psychological Stress Evaluator—Two tests of a vocal measure. *Psychophysiology,* 1979, *16,* 351–357.
7. Lynch, B. & Henry, D. A validity study of the Psychological Stress Evaluator. *Canadian Journal of Behavioral Science,* 1979, *11,* 89–94.
8. Nachshon, I. *The Psychological Stress Evaluator: Validity study.* Final

report, Grant #953–0265–001, Israeli Police. (Department of Criminology, Bar Ilan University, Ramat Gan, Israel)

9. Polygraph Control and Civil Liberties Protection Act. *Hearings before the Subcommittee on the Constitution of the Committee on the Judiciary*, United States Senate, September 19, 1978.

10. Heisse, J. *Senate Hearings* (see #9 above).

11. Kubis, J. Comparison of voice analysis and polygraph as lie detection procedures. *Polygraph*, 1974, *3*, 1–47.

12. Nachshon, I. *op. cit.*

13. Horvath, F. Effect of different motivation instructions on detection of deception with the PSE and the GSR. *Journal of Applied Psychology*, 1979, *64*, 323–330.

14. Lykken, D. T. The validity of the guilty knowledge technique: The effects of faking. *Journal of Applied Psychology*, 1940, *44*, 258–262.

15. Brenner, M., Branscomb, H. & Schwartz, G. *op. cit.*

16. Barland, G. Use of voice changes in the detection of deception. *Polygraph*, 1978, *7*, 129–140.

17. Tobin, Y. A validation of voice analysis techniques for the detection of psychological stress. (Unpublished paper cited in Nachshon, I., *op. cit.* above).

18. Nachshon, I. *op. cit.*

19. *ibid.*, page 49.

LIE DETECTION: THE APPLICATIONS

(Interview with Roc, age seven): What happens when you tell lies? *You get punished.* And if you didn't get punished, would it be naughty to tell them? *No.* I'm going to tell you two stories. There were two kiddies and they broke a cup each. The first says it wasn't him. His mother believes him and doesn't punish him. The second one also says it wasn't him. But his mother doesn't believe him and punishes him. Are both lies they told equally naughty? *No.* Which is the naughtiest? *The one who was punished.*

—Jean Piaget
The Moral Judgement of the Child

Listen, I don't know anything about polygraphs and I don't know how accurate they are, but I know they'll scare the hell out of people.

—President Richard M. Nixon
Oval Office Tape, July 14, 1971

This section begins with an examination of the widespread but seldom discussed practice of modern American business to do its own police work. Many American businesses, large and small, deal with intramural crime by hiring private investigators or by maintaining their own security operatives. These private investigators lean heavily upon the polygraph as a chief tool in their work. As Chapter 14 makes clear, this private police work is frequently effective, but any civil libertarian will find other consequences of this trend disturbing.

By far the most common use of lie detection is in the screening of job applicants and the periodic screening of current employees, not only by federal security agencies but by an increasing proportion of employers in the private sector. Chapter 15 discusses the arguments for and against this practice. A related issue is the use of paper-and-pencil tests, questionnaires, that are alleged to measure "honesty" or "trustworthiness." These developments are critically reviewed in Chapter 16. Chapter 17 is devoted to what I believe is the most effective feature of the polygraph examination, its indisputable ability to elicit damaging admissions or confessions.

In recent years, the legal barriers against the use of lie test results as evidence in court proceedings have weakened. In an increasing number of U.S. jurisdictions, polygraphers who have tested witnesses or the defendant himself are being accredited as expert witnesses and permitted to offer their opinions as to the credibility of the person tested. An analysis of this difficult and important problem will be found in Chapter 18.

Chapter 19, entitled "How to Beat the Lie Detector," is not really intended as a handbook for hoodlums. I explain earlier (in Part II) why I think that the lie detector tests do so poorly in identifying truthful responses, and Chapter 19 thus begins with a recipe that, in theory, could also defeat the lie test's relatively better success in detecting deception. But this chapter is primarily concerned with my personal evaluation of the probable effects upon American society of the growing uses of modern Truth Technology and my own recommendations about what should be done. If, as I think, the lie detector can be beaten by a guilty criminal who has been schooled by some knowledgeable Fagin or unscrupulous lawyer, then this is just an additional reason why we should consider legislation and other ways to "beat"—or to beat back—the metastasization of the lie detector throughout the tissues of our social system.

14

Truth, LTD.: The Polygrapher As Private Detective

PAUL ALTMEYER: "Do you think an employer should rely solely on the results of one of these tests?"

JOHN REID: "Well, true, I suppose they could put a person back to work and say, 'Now don't do that again.' "

ALTMEYER: "Well, you're the judge and jury then?"

REID: "Well, true in that particular thing, except that the penalty is just losing your job. . . . "

—NBC News Interview with
John Reid, 1977

Someone must have been telling lies about Joseph K. for without having done anything wrong he was arrested one fine morning.

—F. Kafka, *The Trial*

The Coker Case

Extracts from a letter dated February 17, 1975:[1]

My spirit is broken and my mind weary, but I am going to do my best to tell you just what happened, out of love for my wonderful husband and the hope that you can help him. He has always been a quiet, easy-going, humble person and the shock of his being blamed for something he is not guilty of has put him in a state of depression that worries me every moment. I am trying to let him know how much I care, know without a shadow of a doubt he is innocent, and how very much the children and I need him. So far, none of my assurance has seemed to help very much.

Sometime in December, 1974, Willis Foster came to my husband and told him he had been sent from Charleston to find out what was going on in the store. The Lake City Piggly-Wiggly, where Mack was the assistant manager, had been having some shortage problems before, but in the past two quarters, they said the shortage reached a peak of $13,000 one quarter and $10,000 the last quarter. Near the end of January, Mr. Lewis, the manager, was called to Charleston and returned with the news that the people from Truth Associates, Inc. were coming to talk to all the employees. At the meeting of all 52 employees, the two polygraph men reviewed the situation in the store and said it would be appreciated if all would take the tests. They said information given during this test would not cause anyone to lose his job nor would anyone be prosecuted.

Mack came home for the first time in months with a light heart and stated, "Well, thank the Lord, for once, people will truly know me for what I am!" He was so confident his test would be good because he knew he had nothing to hide. For people to finally know for a fact how clean he lived made him feel good inside. Tuesday was his day off, and he was anxious to get to work on Wednesday and take his tests. But then he learned that everyone who had taken the test Tuesday was jumping up and down. No one agreed with their test and Mack began to get concerned, but he still knew he had nothing to hide so he tried not to worry. I went to pick up my husband for lunch on Wednesday (we only have one car, a 1968 Buick), and it was after noon when he was released from the motel room where the test was given. He came out holding his chest, and I immediately knew something was wrong. I called to him and he just leaned against the car for awhile, got in and stared into space. After what seemed to me like an eternity, he said, "I have to go back to the store and clock out for lunch." That's all he said, just stared as if in shock. He's a quiet person anyway and I could sense he was too full to talk. About half-way home (we live in the country on my father's farm) he said, "There just *ain't* no way—there just ain't no way! Honey, tell me this is just a bad dream and I'm going to wake up in a few minutes." I asked if he felt like talking about it—he just stared (I was driving). When we got home, he went straight to the bedroom, threw himself on the bed and just lay there, no motion at all. I let our little girl, Dawn, age 4, go out and play—our three boys were in school—so it might be easier for him to find the right words to begin. Finally he began to tell me as best as he could remember.

The polygraph men had told them all Monday that they were supposed to decide over night how much of the losses each one might be responsible for himself over the past six months. Mack had decided $100. How he came up with that figure is when bags of merchandise such as grits, sugar, rice, detergent, dog food, flour or meal is damaged in shipping or in the stock room, instead of just throwing the good part away, Mack will bring the balance home for me to use. Everyone in the store knows this and he divides any of these things with his men if any of them want it. But the man asked if he was responsible in *any* form that might have cost the store, and this is what he felt he might owe, even though these items were charged off to damaged. The first test that the man give him went like this.

QUESTION 1. *Are you ready for this test to begin?*

Mack answered, "No." (This is because on Monday night at the meeting the polygraph people said everyone would have to answer "No" on this question.)

QUESTION 2. *Are you completely convinced I will only ask you the questions I read to you?*

Answer, "Yes."

QUESTION 3. *Other than your job, is there anything else you are afraid I will ask you a question about?*

Answer, "No." (Mack told me—"why should I care if he knew anything about me? I had never laid eyes on him until this day." All people, sometime in their life, if it's nothing but jokingly making a comment about some sexy model or something, maybe wouldn't want his wife or his mother to know about it, but certainly he could care less if this man knew.)

QUESTION 4. *Between the ages of 10 and 30 do you remember stealing anything from someone who trusted you?*

Answer, "Yes." (Mack said he couldn't remember anything right off hand, but while in school he traveled with the baseball team—his school was State Champions for 3 years in a row—and he said, "You know how a bunch of boys are away from home; we'd do anything we thought was funny," and it was possible during all this time he had picked up something or was responsible for destroying something of value to someone—so to be sure to given a 100% truthful answer he said 'Yes.' He was the team's first baser for East Clarendon High in Tubeville, S. C. and graduated the same year I did in Lake City, 1960).

QUESTION 5. *Are you sure that $100 will pay Piggly Wiggly for all of the things I asked you about?*

Answer, "Yes." (Mack said his responsibilities cover so much of the store that he said $100 just to be sure everything would be covered.) Then the polygraph man tore the paper from the machine and he said, "That figure of $100 that you gave me is incorrect." Mack said he got upset and asked, "Well, well if $100 isn't right, can you find out what is and and tell me?" The man told Mack to pick another figure. Mack said, "I have no idea. I was sure $100 would more than cover it. For *sure*, in only six months, no more than $200." So then he did another test.

QUESTION 1.   *Do you believe $3,000 will cover what you have contributed as shortages to this store?*

Answer, "Yes." (Naturally this figure would cover Mack's part and lots of other people's part too, as far as he was concerned.

QUESTION 2.   *The same question, but $6,000.*

Answer, "Yes." (Same reason.)

Then Mack said they asked him all sorts of figures like $50,000, $125,000, and he is almost certain they got as high as $175,000. I told Mack, 'My Lord, Honey, why didn't you think to tell him to ask you one million dollars?' He just said he was so shocked he couldn't even remember his name, he doubted. Mack said then he tore the paper from the machine and shook his head and he said, "There is something bad wrong here, *bad* wrong! Let's take another test." Mack said okay. This test was like the first one, but this time the last question was, "Are you working in collusion with anyone to steal from Piggly Wiggly?" Mack said the man explained he meant was Mack in with vendors and would sign for merchandise not delivered to the store. Mack said of all the questions he was asked before, he was more sure of the truthfulness, as 100%, of this question than all the rest because some could have been answered as "maybe" instead of "yes" or "no." He said the man told him, 'The needle went *wild* on that one!'

And then after all that, the polygraph operator said, "Son, if I were you, I'd go back around to that store, sit down and *confess* to Mr. Lewis about the things you've done—and maybe, just maybe, you and Mr. Lewis can work things out and help you keep your job." When he went back to the store that afternoon, Mack sat down and told Mr. Lewis all he could remember about how he did and what the man said. On Thursday after school, a boy that works part-time in the store came to my husband and told him, "Today, little Billy Lewis (he's 17) sat up in the classroom and said Mack Coker had stolen $23,000 worth of stuff." Another boy, Mark, was in that class and Mack called Mark to the office and said, "Mark, you don't have to say anything except yes or no. Did little Billy say that in class today?" and Mark said yes, he did, and when someone said where in the world is he hiding all that stuff, little Billy replied, "Oh, he has a brother-in-law that owns a store in Myrtle Beach." Later that same day, two female part-time employees attending our only private school, Susan and Marian, went to Mack and told him that Connie (Mr. Lewis's only daughter, 18 and a senior in the private academy) told stories something to the same effect. By the time the students got home, can you believe my mother's phone was constantly ringing? (We don't have a phone ourselves, just go next door and use Mama's.) Some wanting to help, some wanting to find out what in the world has caused Mack to do something like this?

The next two days, Mack continued to go to work as usual and talked to no one but me. He was in such a state—I'd wake up in the middle of the night to find him sitting on the steps or standing in the yard. I prayed, "Dear Father, please don't let me wake up one night with no life in his body!" On Friday, Mr. Lewis came to him and said, "Mack, get a cup of coffee, we've got to talk!" He told Mack that Mr. Gober (he's Vice President of Piggly Wiggly in Charleston) said that Mack was *solely* responsible for the mess in that store. Mr. Gober said, "These tests are *right,* because every time we've had trouble in any of our stores and sent the polygraph in there and fired the people, that store always straightens up."

But I think when I really "hit bottom" was after Mack was let go and we went to see this lawyer and he said without a written contract an employer can just fire you out of the clear, blue sky for your looks, or because you had your hair parted wrong. He informed me that polygraph could not even be mentioned in the courtroom concerning a case. Mack even signed a paper permitting them to give a test, he was so sure it was the thing to do at the time, and he truly had nothing to hide. But since it turned out the way it had—why didn't he have the right to prove it as non-truth and clear his name? I thought everyone is innocent until proven guilty? Dear God, help us all, if this is the justice in law we have to live by!

REPORT OF POLYGRAPH EXAMINATION, H. ROACH,

EXAMINER FOR TRUTH ASSOCIATES, INC.,

TO MR. JOHN GOBER PIGGLY WIGGLY CAROLINA.

STATEMENT OF VOLUNTARY CONSENT TO A POLYGRAPH EXAMINATION

I, *Mack Coker,* do hereby, voluntarily, without duress, coercion, promise of reward or immunity, agree to a polygraph examination in reference to *Job Honesty.* I have been advised of my rights under the Fifth Amendment to the Constitution of the United States. I further authorize the placement of the polygraph attachments to my person in order that the proper recordings may be made on the polygraph chart. I hereby release Truth Associates, Inc. and *Piggly Wiggly #48* from any and all claims or causes of action of any kind that may result from, or arise out of this polygraph examination. I authorize the release of the results of said examination to *Mr. John Gober Piggly Wiggly Carolina.* I further agree that the results of this Polygraph Examination may be used as evidence in a Court of Law if the need arises.

WITNESSED BY: *H. Roach,* Examiner   SIGNATURE: *Mack Coker*

EXAMINATION RESULTS: Prior to the Polygraph Examination, COKER admitted that his theft of money and merchandise from the store since July, 1974 amounted to $100. The results of the initial Polygraph Examination reflect that he was untruthful in the estimate of $100. Additional tests reflect that the actual sum to be between $8,000 and $10,000. One of the questions asked COKER during the Polygraph Examination was, "Are you working in collusion with anyone to steal money or merchandise from the Piggly Wiggly?" Answer: NO. The polygrams indicate that he was untruthful in his answer to this question.

PAID ADVERTISEMENT ENTERED IN THE LAKE CITY CLARION FOR MARCH 18, 1977.

A slander suit brought by Douglas M. (Mack) Coker involving the Piggly Wiggly Store in Lake City, South Carolina, was settled out of court recently for an undisclosed sum.

The suit arose because of certain defamatory statements about Coker that were circulated around the community some two years ago.

In settling the case, the defendants admitted that various rumors had circulated throughout the community about Coker and that from an investigation into this matter, it was determined that these rumors were absolutely false and had no factual basis.

A spokesman for the Piggly Wiggly Store said he did not understand how the stories could have spread over Lake City, but that the store is glad for Mack Coker that the matter has been cleared up.

Intramural Crime

Employee crime—pilfering, theft of merchandise, tools or equipment, embezzlement, sabotage, and vandalism—is an epidemic problem in the United States. Annual losses to American business are counted in the billions of dollars. "Epidemic"—in the people—is particularly appropriate because not only do the people in general pay for these losses, but, it would appear, people in general are responsible for them. Under the stress of pre-employment polygraph testing, as many as 75% of job applicants admit to some sort of thievery from previous employers.[2] In view of the tax monies paid out for police protection, it comes as a surprise to learn that official police agencies are never even notified in most of these affairs. Increasingly, business is doing its own police work, hiring security personnel or engaging the services of private detective agencies. We are seeing a return to the conditions of the Middle Ages when the nobility and the rich merchants, represented now by the corporation and the private company, provided their own guards and police, small private armies in some instances, to protect themselves and their property. The reasons for this trend, like most business decisions, are pragmatic. If the corporation is experiencing unexplained losses, if someone is sabotaging the assembly line, if some substantial theft bears the earmarks of an "inside job," the official police are unlikely to provide efficient and effective help. The company wants the losses stopped, wants the culprit identified so that he can make restitution if possible and, in any case, be eliminated from the payroll and from the plant. So, the private police are called in and, more than likely, they will bring with them a polygrapher.

This private detecting is frequently successful, which is precisely why it is increasingly utilized. Let us look at it in action. In 1976, a commercial bakery in Southern California was facing ruin, its 125 employees about to lose their jobs. Outraged retailers were returning bread shipments, loaves found to contain shards of glass, bits of barbed wire. Frantic checking of the raw materials, the mixing and baking processes, made it plain that this could be no accident caused by faulty equipment or simple carelessness. It was sabotage, the work of someone deliberately contaminating the mixing dough. After consultation with the employees' union, the bakery called in Intercept, a private polygraphy firm in Hollywood. Two examiners traveled to the bakery, portable polygraphs in hand, and began testing the employees. The eighth person tested, a man of 18 years' experience, confessed in the course of the examination that he had been responsible for all the damages. Angered because someone else had received a promotion to which he thought he was entitled, this man had brooded for two years and then began on his revenge. The police had been no help at all. What could they have done? The dozen employees with easiest access to the mixing vats might have been interrogated officially, their background searched for some motive, their families and friends questioned. Rigorous security measures might have been imposed to restrict access to the mix, to require pocketless work clothes, and so on. A smart policeman might have discovered that two-year-old resentment and followed up the clue. Just having a police detective prowling around, asking question, might have produced results. But the two polygraphers *did* produce conclusive results within 24 hours, and at relatively little cost.

During November of 1978, a gasoline service station in Salt Lake City experienced the loss of about $700, primarily in cash. After $290 disappeared from the till in one night, Polygraph Screening Service of that city was engaged to test the employees. During the pretest interview, a young man hired only two weeks previously admitted pocketing an average of $30 to $40 a day in sums collected for service or gasoline and never rung up. After a polygraph test of the LCT type on which he showed considerable reaction to the questions concerning the $290 theft, he said that he had inadvertently left the key in the cashbox that night while visiting the toilet and found the money missing when he returned. Thus, while continuing to deny the major theft, he admitted stealing an aggregate of several hundred dollars over a period of two weeks, losses that stopped when he was fired. He could have been caught, perhaps, by surveillance or by having professional "shoppers" give him the exact change for a purchase while a confederate watched to see what he did with the money. The city police probably would not have helped. As in the previous example, the polygrapher solved the problem expeditiously and by inducing a confession. The only use made of the examiner's diagnosis that this young man was lying about the major theft was that suspicion was diverted from the other employees.

In some instances, polygraph testing not only catches the culprit, but also exonerates innocent employees whom management is prepared to discharge on the basis of suspicion alone. An art dealer in Beverly Hills was losing trade secrets—names of clients and contacts —to a competitor and had accused a new assistant. A polygrapher cleared this assistant (another case of the LCT producing the sort of truthful chart that one would seldom expect) and then proceeded to obtain a confession from a long-time, trusted employee. A theater manager, citing losses, recommended that all the cashiers, concession clerks, and ushers be polygraphed. The examiner concluded that none of them were responsible for the losses and recommended that the manager himself be asked to take the test. Thereupon the manager confessed a plan to cover up his own thievery by shifting attention to his part-time help. I have no evidence that all of these young people "passed" their tests in the sense that all of their charts would be blindly scored as Truthful. But at least the examiner was not persuaded that he had found his thief until he got to the manager. Scores of similar examples could no doubt be accumulated by polling private polygraphers around the country. The cases I have cited were obtained from two firms run by men whom I know and trust.

But these successes must be balanced against scores of examples like the Coker case, where employees were victimized in a kangaroo court with a machine serving as the jury. An Indiana minister wrote me about one of his parishioners, Wayne K., a religious young man who had continued to tithe to his church while putting himself through college. Now a graduate accountant, a family man, and coach of the church baseball team, Wayne had a record of six years' loyal service in the local bank. When $2,000 turned up missing from the bank vault, a private detective agency urged that all employees be given lie detector tests. Wayne was the third person tested; he failed the test and he was fired. Community protest forced the bank to have him retested by the Indiana State Police. This time he passed and was reinstated. But on the principle of best two out of three, the bank sent Wayne to the Reid firm in Chicago, where he flunked again and again was fired. His pastor asked me what Wayne might do to prove his innocence. His condition was desperate. After more than a year, each time he thought he had found a new position in the only field he knew, word came from his previous employer and the door slammed in his face. In this instance, I cannot prove that Wayne did not suddenly set aside the habits of a pious lifetime and decide to heist the bank vault, but let us remember first principles: *Neither Wayne nor his pastor nor I have to prove that he is innocent.* There has been no indictment here, no trial before a jury of his peers, not one shred of legally admissible evidence against him—in short, no due process as prescribed by the Fifth, Sixth, and Fourteenth Amendments to the Constitution. And yet, Wayne K. was summarily punished, punished indeed more severely than the law typically punishes the first-time felon who has been properly tried and convicted in criminal court. He has lost his job, been shamed in his community, and effectively blacklisted from the profession for which he had trained himself in college and in six years at the bank.

Linda K. worked as a bookkeeper for the Kresge Company in Michigan. A polygrapher was called in to investigate losses and he summoned Ms. K. to his motel room for testing. After the lie test was completed, first the polygrapher and later Kresge's security officer put the pressure on, telling Linda that the polygraph showed she was guilty, insisting that she sign a confession and make restitution. Ms. K. refused, denying any theft from Kresge's, and that was her last day in their employment. Feeling branded by the voodoo of the lie test, Linda was afraid at first to tell her mother what had happened. For two weeks she left the house each morning as if going to work and then spent the day weeping at the home of her married sister. Like Wayne K., Linda K. discovered that having lost one job after a trial by polygraph makes it very difficult to find another. After nearly two years, she finally found an employer who did not believe in the lie detector and would hire her as his receptionist. (She also found an attorney who sued Kresge for "reckless infliction of emotional distress" and for "malicious libel." In November of 1979, the jury returned a judgment against Kresge for $100,000 in damages.)

What happened to Mack Coker, Wayne K., and Linda K. was wrong, un-American in the literal sense of that much-abused term, whether the lie tests were invalid (as I believe) or not. If the reader finds himself musing, "Well, maybe they did take the money, in which case they got what was coming to them," consider the case of John K. John is a deputy sheriff in Minnesota, who, in 1975, was serving as a jailer at the county jail. A federal prisoner, a bank robber, was being boarded at the jail while serving as an informant in another investigation. One day he handed over to the federal marshall a loaded gun and a hunting knife, asserting that he had bribed a jailer to smuggle them in, but had changed his mind about escaping. He named John K. as the arms smuggler and offered to prove his story on the polygraph. The sheriff asked Deputy K. if he also would submit to a lie test and, of course, he agreed. Both men were tested at the Minnesota Bureau of Criminal Apprehension; the bank robber passed his test with cool aplomb but John K. flunked his.

Fortunately for John, the sheriff had received a letter just a few weeks earlier from a local merchant commending this deputy. John had been shopping for a present for his young son and the gift was accidentally wrapped in a paper bag in which another clerk had placed the cash register receipts, several hundred dollars in cash, and checks. Discovering the error when he got home, John called the store and explained, offering to drop off the money on his way to work. "I always thought these lie tests were just about infallible," the sheriff told me, "but why would a man like that accept a bribe to smuggle weapons into the jail?" The bank robber, meanwhile, had been moved to another jail and had escaped from that less-secure facility, suggesting a motive for his charge against John. I told the sheriff that the lie detector itself could lie, and often did, and he proceeded with a conventional investigation. Through an informant, he learned that another prisoner, a young man on a work-release program who spent nights and weekends actually in jail, had been running a smuggling operation. That young man confessed that he had brought in the weapons. Ultimately, the bank robber was apprehended and he also confessed that he had fabricated the charge against Deputy K. *Both* lie tests were wrong.

An interesting feature distinguishes those earlier examples in which the polygrapher moved in like Sherlock Holmes and solved the crime with certainty and dispatch, from these other, Kafkaesque trials-by-polygraph in which citizens have been cut off from their employment, branded as Deceptive. In the earlier examples, the polygrapher elicited a confession from the guilty person. In the horror stories, the only "evidence" against the victim was the opinion of the polygrapher. We are dealing here with specific-issue situations where the examiners used either the "human lie detector" approach or the more respectable Lie Control Test, which, as we have seen, is strongly biased against the innocent respondent even when the tests are conducted and the charts evaluated by experienced examiners with Ph.D. degrees.

A Question of Rights

If my employee steals from me or deliberately damages my property, no one will dispute my right to discharge him whether or not I also bring a criminal complaint against him. Unless some contractual agreement between us intervenes, I may also fire my employee merely because I suspect that he might have been guilty of such an action or, indeed, I may fire him for no reason at all. Apart from humanitarian considerations, there are two factors that work to prevent me from using capriciously this power that I have over his job security. First, it is inconvenient and expensive for me to replace an experienced worker. Second, such arbitrary behavior would damage my reputation as an employer and lower the morale of the rest of my work force. Therefore, I will not fire him unless I think he has given me cause and I will prefer that my action will also seem justified to others.

Enter the private polygrapher. The employee's confession of theft or vandalism will satisfy both of my requirements. But suppose he does not confess but merely "fails" a lie test? That is likely to satisfy my requirements also. Put yourself in the position of my neighbor, the president of a large Minneapolis advertising agency, when an $8,000 movie camera used in filming TV commercials was discovered missing from a locked cabinet. To avoid adverse publicity—and to have some hope of prompt action—he called in the private detectives and they brought along their polygraphs. Three employees who had keys to the camera cabinet were given polygraph examinations. Two of them passed but one, Walter K., was diagnosed as Deceptive. Walter K. was a talented young film producer, the highest ranking black employee in the agency, and my neighbor hated to think of losing him. "I wish I'd just written off the camera. Now I'll have to fire Walter and it will be the end of him in this business." In this instance, the polygraph itself undid the mischief it had almost caused. Before any action was taken against Walter, a fourth person was located who had access to the camera. In the course of his lie test, this man confessed that he had taken the camera, which was later returned. Walter was exonerated. Except for this lucky circumstance, Walter would have lost his job and perhaps his career. This particular employer was reluctant to take that step, but he would have felt not only justified but obligated to take it, and his other employees would have endorsed it. Walter had, after all, been found guilty—by the mysterious machine.

What if the real thief had not confessed, Walter had been fired, applied for work at another agency, and that agency had called my neighbor for a reference? "A camera was stolen and Walter flunked the lie test so we had to let him go." That would guarantee to blacklist him, would it not? On the other hand, believing him to be a thief, would my neighbor have the right to hide that "knowledge" from his colleagues in the industry?

Let us now consider Walter's rights. He could have refused to take the polygraph test in the first place, refused to sign that "voluntary" agreement form permitting the polygraph company to report the results to his employer and waiving all rights of redress. But this is a hollow right since, under the circumstances, refusal to submit to the lie test must inevitably appear to Walter's colleagues and his employer almost as an admission of guilt. The circumstances that thus constrained Walter's decision to submit were these: (1) the polygrapher represented the lie test as being nearly infallible; (2) this representation was accepted by Walter's employer and colleagues; and (3) Walter was innocent of wrongdoing and therefore expected that he had nothing to fear from submitting to the lie test. This acceptance by all parties of the validity of the lie test is the central issue. If Walter had been asked to stake his career on a role of the dice or the verdict of a ouija board, his common sense would have informed him to refuse, nor would his refusal have condemned him in the eyes of others.

What if the examiner had actually used a ouija board, gone through the forms of a standard polygraph test, but based his diagnosis on magic or chance? More specifically, suppose that the polygrapher reported to Walter's boss that Walter's denial of having stolen the camera was Deceptive according to the criteria of an accepted lie detection technique of proven high validity, when if fact, the diagnosis had only chance validity. Under these circumstances, the polygrapher's report would appear to constitute defamation and the examiner would be liable for damages. If the employer is negligent in engaging an irresponsible or incompetent examiner, then the employer might himself be liable.

But polygraph examiners do not use ouija boards. They use instead a procedure—either the clinical lie test or the polygraphic lie test—which is generally more valid than chance but less accurate than the 99, 95, or 90 percent that is typically claimed. Suppose that Walter K. had been granted the right of *informed consent* and that the release form he was required to sign had contained a paragraph like the following:

I have been informed that, according to the best available evidence, the polygraph test I am about to take has an average accuracy of from 63% to 71% and that, if I am truthful, the probability of my being diagnosed as Deceptive may be as high as 50%.

It seems safe to say that most people would not submit to testing if they were provided with this information. Suppose, alternatively, that Walter had been encouraged (as he was) to believe that the lie test is "almost infallible," but that the polygrapher had then reported his diagnosis to the employer together with an acknowledgement that about one out of three Deceptive diagnoses are erroneous, false-positives. This might protect Walter in some measure but it would have the disadvantage of ruining the polygrapher's business; what employer would pay from $35 to $150 for such ambiguous information?

Thus, a question of rights seems to turn on the issue of validity. If you confess that you stole the camera, or if the polygrapher actually sees you take it, then he does not violate your rights by reporting your guilt because his information is valid. Should he report that you are guilty or deceptive without any evidence at all, then he has defamed you and is vulnerable to civil suit. Somewhere between these two extremes, not yet clearly defined in law, there is a crossing point, a degree of validity that would justify a reasonable and prudent man in making such an adverse report about you. If the polygrapher makes such a report and, either mendaciously or through ignorance of the relevant research, if he indicates that his report is based on an extremely valid test when the best evidence shows only marginal validity, then that misrepresentation might itself be considered a cause for damages.

There have been surprisingly few lawsuits brought on behalf of plaintiffs who had been subjected to trial by polygraph, adjudicated Deceptive by the machine or the examiner, and then punished by their employers. Many attorneys, like the first one whom the Cokers approached, seem to assume that there is no cause of action in such cases. Without a contract, the employer can fire whom he wants to. The polygraph tests were, after all, taken "voluntarily." Many victims of such lie test miscarriages, like Wayne K., feel dishonored and on the defensive and assume that they must somehow prove their innocence or take the consequences. If more persons who have been victimized in this fashion were to bring suit against their employers and the polygraphers involved and were successful in obtaining damages, then this particular misuse of the lie test might become less frequent.

To Catch a Thief

But what about all those confessions, those cases of internal crime solved expeditiously by polygraphic interrogation leading to confession by the culprit? If we are to protect the innocent from victimization through trial by polygraph, shall we have to do so at the cost of prohibiting private polygraphic investigation of this type of crime? It seems to me that there are two alternative approaches, either of which might provide the needed safeguards for the human rights of employees while, at the same time, giving some measure of additional protection to the property rights of employers. One method would allow the present system to continue but would enact strict statutory requirements for licensure of polygraph examiners, including provision of civil remedies for damages suffered as a result of unethical, incompetent, or inaccurate testing or reporting by a polygrapher. This is the proposal of Dr. Martin Orne, an eminent research psychiatrist and student of polygraphy, who draws an analogy to the legal accountability required of physicians and other professionls who are subject to malpractice suits and are expected to be both professionally and financially responsible for their actions.

The other alternative, which I am inclined to favor, is to place employee crime, like other categories of crime, in the hands of the official police, providing such additional facilities to the police as may be required for them to handle this additional responsibility. We are talking here about crime and punishment, deep matters that liberals and conservatives alike have regarded as responsibilities of the State. "To establish justice and insure domestic tranquility" are among the reasons why men establish governments in the first instance and, in the Preamble to the American Constitution, are even given priority over such objectives as providing for the common defense and promoting the general welfare. Private vendettas, vigilante justice, lynch mobs, and hired guns are universally regarded as uncivilized, as symptoms of a society out of control. A business trying to protect itself from internal thievery or sabotage is hardly a "lynch mob," nor is a private polygrapher a "hired gun." But it is manifestly dangerous to delegate the police powers of the State to private agencies.

This line of argument assumes that the innocent employee's rights will be better protected if internal crimes are turned over by his employer to the official police. It assumes that the police will not communicate unproven suspicions or inadmissible evidentiary details to the employer, but will investigate each matter in an orderly fashion leading to the detection and prosecution of the guilty. The police may use polygraphy or may elicit confessions by skillful direct interrogation. But their responsibility is to society generally rather than to the employer in particular and there are established—if not always effective—methods of monitoring the behavior of the police and curbing abuses of police authority. If anyone doubts society's ability to control the police, these doubts make a poor argument for wider delegation of police power to private and still less accountable hands.

The present apparent inability of the official police to cope with the internal crime problems of American business appears to stem mainly from economic considerations. It seems probable that those businesses with the greatest problems do not contribute enough in local taxes to sustain the expanded police facilities that this plan would require. But tax rates can be modified to meet the need. A manufacturer whose product is being sabotaged, a business that experiences the theft of an expensive piece of equipment, a retail merchant whose records indicate recurrent losses of internal origin, all of these, in a well-regulated society, should be able to obtain prompt and effective police service. Much has been said, by advocates of private polygraphy, about the rights of business to protect its plant and property. I agree with these claims, but I would argue that business, like the ordinary citizen, should turn to the officially constituted police agencies for the protection of those rights rather than taking the law into its own hands.

Notes

1. Except for the Coker family and Roach, the polygrapher, the names of the participants in this affair have been disguised.
2. Barefoot, J. Kirk. Testimony on behalf of the American Polygraph Association. *Hearings before the Subcommittee on the Constitution of the Committee on the Judiciary, United States Senate, 95th Congress, 1977–78*, p. 60.

CHAPTER 15

Pre-And Post-Employment Screening

The whole process smacks of 20th century witchcraft. . . . The burden of proof should be on those who assert the efficacy of polygraph in predicting the behavior of prospective . . . employees. There have been practically no efforts to compile this proof. . . . Why then do [employers] have such blind faith in these devices? In my opinion, it is directly related to the role of science and technology in our society—the cult of "the expert." There is an increasing belief that anything scientific must be more reliable and rational than the judgment of men. . . . Even if [polygraphs] could be proved 100 percent reliable and valid, there is no necessity for these infringements of freedom and invasions of privacy: but even if there were a necessity for them, I believe every citizen should answer with William Pitt: "Necessity is the plea for every infringement of human liberty. It is the argument of tyrants: it is the creed of slaves."

—Senator Sam J. Ervin, Jr.

We drove to a little restaurant in Hollywood in our host's new Cadillac Seville. The dinner was superb. The conversation touched on the problems of foreign travel, the pleasures of child-rearing; we had been talking polygraphy all day. Our host, a former police lieutenant, is the head of a flourishing private polygraphy firm in Southern California and was the current president of the American Polygraph Association. He is intelligent, prosperous, and highly professional. His firm does a considerable amount of specific-issue testing for defense attorneys, public prosecutors, juvenile court judges, and the like, and they are frequently engaged for private investigations. But their bread-and-butter business is screening job applicants and the periodic interrogation of current employees for some 300 corporate clients. Their six full-time polygraphers conduct 800 examinations per month, of which about 70% are the pre-employment type and take about one hour's time, including interview, testing, and the preparation of the report to the customer, who pays $45 per applicant for this service. The examiners, who earn salaries of from $12,000 to $32,000, depending on experience, thus generate an average gross annual return of over $50,000 each on pre-employment work alone. Another 15% of this company's total activity is devoted to postemployment screening. Many companies require employees to undergo polygraph tests at least once or twice each year on the belief that such periodic screening will act as a deterrent. Pre- and postemployment screening is the life's blood of the polygraph industry.

In 1977, Senator Birch Bayh of Indiana promulgated a bill that would outlaw polygraph testing of employees and job applicants in the United States.[1] At least 16 states have already enacted legislation designed to prohibit polygraph testing of employees, but many of these statutes are toothless and easily circumvented. Even apparently strong, well-drafted laws seem to have little effect at the state level, as the Minnesota experience attests. The Minnesota law, passed in 1976, is clear enough:

No employer or agent thereof shall directly or indirectly solicit or require a polygraph, voice stress analysis, or any test purporting to test the honesty of any employee or prospective employee. No person shall sell to or interpret for an employer or his agent a test that he knows has been solicited or required by an employer or his agent to test the honesty of an employee or prospective employee. An employer or agent or any person knowingly selling, administering, or interpreting tests in violation of this section is guilty of a misdemeanor.[2]

But the 1979 Minneapolis Yellow Pages carried ads for 5 lie detector firms (there are 30 in New York City), and business is apparently booming. One problem, from the preventionist point of view, is that few Minnesota citizens know that such a law exists and no complaints are brought to the authorities.

Enactment of the Bayh bill, followed up with strict enforcement by federal authorities, should certainly have a greater impact than these ineffectual state statutes, but would that impact be desirable? Is it in the national interest to prohibit polygraph screening of employees and to put the lie detector industry out of business? ("Out of business" literally: the Bayh bill would restrict the use of polygraphy to official law enforcement agencies and the selection of candidates for high-security jobs in government.) Or is the burgeoning of this industry a response to a legitimate need of American business? Does the social and economic structure of our increasingly complex society require the technology and skills of the polygraph examiner?

The Case for Polygraphic Screening

No matter what it is called—internal theft, peculation, embezzlement, pilferage, inventory shrinkage, stealing or defalcation—thefts committed by employees are behind at least 60% of crime-related losses. So many employees are stealing so much that employee theft is the most critical crime problem facing business today. The best way to stop employee theft is simply not hire those employees inclined to steal. The best way is also impossible. What the employer must do is to set up a screening process that will weed out the obvious security risks. Many experts believe that personnel screening is the most vital safe-guard against internal theft.[3]

We have already noted that employee theft in the United States amounts to billions of dollars annually. Estimates range from $9.2 billion by the Department of Commerce to as high as $50 billion by spokesmen for the polygraph industry. It is said that 3 out of 4 job applicants, under the stress of polygraphic screening, admit to having stolen from previous employers.[4] Admittedly one should be cautious about interpreting these figures. As it appears in the flat language of the polygrapher's report, an admission of a small misdeed can sound more serious than perhaps it really is. I used a University stamp the other day to mail a personal letter, my own stamp supply having run out. Let us not hedge about it: that constituted "stealing from his employer." Still, I have never pilfered from the petty cash or made off with a typewriter for resale. One cannot believe that three-fourths of our fellow citizens are thieves in any useful, reasonable sense of that term. But there seems to be no doubt that many Americans, who would never contemplate a holdup or a burglary and who do not think of themselves as criminals or outlaws, play by rather different rules at the office or shop than they do elsewhere and tend to make free with their employer's property in a way which they recognize at least as being forbidden (they don't do it when the boss is watching), if not actually dishonest. The $5 per hour secretary who called in "sick" so as to have a day free for personal business has stolen $40 from the company, but that same secretary might never purloin a $40 item from a department store. A factory worker borrows a wrench for use on a project at home and then never bothers to return it: Lockheed has thousands of wrenches and will never notice one is missing. That same man would never similarly "borrow" a tool from his neighbor's garage; that would be stealing. And there are undoubtedly a great many real thieves, deliberate, self-acknowledged embezzlers, in the work force as well. However one adds it up or interprets its origins, employee theft in this country is both common and costly.

The cost of most of this embezzlement is of course passed on to all of us. Some individual employers may not survive long enough to pass along the costs to the consumer. As many as 3 out of 5 small business bankruptcies have been attributed to losses due to employee theft although, again, this estimate is probably inflated by the reluctance of the failed businessman to acknowledge poor management, including inadequate security precautions.[5] The businessman, whether construed as acting in his own interest or indirectly, for us all, has a clear right to strive to protect his proceeds and property. The personnel manager has not only the right but the obligation to attempt to hire employees who will prove both competent and honest. He will attempt to collect information about job applicants that is relevant to both of these qualities, using tests, interviews, and background investigations. If a previous employer reports that Jones was fired for stealing, it is unlikely that Jones will be hired to the new job he has applied for. If Smith seems shifty and evasive during the job interview, it is unlikely that Smith will be put on the payroll. Employers have always considered honesty to be an important desideratum, have always been alert for evidence that a job applicant is not to be trusted. Polygraphic screening is merely a direct, explicit, and efficient means of doing a job that employers always have and always will do, one way or another. A manager may hold the private conviction that blacks or homosexuals or all males between 18 and

26 are not to be trusted: is it better to entrust the hiring decision to his subjective interview evaluation or to a polygraph that entertains no prejudices?

As we have seen, the Relevant Control Test format generally used in employee screening may be more valid than the typical Lie Control Test used in criminal investigation. While there is no actual evidence on the screening test's validity, one way or the other, the assumptions on which this test format depends seem rather more plausible than those required by the LCT. If a job applicant consistently reacts to questions about previous thefts of merchandise but not to questions about thefts of money or use of drugs or alcohol on the job, then this establishes at least a *prima facie* case that he has a "problem" in this specific area and some explaining to do. Moreover, the actual validity of the RCT polygraph test is not really of central importance. The most professional and best regarded private polygraphers seem agreed that from 90% to 95% of the adverse reports that they submit to their employer clients are based, not on interpretations of the polygraph charts, but on the respondent's own admissions.[6] If he doesn't get the job, it will almost always be because the invisible pressures of the polygraph situation have led him to admit damaging facts, to prior thefts or chemical dependency or to having made false statements on his application form. The main value of the periodic testing of established employees lies in its deterrent effect. Knowing that they may have to face the polygraph within the next six months prevents little lapses that might otherwise proliferate. This is to everyone's advantage and also helps each employee keep clear in his mind that stealing from the company is, in fact, stealing sure enough. In these periodic tests, as in pre-employment screening, adverse reports are most often based on the respondent's own admissions. If someone is fired as a result of a polygraph session, it is usually because he has admitted some dischargeable offense and not just because of the pattern of his chart reactions.

Some spokesmen for the polygraph industry permit themselves to argue that all polygraph testing is done on a voluntary basis,[7] that one cannot get a valid test from an uncooperative subject, and they point to the invariable waiver that all respondents sign before the test proceeds. All this argument means is that a subject cannot usefully be carried kicking and screaming into the polygraph room. Clearly, real-life polygraph tests are seldom truly voluntary in the sense that the subject would rather take the test than not or feels that he or she stands to benefit from taking it. But employees every day do things that they would rather not do if they had completely free choice, unconstrained by a desire to get paid or keep their job or make a good impression on the boss. Coercion of some sort is part and parcel of the employer-employee relationship. Employees and job applicants admittedly are not free to refuse to take required (or "suggested") polygraph tests—not if they want to keep or get the job—but their behavior is similarly constrained in many other ways by the same sorts of implied coercion.

Polygraph tests are said to involve an invasion of the respondent's rights to privacy—and yet it is difficult to imagine legislation being proposed to prohibit an employer from asking the same sorts of questions in the context of an ordinary job interview. "Have you ever stolen money from a previous employer?" "Are you addicted to any street drug?" Do we object to the asking of these questions during a polygraph test because the machine intrudes upon the respondent's "right" to answer deceptively? Professional polygraphers freely admit that many of their fraternity are incompetent or unethical or both, that there are some who take advantage of the polygraph interrogation situation to ask questions that are irrelevant and intrusive. But, they argue, this problem can best be handled by raising professional standards through the enactment of state licensure laws. California, for example, licenses astrologers—but not polygraphers.

Personnel interviewers are free to ask the same types of questions used in typical polygraph screening sessions and then base employment decisions on the respondent's answers or on whether he blushes or "trembles and looks pale" when he replies. How can the addition of a polygraph machine, which provides an accurate, quantitative record of what might be called "internal blushes," change a licit inquiry into an improper assault on the employee's human rights?

The Case Against Employee Screening

I have joined with other Members of the Senate to formulate legislation which is designed to put a stop to a growing and disturbing job requirement in the working lives of Americans—lie detection tests administered by their employers on a periodic basis. Each year in this country, thousands of ordinary workers and job applicants are forced to submit to mass lie detector sweeps of the plant or shop where they are employed or seeking employment. These truth-testing sessions are not necessarily the result of a specific theft or loss or even of suspicion of such crimes. Rather, they represent the indiscriminate and randon instrusion of so-called truth-testing machines into the daily lives of Americans. Failure to submit to these tests, or unsatisfactory responses to questions, are often punished by loss of employment, or summary transfer to a less desirable position. It is interesting to note that the people most likely to be forced to take these tests or suffer the consequences are lower level, nonunion workers—precisely those individuals least able to assert their rights.[8]

The original publication of the Kinsey studies of human sexuality created quite a stir because Kinsey's findings indicated that most Americans were perverts and even, in many jurisdictions, sexual criminals guilty of adultery and fornication, sodomy or bestiality, not to mention solitary vice. The initial shock caused by these revelations stemmed in part from an implicit assumption that they indicated a recent breakdown of morality, that our society was changing suddenly and drastically and for the worse. No one is shocked any more. We have assimilated the Kinsey statistics by realizing finally that the only sudden change had been in our perceptions, that human sexual behavior had matched Kinsey's descriptions probably for centuries, hidden behind a screen of ignorance and social hypocrisy. Polygraphers' reports that 75% of job applicants admit to thefts of goods and money, drug abuse, and the like should be interpreted in a similar way. We have all told lies, taken things that did not belong to us; we are all sinners. It is probable that every reader of this book has committed at least one undiscovered crime. But the same could doubtless have been said of our ancestors one, two, or five centuries ago.

Whether employee theft has increased in recent years is difficult to say. Modern statistics are not very accurate, and we have no comparable figures at all for, say, the 19th century. It has always been true that things left carelessly about are likely to disappear. A business with poor security arrangements will show greater inventory losses than will a business that is more competently organized and managed. Large, impersonal companies, shops or factories with bad employee morale, provide ready rationalizations for employee theft or even sabotage. "The bosses squeeze everything they can out of me; I'm just getting a little of it back." Where security is lax, there is the added rationalization: "Everyone else does it; if I don't help myself too it's like taking a voluntary pay cut." There is no persuasive evidence that we are any more a nation of thieves now than in 1776. No one can prove the current losses to employee theft are proportionately greater than during the beginnings of the industrial revolution. There is a problem, but it is an old, familiar problem; there is no emergency.

The RCT test format used commonly in employee screening may indeed be more plausible in theory than the LCT, but that is weak praise. The total lack of scientifically credible evidence of validity of the RCT in real-life applications represents a burden of proof that the polygraphy profession has simply shrugged away. The ethical standards of the American Psychological Association would clearly prohibit the sale of interpretations of tests that are claimed to be highly valid when these claims, in fact, rest upon sheer speculation. It is not good enough to say that only 10% of adverse reports are based on the polygraph results alone; until the polygraph results can be shown to provide a dependable basis for branding the respondent as deceptive or dishonest, then 10% is 10% too many.

There is reason to believe that many of the "damaging admissions." elicited during polygraph screening and which form the basis for most adverse reports to the employer, are overstated and misleading. In the Coker case, for example, supermarket employees were told in advance to estimate "how much of the store's losses you might personally be responsible for." Mr. Coker estimated $100, having in mind his responsible position as assistant manager and the many possibilities for damage, breakage, and other accidental losses that might be technically within his domain of responsibility. He did not believe that he had ever stolen anything from the store. But the polygrapher's report asserted that "Coker admitted the theft of money and merchandise amounting to $100," a "damaging admission" indeed, well calculated to persuade the home office that they were getting good value from Truth Associates, their polygraph firm.

But suppose that an extraordinarily scrupulous polygrapher were to adopt the practice of reporting back to the employer only the respondent's own words, perhaps in the form of tape recordings of the interviews, so as to ensure that their "admissions" were never exaggerated or distorted in the process of paraphrasing or abbreviating for purposes of the report. There would still remain the problem of what the employer is to make of these admissions, the possibility that he or she will exaggerate their significance due to lack of familiarity with what the people are inclined to say under the unusual circumstances of the polygraph examination. Upon learning that some person enjoyed a sexual practice outside one's own experience, someone in the pre-Kinsey era might well have classified that person as perverted, abnormal, and an execration. To a manager unused to hearing the confessions of the staff, the small sins of one or two employees might appear similarly magnified in importance. The fact is that many employers do hire applicants in spite of their having made "damaging admissions"; with 3 out of 4 applicants branded in this way, the employer may not otherwise be able to maintain a full staff; so he tries to discriminate those admissions that are damning from the merely damaging.

What about those 25% who do not make damaging admissions?—they are the interesting minority, the literally abnormal ones. This group will include those saintly persons who have nothing to confess and also, undoubtedly, most of the real sinners, the habitual liars and deliberate villains who expect to cheat and steal at every opportunity —and to whom it would never occur to volunteer an admission of any kind. It is not as if the polygraph or the clever examiner elicits the damaging admission against the will and resistance of the respondent. In most instances, one must assume, the damaging admissions that emerge in a polygraph session reflect impulses of guilt and shame, the normal pangs of conscience, the urge to be honest and straightforward. For many of those who receive adverse reports one might argue that their damaging admissions should have been evaluated in their favor rather than against them. The basic question is this: Do those who offer damaging admissions on the polygraph interview prove to be less satisfactory, less trustworthy employees than those who do not? It is at least possible that the main effect of pre-employment screening is to assist the worst scoundrels, who know better than to admit anything, to be the first ones chosen for employment. Where is the proof that such screening actually reduces losses?

The claim that "business *needs* the polygraph" is simply not true. Sears and Penney's, the nation's two largest retailers, do not use the polygraph at all but seem to flourish (compare Sears' performance with its most direct competitor, Montgomery Ward, which uses polygraphy routinely). Ford Motor Co. manages to compete without polygraph screening as does the aerospace-military giant, Rockwell International, in spite of its highly sensitive line of business. One of the largest American banks, Manufacturers Hanover Trust Co., has not found it necessary to subject its employees to polygraph screens and sweeps.[9] The fact that many large, well-managed companies have resisted the trend toward routine use of polygraphy suggests either that effective alternative methods of coping with employee misconduct must be available *or* that polygraphic screening in fact is not effective. I believe that both of these conclusions are correct. There is certainly no persuasive evidence that polygraphic screening actually reduces employee theft. The American Polygraph Association asserts, "The best way to stop employee theft is simply not to hire those employees inclined to steal," but this goal is unachievable. I find no reason for supposing that polygraphic screening helps at all. The polygraph examination *is* intrusive, an invasion of one's privacy, one's inner space; it puts the respondent in a uniquely vulnerable position that, as the American Management Association agrees, is open "to much abuse." The reason that the polygraph is successful in eliciting all those damaging admissions is precisely because, for most people, taking a polygraph test is a stressful, often a traumatic, experience, a "bloodless third degree." Yet, if the practice prevented $10 or $50 billion in employee theft each year, then America's work force might well be asked to bite the bullet and submit. But, absent any solid proof that all those millions of screening tests have prevented any theft at all, it is difficult to see why prudent businessmen would want to invest in this approach or to subject their employees to such a dehumanizing experience. There are better ways of coping with employee misconduct.

Coping with Employee Theft

An employer might consider four approaches to minimize employee theft:

(1) *Selective Hiring.* This is the polygrapher's preferred approach, but it remains to be demonstrated that having a polygraph guarding the factory gate does any good. Another method, using paper-and-pencil tests of "honesty," will be considered in Chapter 16. The old standard method of checking references seems to have fallen out of fashion.

(2) *Security.* Every employer can follow the same principle for preventing theft that you and I use when we lock our house or car—he can take steps to minimize the opportunities for stealing. He can keep track of inventory, maintain good records, restrict access to valuables, lock things up, fasten things down. There are two multipump gasoline stations that I frequent, both still using attendants to pump gas. At one station, the amount of each sale is called into the office/store by intercom

and the customer pays there at the cash register. At the other station, each attendant collects and makes change from his pocket. This second arrangement clearly invites theft; the first one makes it considerably harder.

(3) *Employee Morale.* It would be naive to suppose that good employee relations will eliminate employee misconduct. But one can hardly doubt that it will pay in the long run to treat one's employees with consideration and respect, to pay them adequately and treat them fairly. For the great mass of people stealing comes hard and requires some sort of rationalization. If management can be regarded as the enemy, selfish, indifferent, unfair, then a ready excuse is provided. One of the best techniques might be some form of profit-sharing arrangement, ideally one that is focused on relatively small groups of employees who are in daily contact, so that each person will be encouraged to feel that to steal from the company is to steal from one's friends and colleagues. The success of South Bend Lathe Corporation in Indiana is instructive. Through the Employee Stock Ownership Plan, sponsored by the U.S. Commerce Department, the employees and management of South Bend Lathe bought the company in 1974. Earnings per share more than tripled in the next three years—and there is no problem with employee theft or sabotage. This result is typical of 75 firms with similar plans surveyed by Senator Russell Long and the Senate Finance Committee in 1979.[10]

(4) *Surveillance and Sanctions.* Finally, of course, good management will make use of the same deterrent methods used by society at large in effort to minimize crime. Good organization and record keeping will help to ensure that theft is promptly discovered. Retail merchants can hire professional "shoppers" to provide periodic checks on the competence and conduct of their clerks and a good team of shoppers will readily detect failures to properly ring up purchases and the like. If valuables are hard to get at, difficult to remove and spirit away, if losses will be quickly detected and closely investigated when they occur, and if one's individual actions are periodically and unpredictably subject subjected to special scrutiny, the ordinary person will be disinclined to take the risk.

One must first acknowledge that there will always be employee theft, that in the shop as on the street there will never be perfect discipline, total security. Next, one should reject the notion that the problem of employee theft is analogous to the old war-time problem of keeping spies and saboteurs out of the arms factories. All the statistics indicate that the majority of employees will help themselves to company property if everybody's doing it, if it is easy to do and little risk is entailed, and if poor pay, bad working conditions, or unfair treatment provide easy rationalizations. If this is so, then pre-employment screening cannot be an adequate solution, because few people would survive a truly valid screening process. And there is no evidence that polygraphic screening has any validity; indeed, the small proportion of real thieves among the applicants may be the most likely to "pass" the screening. Therefore, the solution—which can only minimize the problem, not eliminate it altogether—lies in well-planned security precautions, attention to working conditions and employee morale, and appropriate surveillance. In short, good management.

Notes

1. Polygraph Control and Civil Liberties Protection Act. *Hearings before the Subcommittee on the Constitution of the Committee on the Judiciary, United States Senate, 95th Congress, 1977–78.* Senator Sam Ervin of North Carolina had proposed similar legislation in 1971 and again in 1973. The fate of the pending bill will depend on the balance of voter opinion expressed to members of Congress. The polygraph industry should be able to muster thousands of letters in opposition to Senator Bayh's proposal.
2. *Laws of Minnesota for 1976, Chapter 256, H.F. No. 1330.*
3. American Polygraph Association. *Hearings before the Subcommittee on the Constitution of the Committee on the Judiciary, United States Senate, 95th Congress, 1977–78.* p. 142.
4. J. Kirk Barefoot, Testimony on behalf of the American Polygraph Association, *Hearings,* p. 60.
5. *ibid.*
6. *ibid.* p. 55.
7. *ibid.* p. 62.
8. Senator Birch Bayh, Opening statement, *Hearings,* p. 2.
9. Jenkins, J. Bloodless executioners. *Student Lawyer,* May 1979.
10. McCarthy, C. Employee stockholders bring profits. *Washington Post,* Nov. 10, 1979.

Questionnaire Measures Of "Honesty"

After years of catching thieves with the lie-detector, we've perfected a way to catch them with paper and pencil.

—Headline of advertisement for the
Reid Report, received by mail, 1979.

We all, like sheep, have gone astray.

—Handel, the *Messiah*

In the fall of 1976, the Minnesota Legislature was considering a bill to ban polygraph testing of employees. An unexpected witness at the first committee hearing was Sister Terressa, a member of a teaching order, whose forthright and determined manner carried no suggestion of the cloister. She told the committee that some months earlier she had applied for a part-time job with B. Dalton Bookstores in Minneapolis. The application procedure included a disconcerting questionnaire called the Reid Report. Inquiry revealed that B. Dalton used the results on this test, scored by John E. Reid Associates in Chicago, as their basis for assessing the trustworthiness of potential employees. After weeks had passed without further word, Sister Terressa called the bookstore to learn the fate of her application. She was told that she had been rejected because of her performance on the Reid Report. "They said I had the lowest score on the 'honesty test' that they had ever seen!" Partly because of Sister Terressa's indignant and effective testimony, the present Minnesota statute forbids the use in employment applications of polygraph tests, voice stress analysis, or "any test purporting to test the honesty of any employee or prospective employee."[1]

The misclassification of one outraged nun is not a sufficient reason for the statutory prohibition of a test. B. Dalton, like every other retailer, suffers losses from employee theft. If the Reid Report is generally accurate as a predictor of trustworthiness, then its use will diminish these losses. No test, no predictor, is perfect; if an employer uses any selection criterion whatsoever, then there will be a few persons rejected, like Sister Terressa, who would have been entirely satisfactory employees.

While few would contend that one has an absolute right to any job for which one is qualified, most of us now accept the view that people do have a right to be fairly considered for any job to which they aspire. "Fairly considered" means, among other things, that one will not be rejected for irrelevant reasons. Fair employment opportunity legislation has designated some criteria, like race and gender, as statutorily irrelevant. One can think of many other criteria that are equally irrelevant at least in respect to some types of jobs. I should not be denied an academic position because my grandfather came from Norway, or because my eyes are blue, or because I cannot climb a 30-foot rope in 30 seconds. But the Hibernian Insurance Company might reasonably refuse to hire me as a salesman unless my grandfather was Irish; a film company might insist on a brown-eyed actor for a particular role; or the fire department might demand someone stronger and more agile than I am. Relevance is relative.

Trustworthiness is relevant to most jobs but especially to those that involve the handling of money. A test that is alleged to measure honesty, to predict trustworthiness, will be relevant—and, hence fair—to the extent that it is valid. Here we must think in terms of cost/benefit ratios. In screening job applicants for honesty, the benefit to the employer is measured by the reduction in the proportion of potential thieves among the persons hired, as compared to the proportion of potential thieves among applicants generally. The cost is measured by the number of potentially good employees who are rejected by the screening—and whatever unpleasantness this may mean to them—plus the actual dollar cost of administering the tests. Only the latter, relatively insignificant, cost is born by the employer himself and he may therefore be less strongly motivated to minimize the human cost factor in the numerator of this ratio.

What is the human cost of an (inevitably imperfect) employee screening program? It was a disappointment to Sister Terressa to be refused the job with B. Dalton because of her false-positive score on the Reid Report. It is difficult to translate such a cost into dollars. If all employers used the Reid Report (and if that test is reliable—as distinguished from valid—so that Sister Terressa would be doomed always to get a failing score), then she would be forever denied any job anywhere, a substantial cost indeed. How large a reduction in employee theft would be required to justify barring some proportion of honest citizens from the possibility of employment? An extremely liberal viewpoint might suggest one easy answer: no mere economic benefit to an employer is sufficient to justify any harm done to an innocent, honest, and potentially satisfactory employee. Since no selection system is perfect, this stance would require that all selection systems be prohibited, that all job applicants be hired in the order in which they apply. Another easy solution derives from the opposite ideological extreme; a strict Libertarian would deny to the state all powers of intervention so than an employer would be free to use any form of screening that he though would decrease costs and increase profits, without regard to what I have called the "human cost factor."

I find both these easy answers unacceptable. The Libertarians may be right when they tell me I have more to fear from the State than from Dow Chemical or Mobil Oil or Amalgamated Behemoth, Inc., but when they propose to eliminate all governmental regulation and leave me to fend for myself in the corporate jungle, I rebel. Conversely, if only 10% of applicants can make it through Amalgamated's executive training program, while an aptitude screening test would increase the survival rate to 80%, then I think Amalgamated should be allowed to use the test. Therefore I am committed to the difficult task of computing cost/benefit ratios for each screening method that might be proposed.

One could adopt guiding principles to simplify the task. A procedure that results in a small harm to many people might be said to be less costly than one that results in great harm, like permanent unemployment, to a few or even to one innocent person. This is the principle of "distributed injustice" or "harm sharing." One might also attribute lower costs to a selection method that distributed its errors randomly over the population, than to a test that made more false-positive errors in rejecting, say, blacks than whites. This is the principle of "unbiased error." Some jobs, like police work or employment in a federal security agency, involve unusual potential for harm to the general welfare if the wrong person is hired. For this reason, and because these positions are such a small proportion of the total job market, one might be more tolerant of high rates of false-positive errors as long as the frequency of false-negative errors can be kept down. This is the "public interest" principle. One might be able to mitigate the harm done to persons erroneously rejected by the screening test by using an appeal procedure through which an applicant could be retested or re-evaluated by a different method. I would favor governmental prohibition of any selection procedure that did significant harm to many people, or substantial harm to a few people, no matter what financial benefits might be entailed. But if the harm done to those erroneously rejected was temporary or trivial, and if only a small number of good applicants were mistakenly rejected by the test, and if a large proportion of the unsuitable applicants were correctly rejected by the screening procedure, yielding a suitably small cost/benefit ratio, then I would have to favor such screening.

Once again, the argument leads back to the question: How valid is the test? A perfect test would do no harm and substantial good; its cost/benefit ratio will be insignificant. An invalid test will do no good; hence its cost/benefit ratio will be unacceptably high even if its human cost is relatively small. How valid is honesty testing?

The Prediction of Honesty

More than 50 years ago, psychologists Hartshorn and May reported what has come to be regarded as a classic study of honesty in school children.[2] A variety of ingenious tests were devised in which these students were confronted with opportunities to cheat, or to lie, or to steal, in a number of different situations and for different stakes. The children did not know that they were being tested nor did they know that the investigators had secret methods of detecting who was behaving honestly and who was not. The unexpected finding in this research was that the tendencies to cheat or lie or steal were poorly correlated with one another. The children who most easily succumbed to the temptation to cheat were not the same children who most readily pocketed coins that seemed to be there for the taking. The students who stole were not necessarily inclined to lie when indirectly tempted to do so. Cheating in one situation did not even predict very accurately who cheated in a different situation. A student who would cheat in a game might not inflate his score on a test of athletic ability; the child who claimed more sit-ups than he actually accomplished might not cheat on a spelling test. What one might have thought to be component parts of a general trait of "honesty" did not prove to hang together very well; honesty turned out to be surprisingly situation-specific. Whether a child behaved honestly on a given test seemed to depend more on his motivation and opportunities in that situation than it did on how much of some supposedly general moral imperative he happened to have internalized.

It may be that the components of honesty are better correlated in adults than in children. Nevertheless, since the publication of Hartshorn and May's *Studies in Deceit* in 1928, psychologists have been pessimistic about the possibility of predicting honesty in any general way. The polygraphic screening test, discussed in Chapter 12, does not attempt to measure honesty as a trait of personality. It is based on the proposition that people who have stolen from their employers before are more likely to steal from their employer in the future. The weakness in polygraph screening is the lack of evidence that it can accurately assess an applicant's prior stealing proclivities. People classified as deceptive by the polygrapher may not be deceptive in fact; those who admit to previous misdeeds may not actually be less trustworthy than some of those who deny them.

The new honesty questionnaires like the Reid Report, the Stanton Survey, the Personnel Security Inventory, were constructed by polygraphers for use by business clients unwilling or unable to pay the higher cost of polygraph screening. The provenance of these questionnaires is readily apparent when one studies the test items. One group of questions invites the respondent to admit to various crimes misdemeanors ranging from homicide, to forgery, to stealing from the company, to lying to the boss. These yes-no items are supplemented by rating scales such as:

What total value in merchandise and property have you taken without permission from employers? (Circle nearest value.)
$5,000 $2,500 $1,000 $750 $500 $250 $100 $50 $0

Or:

How honest are you? Be objective and do not exaggerate.

| High Above Average | Above Average | About Average | Slightly Below Average | Below Average |

Dr. Philip Ash, research director for the Reid organization, explains: "Incredible as it may seem, applicants in significant numbers do admit to practically every crime in the books."[3]

Supplementing these "admissions" items are sets of questions intended to measure the respondent's "punitiveness" and his "attitudes toward theft." Typical "punitiveness" items are:

> An employer discovers that a long-service, trusted employee has been taking a few dollars out of the cash register every week. Should the employer have him arrested?

Or:

> What should be done if an employee occasionally smokes marijuana on the job? (Circle one)
> Ignore   Warn   Suspend   Fire   Arrest

Some "theft attitude" items:

> How many people that you know are really honest?
> 95%   80%   60%   40%   20%   5%

> How many employees take small things from their employers from time to time?
> 95%   80%   60%   40%   20%   5%

> How many people cheat on their income tax?
> 95%   80%   60%   40%   20%   5%

If you would like to see how you might fare on an honesty test, decide how you would answer these sample questions. Did you recommend jailing that old, trusted employee who's been taking a few dollars from the till each week? And also the young man caught smoking marijuana? Then you are doing well so far. Did you say that nearly all the people you know are really honest? And did you think that almost no one steals from his employer or cheats on his income taxes? Then, unless you have confessed to something serious on the "admissions" questions, you will probably get the job.

The rationale for such scoring is that a thief will be unlikely to recommend harsh punishment for acts he might himself commit and he will probably contend that most people are as dishonest as he. The trouble with this rationale is that the logic does not work in both directions. It is not likely that most people who recommend leniency are thieves. It is not true that all those who see the world as a sinful place are great sinners themselves. Ironically, polygraphers insist that most employees are occasionally dishonest and they are so sure that most people cheat on their income taxes that this situation is often used as a "known lie" control question in polygraph tests. Yet, when a job applicant reveals a similar degree of cynicism on the honesty questionnaire, the report to the employer will be "Not recommended for employment."

We can now begin to understand why it was that Sister Terressa got such a bad score on the Reid Report. We may doubt that she had anything sinister to reveal on the "admissions" questions (although no doubt she honestly confessed whatever youthful misdeeds she could remember). But Sister Terressa was handicapped by Christian charity, which ensured that she would do badly on the "punitiveness" items. And she was an intelligent, educated woman, with some experience of the world, and these qualities prevented her from expressing the naive assessment of humankind required to do well on the "attitude toward theft" items. A clever thief might achieve a good score on the honesty questionnaire—by answering deceptively. But, if the questions are to be answered honestly, then what is required is a punitive, authoritarian personality combined with a worldview like that of the three monkeys who hear-no-evil, see-no-evil, speak-no-evil. Oh, brave new world of work, that has such creatures in it!

Validity of Honesty Questionnaires

As was true for the various forms of lie detector test, the assumptions of the honesty questionnaires do not command immediate acceptance. It is not certain that those who admit to prior misdeeds will be less trustworthy in future than will persons who make no admissions. It is not obvious that punitive or naive employees will be more reliable than will people who are less authoritarian or more sophisticated. If the assumptions are less than compelling, a burden of proof lies on the purveyors of such questionnaires to demonstrate that the assumptions hold or that the tests do in fact predict trustworthiness.

The available evidence consists mainly of reports that job applicants tend to make the same admissions on the questionnaires that they make during polygraph screening examinations, especially if they know, when they fill out the questionnaire, that the polygraph test is in the offing. But to use one unvalidated test as a criterion against which to validate a different test is rather like one vagrant vouching for another. Since there is no evidence that polygraphic screening can distinguish between honest and dishonest job applicants, the new honesty tests must prove their worth some other way.

The accepted standard method of validating any selection test is quite straightforward. One first administers the test to a representative sample of job applicants. Then all these applicants are hired without regard to what their scores might be. At some later time, when job performance records are available on these workers, each employee's test score is compared with his subsequent performance. If most high-scoring applicants turn out to be satisfactory employees, and if most low scorers prove unsatisfactory, then the test has been shown to be a valid predictor. For the honesty questionnaires, only one such traditional "prospective" study has been reported, by Philip Ash of the Reid firm, in the trade journal *Polygraph*.[4] Dr. Ash concluded that his findings were at least moderately encouraging but, unfortunately, he allowed himself to be misled by a faulty statistical analysis. Statisticians will recognize the problem when I explain that Ash's conclusion was based on a "canonical correlation," a notoriously unreliable statistic. Of the 140 job applicants in this study, one single individual admitted on one of the Reid Report items that he had been previously arrested. At the followup of these bank employees (apparently several years later, the report is unclear), two persons had been discharged for theft. One of these two was the man with the previous arrest. If that single subject is removed from consideration, Ash's canonical correlation shrinks to insignificance. (The previous-arrest item, in fact, has since been deleted from the Reid Report.) Meanwhile, buried in the tables of the article, we find the real evidence about the Reid Report's usefulness. Scores on the "punitiveness" and "attitudes toward theft" scales do not differentiate the two known thieves from the other applicants nor are these scores correlated with supervisors' ratings of the quality of the employees' performance. Thus, in contrast to the polygraphic screening tests, there is an empirical answer to the question, "Do the honesty questionnaires predict honesty?" To the extent that this one in-house study can be trusted, the answer is "No."

Verdict

Employees are not neatly divided into honest and dishonest categories with a convenient test at hand to distinguish between them. Employee theft is probably more dependent upon situational factors—easy opportunity, resentment and alienation, special need, etc.—than it is on enduring traits of personality that can be measured by any test. For these reasons it is doubtful that employee theft-proneness could ever be predicted with useful accuracy even by a well-constructed psychological test. Whether the honesty questionnaires under discussion were well constructed is perhaps a matter of opinion; my opinion is negative. They depend in part on the assumption that applicants who admit past misdemeanors will be less trustworthy in future than those who do not make such admissions. This assumption is not obviously true and is unsupported by persuasive evidence. The honesty questionnaires assume that job applicants who think that most people yield to temptation now and then cannot be trusted; they assume that reliable employees are those with punitive, authoritarian attitudes. These assumptions seem implausible and are unsupported by any evidence. The one prospective study of the validity of an honesty questionnaire yielded negative results. Nevertheless, at the 1979 annual meetings of the American Psychological Association, the vice president for personnel of the Graybar Electric Corporation reported that his company used one of these questionnaires routinely in some 15 states.[5] One can only wonder why.

Notes

1. *Laws of Minnesota for 1976,* Chap. 256, H.F. No. 1330
2. Hartshorne, H. & May, M. *Studies in Deceit,* New York: Macmillan, 1928.
3. Ash, P. *Proceedings of the XVIIth International Congress of Applied Psychology,* Brussels: Editest, 1972. p. 986.
4. ⋅ Ash, P. Predicting dishonesty with the Reid Report. *Polygraph,* 1975, *4,* 139–153.
5. Symposium on Polygraphic Examining for Pre-employment Screening. Annual Meetings of the American Psychological Association, September 1979.

CHAPTER

17

The Fourth Degree: Polygraphically Induced Confessions

To obtain a confession where guilt is indicated is the purpose and ultimate goal of the deception [lie detector] test. . . . The instrument and the test procedure have a very strong psychological effect upon a guilty subject in inducing him to confess.

—C. D. Lee, *The Instrumental Detection of Deception*, 1953

We get better results than a priest does.

—John E. Reid, *N.Y. Times*, November 21, 1971

She was a journalism student working as a reporter for the *Minnesota Daily* and she was angry. She had told me on the phone that she wanted to do a story on the lie detector business, but it was plain that she had lost her journalistic objectivity. She wanted to blast them. This young woman had applied for a part-time job in a retail store that required a polygraph examination for pre-employment screening. "I was kind of intrigued; I thought it would be interesting." She was so furious that I thought she must have drawn one of those prurient polygraphers who take advantage of the examination situation to peek under the mental skirts of female applicants. I was mistaken; she had received the standard pre-employment treatment. She was angry because after it was all over (she had "passed" the test) she felt violated. She realized that she had told the examiner things she hadn't told her priest, that she had blurted out all her little secrets, trying to explain why that implacable machine had "shown a reaction" to this or that question.

You come in feeling like an honest, decent person and then he starts telling you that you're showing a reaction to some question about drugs or stealing and you try to think of a reason, things you've done, maybe years ago. You get to feeling as if the all-important thing is to get the machine to say that you're all right. You feel as if the thing can almost read your mind but not really accurately, it exaggerates, gets things mixed up. And you feel that if you tell the man everything you can think of, everything you've ever done that you might feel guilty about, why then finally it might come out with a clean record.

An ordinary employment interview does not have such impact. It may be a mistake to attribute all of the effect to the mystique of the polygraph, however. After all, the ordinary employment interviewer does not ask the same questions: "Have you committed an undetected crime?" "Did you ever steal merchandise from a previous employer?" It is possible that a skilled, tough interviewer could use the pressure of a level gaze, a skeptical expression, and an expectant silence to produce similar results from the same sorts of people who find themselves babbling in the polygraph room. What sorts of people are these? Polygraphers report that they elicit "damaging admissions" from 75% of job applicants. This statistic tells us at once that we are talking about ordinary, average people; it is the ones who do *not* make damaging admissions who are apparently exceptional.

Polygraph examinations are being increasingly used to screen applicants for police work. In Orlando, Florida, during 1961 and 1962, nearly 900 applicants were pruned by aptitude tests and other criteria down to 45 serious candidates who then were subjected to a polygraph interrogation. According to C. A. Romig, 75% of this select group admitted to having committed "serious undetected crimes."[1] From 1963 through 1971, the Kalamazoo Police Department gave polygraph examinations to some 520 applicants who, collectively, admitted to more than 4,500 larcenies, including 89 burglaries. More than 160 admitted a variety of sexual peculiarities ranging from indecent exposure to bestiality, 35 confessed to previous arrests, and 45 admitted falsifying their application forms.[2] A Chicago police detective, applying for a responsible position with the Minneapolis Police Department, admitted numerous instances of illegal intimidation of suspects. One of his favorite methods had been to drive the handcuffed suspect at speed along the freeway, passenger door ajar, threatening to shove him out unless he confessed whatever it was the officer wanted to hear. One wonders whether this detective learned from his experience with the polygraph that equivalent results could be obtained less violently.

Some pre-employment admissions, like these, are obviously significant. An applicant who admits to burglary, arson, assault, passing bad checks, chemical dependency—to list some of the offenses acknowledged by police candidates—should reasonably be turned away. But not all the "damaging admissions" made by job applicants should be taken this seriously, not unless we are prepared to conclude that 75% of Americans are criminals and unemployable. Turn anyone inside out and "who shall 'scape whipping?" B. F. Skinner, a distinguished American psychologist, tells in his autobiography of running next door from the shoestore where he worked as a boy to buy ice cream with pennies taken from the till—"Theft from previous employer." Skinner also mentions incidents of embezzlement, sexual misconduct, and alcohol abuse, all in the course of the relatively sedate, privileged, and productive young manhood of an outstanding scientist.[3] I am not so distinguished as Professor Skinner, but I could a longer tale unfold of juvenile sins. So, indeed, could almost anyone; examine your own conscience. As suggested earlier in this book, one is inclined to wonder about those people who do *not* make "damaging admissions." Some undoubtedly are truly saintly; others have sense enough not to be bamboozled by the polygrapher and his machine and self-disciplined enough to keep their own counsel. What about the real rogues, the deliberate villains who plan to rip off everything they can if they can get the job? Do they make "damaging admissions," or do they bluff their way through this situation as they have learned to do in others?

For many polygraphers, the posttest interrogation and the confession it so often induces is the real object of the whole exercise. A lie test diagnosis is a promissory note, not negotiable in many places, while a confession is pure gold, admissible in court, the finish to a criminal investigation, the commodity the client will be happiest to pay for. The Michigan State Police were among the earliest in this field and, in 1943, LeMoyne Snyder reported on the results of the use of the polygraph in some 900 criminal cases over a period of eight years.[4] More than one-third of these were solved by confessions obtained during or subsequent to lie detector tests. The Los Angeles Police Department maintains a polygraph laboratory with several full-time examiners, who estimate that they obtain confessions from about 25% of the suspects examined. More specifically, about 60% are diagnosed Deceptive (30% Truthful and 10% inconclusive or interrupted) and some 40% of that 60% produce confessions. Criminal investigation involves two equally important—and often equally difficult—aspects: (1) identifying the guilty person and (2) obtaining admissible evidence against that person sufficient to obtain a conviction. A confession solves both of these problems, neatly and inexpensively. Any technique that can produce a confession in from a fourth to a third of those cases in which suspects are apprehended and agree to be tested is an undoubtedly valuable tool.

Certain problems remain to be considered. First, who is it that confesses? There are no statistics to guide us, but it seems most unlikely that the sophisticated professional criminal will be stampeded into a confession by anything a polygrapher might tell him. Many felons, however, are not professional criminals, just victims of passion or impulse or circumstances who never expected to get into such a mess and do not expect to get away with it.

Secondly, is the polygraph really necessary? A recent news story described how one ingenious pair of detectives used a Xerox machine to obtain a confession from an unsophisticated suspect. Each time the man failed to produce the answer they wanted, the machine would groan and whirr and deliver the printed message, "He's lying!" copied from a previously inserted master. Most urban policemen know the trick of wrapping the squad car's microphone cable around the arm of a gullible suspect and then surreptitiously touching the transmit button when he denies their accusation. "You see that red light, George? That red light means you're lying to me. Let's try it again now." Are any of these stage props actually necessary? Are they more important for breaking down the culprit's defenses or for enhancing the interrogator's confidence and aggressiveness? If the St. Paul Police use the polygraph, while those in Minneapolis rely on old-fashioned straight interrogation by experienced detectives, will St. Paul produce a higher proportion of confessions? The experiment has not been tried, and it is difficult to guess the outcome. Perhaps most of that feckless 25% who confess under polygraphy would confess anyway with the help of a little intelligent questioning.

Third, every lie detector test involves deception, or attempted deception, of the suspect, and confessions induced by this procedure are to that extent tainted. Tainted or not, one could argue that a valid confession obtained through trickery is better than no confession at all. There is something offensive about the fact that the ignorant and the gullible are most vulnerable to such devices; educated people with good legal counsel seldom make confessions under these conditions. But the key again is whether the confession is valid. Foolish and gullible people who break the law are more liable to get caught, but society does not owe a stupid man protection in order that his chances for success in crime equal those of someone better endowed. The real problem about depending upon the myth of the lie detector for inducing confessions is that this myth must gradually be eroded. A young policeman may reasonably use polygraphs and Xerox machines as long as they work, but he should, meanwhile, learn to interrogate, against the day when the tricks no longer work and he is on his own.

The Peter Reilly Case

Finally, can we assume that polygraphically induced confessions are always valid? The answer is that we cannot, not as long as some police give too much rein to their amateur notions of psychology and play upon the susceptibilities of the gullible. Most lawyers know of Borchard's *Convicting the Innocent,* in which are reviewed 65 cases of persons imprisoned or executed on the basis of confessions proved later to be false.[5] A vivid recent illustration of how a false confession is born can be found in Barthel's *A Death in Canaan,* a true account of a Connecticut murder investigation in 1974.[6] Peter Reilly, 18 years old, came home one night to find his mother's mutilated body on the floor of the bedroom, her last gasps of breath bubbling from a severed windpipe. The police whom he summoned placed Peter in a squad car, where he shivered alone for three hours while detectives rummaged inside the house. After a few hours' sleep at the State Police Barracks, Peter was given a lie detector test, and the pre-test interview, the test itself, and the subsequent hours of interrogation were tape-recorded, so that we can follow what actually happened. During the lie test, Peter gave strong physiological reactions to questions like, "Last night did you hurt your mother?": hardly surprising under the circumstances, but these policemen had taken classes in polygraphy that apparently corroded their common sense. "Pete, we go strictly by the charts. And the charts say that you hurt your mother last night." The transcripts reveal how Peter, shocked and distracted, wanting to cooperate with the kindly policemen, let himself come to believe in "the charts" rather than in his own memory. "The test is giving me doubts right now. Disregarding the test, I still don't think I hurt my mother." Sergeant Kelly explains that Peter's mother really had it coming; she was always on his back, until he finally blacked out and killed her and now, "You're so damned ashamed of last night that you're trying to just block it out of your mind." And Peter: "I'm not purposely denying it. If I did it, I wish I knew I'd done it. I'd be more happy to admit it if I knew it. If I could remember it. But I don't remember it."

Peter had some doubts at first about the machine. "Have you ever been proven totally wrong? A person, just from nervousness, responds that way?" But Sergeant Kelly was a rock of certainty. "No, the polygraph can never be wrong, because it's only a recording instrument, recording from you."

"But if I did it, and I didn't realize it, there's got to be some clue in the house."

"I've got this clue here [the charts]. This is a recording of your mind."

"Would it definitely be me? Could it have been someone else?"

"No way. Not from these reactions."

There was a problem about the legs, both heavy femurs broken just above the knees. Peter hadn't known his mother's legs were broken. "Did you step on her legs or something? While she was on the floor? And jump up and down?"

"I could have."

"Or did you hit her?"

"That sounds possible."

Can you remember stomping on her legs?"

"You say it, then I imagine I'm doing it."

"You're not imagining anything. I think the truth is starting to come out. You want it out."

And then finally, after several hours, "Well, it really looks like I did it."

Thus, while the real murderer was effecting his escape, Peter Reilly was signing a confession to the mutilation slaying of his mother, and it was two years before that confession was shown to be false, that Peter could not have committed the crime, two years during which the trail left by the actual murderer, still at large, grew faint and cold.

Reading the transcript of the Peter Reilly interrogation, any sensible person should be able to recognize at once that this confession was meaningless, an eruption from seeds planted one by one in the mind of an exhausted and impressionable boy. The police, eager to "solve" their case and blinded by a perverse and groundless faith in the polygraph, apparently were satisfied they had their killer. How the district attorney could have agreed to prosecute such a case is difficult to understand. The Peter Reilly story should be required reading for all polygraphers, every prosecutor, every juror in cases where repudiated confessions figure in the evidence.

Why Do People Confess?

The etymology of "third degree," an American colloquialism going back to the 19th century, is somewhat obscure. It refers to protracted and exhausting interrogation accompanied by threats, intimidation, or actual torture. The "sweat box" was a popular technique of administration, a small cell set next to a furnace. "A scorching fire would be encouraged in a monster stove adjoining, into which vegetable matter, old bones, pieces of rubber shoes, and kindred trophies would be thrown; all to make a terrible heat, offensive as it was hot, to at last become so torturous and terrible as to cause the sickened and perspiring object of punishment to reveal the innermost secrets he possessed."[7] According to this same author, "third degree" is an allusion to Masonic rites and to the trials and rituals administered to those aspiring to the Third Degree or Master Mason level of that hierarchy. "The officer of the law administers the 'first degree,' so called, when he makes the arrest. When taken to the place of confinement, that is the 'second degree.'"

We need not inquire why the third degree is conducive to confession, valid or otherwise, but it may be useful to consider why polygraphic interrogation—the fourth degree—without benefit of sweat boxes or bludgeons is nonetheless so frequently effective. "All men are liars," says the psalmist, but most of us play the game according to established rules, and one basic rule is that when the jig is up, you should resign. When your inquisitor knows the truth, when your story has been shown to be inconsistent or incoherent, when the counterevidence is obvious before you, then you are supposed to admit defeat. Other rules are that one lies only for an important reason, and preferably never to a friend. A good interrogator becomes your friend, helps you to justify whatever it was that you did, making it easier for you to acknowledge the truth. Lying is difficult, tiring. A good examiner makes you see how much easier, what a relief it will be to stop the hopeless battle of wits and get it off your chest. He speaks not of punishment, but of reconciliation. Most important of all, he tries to make you realize that your story won't hold water, that it doesn't square with the facts or is inherently incredible. He may allude to other witnesses, other evidence, information in the light of which your denials are transparent and futile. He is careful from the outset to make you feel that your objective is to make *him* believe you and that if you cannot win him over, then the game is lost. He wants to prevent you from stubbornly repeating the same story, "take it or leave it," because once you have ceased to care whether he believes you, then his leverage is lost. Some people, including many experienced criminals, never expect the examiner to believe them, and this pessimistic attitude protects them from much of the stress of interrogation. This is a rational attitude, since normally it does not matter what the examiner believes, only what he can prove. But most of us, when we are lying, act less realistically, as if our denials were mere paper shields which the examiner's disbelief can shred like a knife, leaving us exposed.

Once he has you playing his game, has you trying to convince him, a good interrogator will devise a variety of methods to persuade you that you have finally lost, that it is hopeless, he has seen through you, and you might as well confess. The polygraph is only one such method, but it is an easy one to use and frequently effective. "We go strictly by the charts, and the charts say you hurt your mother last night." If Peter Reilly had actually been guilty, how could he have stood up to that? Yet, why should anyone care what "the charts say"? Has man evolved some innate tendency to defer to oracles? Or is there some unconscious logic which informs us that if the lie detector knows, then everyone will know, and that a lie that no one believes is of no use?

Confessions and the Courts

Because police are often overeager in their attempts to elicit confessions, American courts have reacted by application of the Exclusionary Rule, suppressing or refusing to admit into evidence confessions obtained by illegal means or under circumstances that the court deems to be coercive so that the resulting confession cannot be considered to have been "freely and voluntarily given." Judges have begun to speak of "psychological coercion," a concept so broad as to include potentially all the tactics of the skilled interrogator that we have considered above. The only confession that would be wholly untainted by psychological coercion might be one obtained from a citizen who walks in off the street and volunteers his story. We abjure torture, threats, intimidation, because (1) such treatment of criminal suspects, some of whom are innocent, is uncivilized and violates principles of human rights that our society holds dear and because (2) such forms of coercion are bound to elicit a high proportion of false confessions. But once we start to talk about psychological coercion (and we have already started when we deplore threats and intimidation), where do we draw the line? Any action, any external stimulus that increases the probability of a confession's being emitted by a suspect, would constitute some degree of "coercion" under this broad definition and the voluntariness of the confession would be to some degree diminished. Merely asking, "Did you do it?" is coercive in this sense because presumably some persons require at least this much external stimulation or help before acknowledging their guilt. To establish a friendly, confiding relationship with the suspect, to discuss the advantages of getting his guilty secret off his chest, to suggest that his alibi appears incredible, are tactics that are more coercive still and will yield confessions that are in some sense less than completely voluntary. To use trickery—to allude to nonexistent witnesses or other imaginary evidence, to pretend that confederates have already confessed, or to indicate that the polygraph charts have somehow revealed the truth—will further increase the proportion of confessions obtained. Such tactics do not seem to me to violate the first canon implied above: such methods are not intrinsically harmful or inhumane. However, trickery and the confessional pressures of the polygraph examination do greatly increase the dangers of eliciting false confessions.

I was recently consulted by a young woman who had signed a false confession to the theft of money from the store where she worked.

The corporation's chief security officer, a man trained in interrogation techniques by the Army, had scorned the polygraph for this $10 matter and had relied instead on standard methods. He indicated that what she allegedly had done was not really so bad: "Everybody slips once in a while." But, at the same time, he exaggerated the magnitude of the charge so that she might more readily confess to a lesser one: "How much do you think you've taken altogether? $1,000? $500?"—although the sum he really had in mind was less than $50. He made her see the futility of continued denial: "I saw you take some money out of the register with my own eyes, Carol," although the view from his distant hiding place was so indistinct that he could not have been sure what he saw. And he contrasted the minor consequences of confession with the dire consequences of obstinacy: "If you sign this statement, we can settle this now between us. Otherwise, of course, I'll have to turn the matter over to someone else." Assuming he meant the police, Carol ultimately signed even though she was innocent.[8]

Another type of false confession results when the suspect is led actually to believe that he is or might be guilty. In the Peter Reilly case we can trace this "brainwashing" process from first to last. However, I have seen transcripts of confessions obtained in the course of a polygraph test that reveal with equal clarity that the confession is valid. The suspect volunteers facts and details of his crime not suggested to him by the examiner. The confession is not a mere acknowledgement of guilt but amounts rather to a narration of a coherent and at least partially verifiable description of the particulars of the event. As someone not learned in the law, I would think it reasonable to give credence to confessions of this latter kind even though obtained partly through trickery, including the deception inherent in a polygraph examination. But the problems of interpreting the Fifth Amendment and of establishing rules to ensure adherence to those interpretations are deep matters and beyond my competence.

To sum up, polygraphic interrogation in the hands of a skillful examiner is a powerful cathartic (emetic?), an effective inducer of confessions. Its confessionary influence may be most effective with the naive and gullible or, among criminals, with the less experienced, less hardened types. In pre-employment or other screening applications, it appears that the majority of ordinary citizens may be led to make damaging admissions in this secular confessional. In criminal investigations, as many as 25% of those cases where suspects are available for questionning may be settled expeditiously by confes-

sions obtained through polygraphy. This aspect of polygraphic interrogation is quite independent of the actual validity of the technique
as a detector of deception. If all polygraphs were stage props it is
likely that just as many admissions or confessions would be elicited.
Certainly much of the popularity and utility of the polygraph derives
from this incidental effect. This may be why so many polygraphers
show little interest in research on the actual validity of the various
forms of polygraph test; even if its true validity is no better than
chance, so long as most people believe in the lie detector or the voice
stress analyzer, these tools will continue to elicit admissions and
confessions, and that is their principal purpose. Because they are so
effective, however, these methods commonly inflict great stress and
emotional disturbance on the innocent and guilty alike. The fourth
degree may leave no cuts or bruises, but it hurts—that is why it
works. And because it works so well, one should distrust any confession obtained by modern interrogation methods, whether the polygraph was employed or not, unless that confession can somehow be
confirmed.

Notes

1. Romig, C. Improving police selection with the polygraph technique.
    Polygraph, 1972, *1,* 207–220.
2. Fox, D. Screening police applicants. *Polygraph,* 1972, *1,* 80–82.
3. Skinner, B. *Particulars of My Life,* New York: Knopf, 1976.
4. Snyder, L. Criminal interrogation with the lie detector: Eight years
    experience with the Michigan State Police. *Polygraph,* 1978, *7,* 79–88.
5. Borchard, E. *Convicting the Innocent,* Garden City, N.Y.: Garden City
    Publishing Co., 1932.
6. Barthel, J. *A Death in Canaan,* New York: E.P. Dutton, 1976.
7. These remarks are quoted from the Presidential Address of one Major
    Sylvester, at the 1910 Meetings of the International Association of
    Chiefs of Police; cited in Larson, J. *Lying and Its Detection,* Chicago:
    University of Chicago Press, 1932, pp. 97–98.
8. Since World War II, military and criminal interrogation techniques
    have become quite sophisticated. Fred Inbau and John Reid, in addi-
    tion to their contributions to polygraphy, wrote one of the several
    textbooks in this field, *Criminal Interrogation and Confessions,* Bal-
    timore: Williams & Wilkins, 1967. If jurors were to read this text, they
    might better understand why even innocent suspects sometimes con-
    fess to things they did not do.

18

The Lie Detector And The Courts

As a tool of persuasion and advocacy, the polygraph stands alone because of its ability to slash the jugular vein of each case which must ultimately turn on whether one or more persons are attempting deception. If the credibility of the defendant can be established or destroyed in a criminal case, or if the plausibility of either party in a civil case can be demolished, there is nothing more to settle, nothing left for judge or jury except the assessment of penalty or awarding of damages. No other courtroom tool possesses this awesome power.

—Marshall Houts, LL.B.,
in Norman Ansley (Ed.),
Legal Admissibility of the Polygraph, 1975

Defendant's offer of polygraph evidence has been accepted in Federal courts three times, twice over-ruled by appellate courts (*U.S. v. Sigler,* 1972, and *U.S. v. Frogge,* 1973) and once not appealed (*U.S. v. Ridling,* 1972). All U.S. courts addressing the issue have excluded the results of unstipulated polygraph tests . . . it remains true in 1978 that the substantial weight of legal authority rejects the admissibility of polygraph evidence.

—Professor E. A. Jones, Jr., 1978

In November of 1920, Dr. R. W. Brown was shot to death in Washington, D.C. The following summer a young black man, James Alphonzo Frye, was arrested and grilled for several days by the D.C. police. Frye finally admitted the Brown murder but repudiated this confession just before his trial, claiming that he had been promised half of the $1,000 reward if he would falsely confess to the killing. Our old friend, Dr. William Moulton Marston, administered his blood-pressure lie test to the defendant and concluded that he was innocent. The defense petitioned the court to allow Dr. Marston to be qualified as an expert witness and to present to the jury the results of his lie test. Judge McCoy, presiding, excluded this evidence and his ruling was later upheld by a federal appeals court in language that for nearly half a century stood as a barrier between the lie detector and the courtroom:

Just when a scientific principle or discovery crosses the line between the experimental and demonstrable stages is difficult to define. Somewhere in this twilight zone the evidential force of the principle must be recognized, and while courts will go a long way in admitting expert testimony deduced from a well-recognized scientific principle or discovery, the thing from which the deduction is made must be sufficiently established to have gained general acceptance in the particular field in which it belongs. We think the systolic blood pressure deception test has not yet gained such standing and scientific recognition among physiological and psychological authorities as would justify the courts in admitting expert testimony deduced from the discovery, development and experiments thus far made.[1]

Ironically, Frye, who was found guilty of second-degree murder and sentenced to life imprisonment, was subsequently exonerated and set free. Marston had been right after all.

In recent years the barrier presented by the *Frye* decision has been eroding. Twenty states now admit the results of stipulated lie tests, polygraph examinations administered after prior agreement by both sides. The rationale here, apparently, is that anything is fair that both sides agree to although, as Attorney Lee M. Burkey has pointed out:

It is difficult to understand how the polygraph method is improved merely because the parties stipulate to be bound by it. Would the court approve a stipulation to be bound by the toss of a coin?[2]

Another recent development flies more directly in the face of *Frye* and is largely a result of the efforts of the celebrated defense counsel, F. Lee Bailey. Himself a former professional polygrapher, Bailey advocates the principle that the defendant should be allowed to "prove his innocence" with evidence of having passed a lie test, introduced even over the objections of the prosecution. Massachusetts and New Mexico already have endorsed this principle.

Earlier (in Chapter 4), we saw that a logical consequence of a highly accurate Truth Verifier would be the elimination of the jury in most criminal trials, replaced by a polygraph examination of the defendant. While most modern polygraphers are eager to be qualified as expert witnesses in court, none of them publicly advocates so radical a step as the substitution of a polygraph machine for the jury box as a standard courtroom fitting. Yet this modesty seems inconsistent in those polygraphers who claim to be able to arrive at the correct diagnosis 95 or 99% of the time; no one seriously believes that judges and juries are as prescient or as accurate as that. If John Reid has examined the defendant, and if his findings involve fewer than 1% errors as he claims, then in the interests of justice—not to mention efficiency of adjudication—the court should hear Mr. Reid first and then issue a directed verdict in harmony with his conclusions.

But we have also seen that, in fact, no lie detector test is 99% or 95% or even 90% accurate and that there is strong reason to doubt that any lie test will ever attain such levels of accuracy, based on what we have long known about the complexity and variability of the human animal. Both the Truth Control Test (which requires that the subject believe he is suspected of an equally serious but actually fictitious crime) and the genuine Lie Control Test (which requires that *we* know the subject to be guilty of an equally serious crime—but that he not know that we can prove his guilt), both of these theoretical variations of the lie test could in principle be highly accurate. But both of them require a complicated deception of the subject and are invalidated if the deception does not work. If courts began deciding cases on the basis of these tests one can be sure that defense attorneys would quickly learn the theory of the procedures and that the necessary deceptions would become impossible.

The forms of polygraph examination actually used in criminal investigations, the clinical lie test of the Reid and Arther schools or the various forms of polygraphic lie test such as the LCT and the PCT, have an average accuracy of from 63% to 75%, according to the best data available, and the polygraphic lie tests at least are strongly biased against the truthful respondent. Basing criminal verdicts entirely or substantially on such evidence would be wantonly unfair and improper. On the other hand, there is good evidence that, in the hands of a well-trained examiner, some forms of the polygraphic lie test such as the LCT do have significantly better than chance validity. Every day criminal court juries listen to evidence that is substantially less than 90% accurate on the average; eye witness testimony is notoriously undependable. Other types of expert witness, similarly, are not held to such demanding standards of near-infallibility. My own profession provides perhaps the worst example. On questions of mental status, competency to stand trial, and the like, one gets the impression that both sides can always find psychologists or psychiatrists of equal status and credentials who will give exactly opposite "expert" opinions. Handwriting and "voiceprint" identification are imperfect art forms and yet juries are permitted to hear the opinions of such experts and make of them what they will. Even ballistics and fingerprint identification are fallible, as is proven every time the defense produces someone who reads the signs differently than did the prosecution's expert. Why should the polygrapher be excluded from this parade of imperfectibility? Research indicates that the Rorschach Inkblot Test is probably less valid than the Lie Control Test; why then should a psychologist who has administered a Rorschach be permitted to state his opinion about the defendant's competency while a polygrapher, who has administered a LCT, is not allowed to testify as to the defendant's veracity?

Two separate lines of argument can be adduced in justification of this seemingly arbitrary discrimination. One has to do with the apparent paradox that the same lie test that averages (say) 70% correct conclusions on the general run of cases may be only 50% accurate (or worse) on the selected subset of cases that will be offered into evidence in court. The other line of argument contends that the polygrapher *is* different from other experts in that his testimony is "improperly preemptive of the act of judgment of the (trier of fact) on the issue of credibility."[3] Let us consider these two arguments separately and in more detail.

The Question of Base Rates

In psychometric parlance, the *base rate* of a condition (such as schizophrenia or being guilty of a certain crime) refers to the frequency of that condition among the members of a specified population. In the Horvath study of the accuracy of the LCT, the base rate of liars in the population studied was intentionally set at 50% by selecting for analysis polygraph charts from criminal suspects half of whom were later determined to be guilty and half innocent. In the Barland & Raskin study, an unselected series of cases was employed of which 78% turned out later to be guilty according to the criterion used; the base rate for lying here was 78%.[4]

What is the base rate of lying among the defendants whose stipulated polygraph tests are admitted into evidence in American courts? In my experience, prosecutors offer a defendant the option of stipulating to a lie test only in situations where the prosecution's case is weak and unlikely to sustain a conviction. Under these circumstances, if the defendant passes the lie test, charges can be dropped and nothing lost. But if the defendant fails the lie test, then the prosecution can proceed with a much stronger case and better chance of winning. Therefore, in the vast majority of those stipulated lie tests that are actually offered into evidence, the defendant *has* failed the test. Thus, we are dealing here not with criminal defendants in general but rather with that subset of defendants against whom persuasive evidence of guilt is not available. Among this select subset, the most likely reason that the prosecution's case is weak may be that the defendant is in fact innocent. For purposes of illustration, I shall assume that 70% of these particular defendants are innocent, which means that the base rate for lying among this group will be 30%. Taking together the two good accuracy studies described in Chapter 8, we can assume that about 90% of the liars will fail these stipulated tests (assuming they have not learned how to beat the polygraph) and that about 50% of the truthful suspects will also fail. That is, out of each 100 stipulated tests, 27 out of 30 guilty suspects will be classified Deceptive and so will 35 of the 70 innocent suspects. Since only the failed lie tests will be presented to the court, 35 of the 62 lie tests offered into evidence on this principle will be erroneous, a rate of accuracy actually worse than could be obtained by flipping coins!

When we think of criminal suspects against whom the State has difficulty obtaining adequate evidence, we are inclined to think of organized-crime figures, professionals with clever lawyers. But those same clever lawyers will not permit their clients to accept the prosecution's offer of a stipulated lie test. The defendants we are now discussing are likely to be small-time or first-time offenders, if they are guilty, and more likely still to be innocent victims of circumstance. If my estimate of 30% guilty is too low, then a larger fraction of the lie tests admitted into evidence will be valid, perhaps half of them or more. Conversely, if the State's polygrapher is more like the ten examiners studied by Horvath then like the two Ph.D. examiners involved in the Barland and Raskin study, the stipulated lie tests presented to the court will have still lower accuracy. We now have an answer to lawyer Burkey's question about "how the polygraph method is improved merely because the parties stipulate to be bound by it": it is not improved but it *is* changed. The fact of stipulation means that courts will see a selected group of lie tests the average validity of which will be substantially poorer than is true for lie tests in general. On the reasonable assumptions employed in the above example, this group of lie tests will have a probative value of about zero.

Suppose instead that the courts accede to F. Lee Bailey's proposal and permit the defense to offer lie test evidence over the objection of the prosecution. The humane intention here would be to compensate for the greater resources available to the State by giving the defendant this opportunity to prove his innocence. We must now imagine every defendant shopping for a friendly polygrapher in the hope of achieving a "pass" that could be offered into evidence—and that no defendants would offer testimony of a failed lie test. That is, we are now talking about criminal defendants against whom the evidence is strong enough for the prosecution to bring them to trial, rather than the subgroup against whom the prosecution's evidence is weak. If we assume that 80 out of each 100 criminal defendants actually brought to trial are in fact guilty, then about 8 of the guilties and 10 of the innocents should present evidence of passed lie tests, evidence that will be wrong 44% of the time.

As a final illustration, consider the use of lie detectors in pre-employment screening. Polygraphers report that some 75% of job applicants make damaging admissions in the course of such screening, admissions offered to clear their consciences in order to obtain a Truthful verdict from the polygraph. We can assume that most of those who make damaging admissions do not then feel required to lie to the polygraph, and that at least some applicants have nothing either to admit or lie about. If only 20% of job applicants try to lie during the actual polygraph test, then about 580 out of each 1,000 applicants should fail the test and 69% of them will be false-positives, truthful victims of lie test errors.[5]

The base-rate problem we have been discussing has to be considered whenever the proportion of liars in the group actually being tested is appreciably different from 50%. In all three examples, each based on reasonable assumptions, asymmetrical base rates would be expected to lower the average validity of those lie tests in which we would actually be interested; for example, those lie tests that would actually be used in court. Given a polygraphic lie test with an average validity of 70%, the best estimate we can make on the research available, the base rate problem reduced the effective validity in all three examples down to around chance levels or even worse. If the courts attempted to minimize the base rate effect by requiring all defendants to take polygraph tests and then admitting the results into evidence whether pass or fail, they would still face the irreconcilable difficulty that about half of all innocent defendants tend to be erroneously diagnosed as Deceptive.

The "Friendly Polygrapher." Dr. Martin Orne has pointed out that the well-established tendency for truthful subjects to fail the lie test may not hold in the special situation where the polygrapher has been engaged by the respondent or his attorney and is in that sense "friendly" to the respondent's interests.[6] The examiner will have a natural inclination to serve his clients' interests. When the respondent on his own initiative requests and pays for a polygraph test, the examiner will be disposed to expect a Truthful result. An attorney who hopes for a Truthful result will be more likely to make subsequent referrals to an examiner who produces this desired outcome. In some cases, only by producing a Truthful diagnosis can the examiner hope to earn subsequent witness fees.[7] For all these reasons, even the most ethical polygrapher will approach such a "friendly" examination with both the desire and the expectation that the respondent will "pass" the test.

Many objective psychological tests are relatively immune to the hopeful anticipations of the test administrator. But the lie test contains large elements of subjectivity. The polygrapher constructs the test questions to suit the particular case; his manner will determine the emotional atmosphere of the interrogation; the inflections of his voice will influence the subject's physiological reactions to the questions. And the polygrapher, in most real-life situations, will also score the polygraph charts, a subtle process in which the examiner's predispositions can easily determine marginal decisions. Psychologists know of a large body of research on something called the Experimenter Expectancy Effect, of which a typical study might involve recruiting graduate students as experimenters and then telling them (erroneously) that theory or previous findings indicate that the subjects in this experiment will behave one way rather than another.[8] Whether the experimental subjects are humans or white rats, such experiments tend to produce the results that the student-experimenters (the actual subjects of the true experiment) have been led to expect. Sometimes, no doubt, these biased outcomes are a result of actual cheating; the student-experimenters fake the data so that the senior researcher will be pleased with their work. But this bias will occur without any deliberate falsification. Expecting (and hoping for) a certain outcome, the student-experimenters unwittingly influence the subjects' behavior in the expected direction. Or they recheck findings that come out "wrong" but not those that come out "right"—so that errors in the desired direction are selectively retained. Because of this research, most psychologists would agree with the following generalization: If a test procedure is sufficiently subjective and unstructured so that an unethical examiner *could* easily bias the results, then it is likely that an ethical examiner, expecting or hoping for one outcome rather than another, *will* bias the results without any conscious intention to do so.

These considerations are especially relevant to the proposal that criminal defendants be permitted to offer evidence of having passed polygraph examinations. Such a practice would unquestionably generate an active market for "friendly" polygraphers—and one must doubt that the interests of justice would be well served by the result.

The Polygrapher as Expert Witness

Professor Edgar Jones cites a query by an appellate court justice that poses the theme for this section; this justice wondered "why there was any difference between the testimony of a polygraph operator who believes the defendant is telling the truth, and of a physician who gives his expert opinion on a medical condition."[9] I was asked a similar question by a judge presiding at a murder trial in Anchorage, Alaska, in 1977. I had not thought that particular matter through before and my extemporaneous reply was halting and unsatisfactory. Here is what I should have said.

The law recognizes the special category of expert witness because courts often require information that is available only in the form of the opinion of some specially trained and knowledgeable person. Juries and judges are not competent to give medical tests or to interpret the results, to take fingerprints and then match them, or to determine whether a defendant is afflicted with a mental illness. Therefore, while ordinary witnesses are restricted to reporting what they did or saw or heard, a qualified expert witness is permitted to offer his opinion, based on his special fund of knowledge and experience. These opinions are inevitably fallible but they provide items of evidence that would be wholly inaccessible to a lay jury without the expert's help, pieces of the final puzzle which it is the jury's job to assemble into the most coherent picture that it can. But the polygrapher's evidence, also fallible, goes directly to the heart of the issue; it is offered, not as a piece of the puzzle but as the final picture complete. If the defendant was truthful on the lie test, then he is innocent; if he was deceptive, then he is guilty. Admittedly, there are cases in which another kind of expert's testimony may be crucial; if the fingerprints on the gun are those of the defendant then, given the other facts in evidence, logic may compel the jury to bring in a verdict of guilty. But, even here, it is the jury's job to draw the necessary inference. When, on the other hand, a polygrapher asserts that, in denying his guilt on the polygraph test, the defendant was deceptive, there is nothing left for the jury to do but rubber-stamp this predetermined verdict or else to reject the polygrapher's testimony altogether.

Moreover, judges and juries *are* quite capable of assessing the credibility of a witness without any help from a polygraph examiner. Indeed, assessing credibility of witnesses is traditionally one of the main responsibilities of triers of fact. What I have called "clinical examiners" of the Keeler-Reid-Arther tradition use much the same sort of evidence in deciding credibility that courts customarily employ, including "behavior symptoms" and evidentiary considerations and, sometimes, polygraphers use the sorts of unverifiable or hearsay evidence that our courts specifically reject. It is unlikely that any court would permit some Certified Public Logician, as an expert witness, to tell the jury how it ought to *combine* the facts in evidence in arriving at its verdict; making rational inferences from the facts at hand is another responsibility traditionally reserved to judge and jury. Accrediting as an expert witness a clinical polygraph examiner is an equally radical break with the basic principles of our system of justice.

Admittedly, the average juror cannot administer a lie detector test or interpret a polygram. A polygraph examiner of the school that bases its conclusions entirely on the charts, eschewing "behavior symptoms" and other sources of information, could claim that his training allows him to assess credibility in a special way, not available to the court except through his opinion. Here again, it seems to me, the question of validity is central. If the polygraphic lie test were as nearly infallible as some of its advocates contend, then perhaps the polygrapher should be qualified as an expert witness (*the* expert, indeed, making all others redundant) even though his testimony goes to the heart of the issue and usurps the traditional function of the trier of fact. But the evidence suggests that the polygraphic lie test has only modest validity, that it is correct from perhaps 60% to 75% of the time. The base rate considerations of the preceding section indicate that, for the courtroom applications now used or contemplated, this average validity may be reduced to chance levels of 50% or even lower. Instead of improving the jury's assessment of credibility, such evidence seems far more likely to pollute it.

The polygrapher clearly is a unique kind of expert witness, one whose presence in the courtroom constitutes an abrupt departure from traditional principles. For an institution as wedded as the law is to precedent and to the deliberate and prudent pacing of its own evolution, one would expect such radical steps to be taken only at the prodding of compelling evidence that these steps are in the right direction.

How Juries React to Lie Test Evidence

During the summer of 1974, James Ray Mendoza, age 19, was tried in a Wisconsin court on two counts of murder in the first degree. Two off-duty policemen, dressed in plain clothes, were shot on the street across from a Milwaukee barroom at about 2 A.M. Both fatal bullets were fired from a service revolver carried by one of the officers, who, postmortem tests indicated, had been drinking heavily. Mendoza admitted the killings, pleading self-defense. He said that the men had accosted him after the bar closed, that they had beaten him, bending him back on the hood of a parked car and beating him with a gun butt. Eyewitnesses corroborated this account. Mendoza's hairs were found on the hood of the car. The defendant contended that, in the melee, he was able to seize the policeman's revolver with which he then shot both his assailants.

In view of the evidence, the prosecution offered to reduce the charges to second degree murder and manslaughter if Mendoza passed a lie detector test. In return, he had to agree that the lie test evidence could be used against him if he was diagnosed to be deceptive. The prosecution's offer was accepted. Mendoza was tested by the chief polygrapher of the Wisconsin State Crime Laboratory. The examiner's verdict was "deceptive."

Over defense objections, the trial was moved from Milwaukee to the rich farm country of Sparta, Wisconsin. An all-white jury was impanelled. The defense brought in two other experts to dispute the validity of the lie test results but the trial judge interpreted Wisconsin case law to forbid disputing the polygrapher's findings through the testimony of rebuttal witnesses.

This jury was faced with an unusually clear choice. On the one hand, much of the physical and eyewitness evidence clearly supported the defendant's claim of self-defense. On the other hand, the polygrapher testified that a lie detector test had shown Mendoza's account to be deceptive. The jury chose to believe in the lie test. Mendoza was found guilty as charged. The judge, also apparently persuaded by the polygraph, sentenced the defendant to two terms of life imprisonment—to be served consecutively.

On appeal, the Wisconsin Supreme court ruled that the proceedings should not have been arbitrarily moved to Sparta and ordered a new trial. Released on bail, James Ray Mendoza disappeared and was still a fugitive four years later. Who can blame him?

It is doubtful that even the prosecution believed that Mendoza had premeditated these killings, that he had planned to steal a gun from one of these plainclothesmen, shoot them both, beat himself with the gun butt, and then bribe several witnesses. As is generally true in such cases, the offer of dismissed or reduced charges in return for stipulation to the lie test suggests that the prosecution knew that the defendant's explanation might be persuasive without the polygrapher's expert opinion to refute it. By itself, the Mendoza case demonstrates that an American jury can turn its face from other evidence and allow itself to be guided by the verdict of the polygraph.

There are other clues as to the way in which juries may react to the testimony of polygraphers. In the first reported case in which lie test evidence was admitted, jurors were subsequently questioned by mail as to what importance they had attached to the polygraph findings. Six of the 10 jurors who responded said that they considered the lie test results to be conclusive.[10] In another study, 20 third-year law students were asked to decide an imaginary case; all 20 found the defendant not guilty. They were then asked to suppose that there had been testimony that the defendant had failed a lie detector test. When told that the lie test was 99.5% accurate (roughly the accuracy claimed by Reid and by Arther), 17 of the 20 changed their verdict to guilty.[11] A similar study in Canada employed an imaginary murder case in which the defendant was reported to have confessed his guilt.[12] In spite of psychiatric testimony that this defendant was unstable and prone to false confession, more than half of a group of 50 mock-jurors found him guilty. The case was then presented to another group of mock-jurors, this time including testimony that the defendant had passed a lie detector test. With this one change, 72% now considered him to be innocent. For a third group, a statement by the judge was added, asserting that the polygraph was only 80% accurate and that they should be cautious in evaluating that evidence. Nonetheless, 60% of this group rendered a verdict in accordance with the lie test.

The one remaining study has been interpreted to indicate that juries may not be overinfluenced by lie test evidence.[13] Thirty-one jurors who had participated in moot court or practice trials were contacted by mail after they had already rendered their decisions. They were asked whether they would have voted differently if the evidence had included the results of a lie detector test. Only 20% acknowledged that such testimony would now convince them that they had voted incorrectly. But these jurors had already settled on the opposite verdict after lengthy deliberation. It is obviously more difficult to get people to change a settled opinion than it is to influence that opinion while it is being formed.

The impact upon a jury of lie detector evidence will doubtless vary with the nature of the case, the impression made by the polygrapher, the quality of the rebuttal testimony if any, and by the way in which the judge instructs the jury to interpret such evidence. More and better research on this issue would be useful. But those who scoff at fears that lie test evidence might "somehow be so prejudicial in its weight and impact that the jury will disregard all other evidence and go on the polygraph test results alone,"[14] will have a hard time convincing James Ray Mendoza—if they can find him.

The Psychopathic Liar

Professor Edgar Jones points out that lie detection and truth verification are not quite the same thing, due to the limited capacity "of humans . . . realistically to perceive, and then to store their perceptions as reliable recollections which can later be accurately summoned and recounted." To our capacity to misremember or to misperceive events there are many contributors, including "that ancient sixth sense—the intuitive leap of recognition that so often in fables alights on iridescent truth, while in life as often plunges into some mudhole of surmise."[15] If there could be a dependable lie detector, which Professor Jones considers doubtful, even then the lie detector's diagnosis could not assure us that what this witness says is true, but only that the witness believed it to be true at the time of testing. And most judges understand that there are people, with the best intentions, who are wholly unreliable as witnesses when their own interests and emotions are involved, because they so readily believe what they want to believe.

The psychopathic liar presents a very different problem because his unreliability is entirely conscious and deliberate. Psychiatrist Hervey Cleckley provides a characteristically vivid description:

The psychopath shows a remarkable disregard for truth and is to be trusted no more in his accounts of the past than in his promises for the future or his statement of present conditions. He gives the impression that he is incapable of ever attaining realistic comprehension of an attitude in other people which causes them to value truth and cherish truthfulness in themselves. Typically, he is at ease and unpretentious in making a serious promise or in (falsely) exculpating himself from accusations, whether grave or trivial. His simplest statement in such matters carries special powers of conviction. Overemphasis, obvious glibness, and other traditional signs of the clever liar do not usually show in his words or in his manner. Whether there is a reasonable chance for him to get away with the fraud or whether certain and easily forseen detection is at hand, he is apparently unperturbed and does the same impressive job. . . . During the most solemn perjuries he has no difficulty at all in looking anyone tranquilly in the eyes.[16]

The psychopath's talents as a liar are not due merely to long practice or the cultivation of a beguiling "poker face." Research has shown that the genuine psychopath (the term is carelessly used to include people unlike Cleckley's prototype) is less bothered than the normal person is about danger in general and punishment in particular. He is relatively untroubled by impending unpleasantness, whether of his own making or not. A classic laboratory demonstration of this peculiarity involves connecting the experimental subject to a polygraph and then having him listen to a countdown: "Ten . . . Nine . . . Eight . . . ," knowing that a tremendous blast of noise or a painful electric shock will be presented when the countdown reaches "Zero!"[17] The polygraph shows the normal individual's apprehension beginning early in the countdown, increasing to a climax of high arousal just before the noxious stimulus is due to be delivered. The real psychopath, in contrast, show relatively little premonitory perturbation. He does not look very worried externally and the polygraph confirms that his apparent insouciance is more than skin deep.

The simplest theory to account for these and other characteristics of the psychopath is that he or she has a low "anxiety IQ." Like every other biological characteristic, the innate tendency for fearfulness varies from one person to another. People at the high end of this continuum are easily frightened, timid, predisposed to certain types of neurotic disorder. Those at the low end would appear to be blessed; who needs worry and anxiety? But fear, like pain, has an adaptive function, most obvious in the formative years, and our society depends heavily upon the sequence of punishment-fear-avoidance for the socialization of children. A child with a low anxiety IQ (there is nothing at all wrong with the psychopath's actual IQ, his intelligence) is less influenced by punishment. If his adult community responds by increasing punishment and disapproval, the underanxious child merely becomes alienated from the community and seeks his gratifications elsewhere. And the lack of normal timidity and shyness does have advantages; the latent-psychopathic child tends to be popular with his peer group; he is successfully aggressive, a leader in the gang, learns how to manipulate others, how to get the things he wants through guile or predation. The low-anxiety child responds normally to positive rewards, to success and achievement and the admiration of others. If blessed with insightful parents who know enough to emphasize the positive, he can become socialized through ties of affection and the self-discipline of pride and turn out to be a hero or community leader. Otherwise he may remain unsocialized, a feral creater—and an unusually skillful and confident liar.

We have seen that the normal individual tends to "fail" the standard lie test because he is aroused (actually frightened, worried) by the relevant questions and the polygraph reveals this apprehension. It is natural to suppose that a psychopath would be less aroused by the relevant questions and therefore less likely to be classified as Deceptive—whether he is lying or not. In a properly scored lie control test, the only way to "pass"—to be classified as definitely Truthful —is to respond more strongly to the so-called control questions than to the relevant questions. There is no reason to expect the psychopath to show this pattern. Instead, one might expect the psychopath to show minimal reactions to both the relevant and the control questions and, thus, to produce Inconclusive results. But since the LCT is predicated on the respondent's expected fear of discovery, if he is guilty and lying, and since the psychopath's cardinal characteristic is his attenuated fearfulness, his lack of normal guilt or shame or concern about the consequences of his actions, then it is natural to suppose that the standard lie test should be relatively unsuccessful in detecting lying in the psychopath.

A recent study of this very question has led polygraphers to think that this expectation has been refuted.[18] Inmates of a prison in British Columbia were classified as psychopathic or nonpsychopathic and then invited to participate in the experiment. Half of the participants were asked to commit a mock crime, to "steal" a $20 bill, and then to take a lie detector test while pretending to be innocent. The other group was actually innocent of the "theft" and took the same test. All subjects were offered a prize of $20 if their lie test indicated that they were truthful in denying the theft. In the event, nearly all of the "guilty" subjects were scored as Deceptive and nearly all of the "innocent" subjects were scored as Truthful—96% accuracy overall —and the psychopaths were as successfully classified as were the non-psychopathic inmates. This is truly a remarkable result, especially since these statistics are so much better than this same polygrapher, Dr. David Raskin, achieved when he scored the LCT charts of real criminal suspects in the earlier study by Barland and Raskin, where his average accuracy was only 72%. Raskin acknowledges that the psychological differences between laboratory and field situations are "profound":[19] accuracies obtained in laboratory experiments like this prison study cannot be used to estimate the accuracy to be expected in real-life uses of the lie test. Moreover, Raskin himself both administered the LCT examinations in the prison study and also scored them. If we picture those 44 inmate participants, each trying to win his $20 and half of them hoping to bring back to their colleagues the news that they had "beaten the lie detector," it is easy to imagine that a least a few of them made some revealing comment or exhibited a tell-tale expression, perhaps after the formal test was over and they were being disconnected from the polygraph. For example, if a "guilty" subject asked before leaving the experimental room, "Well, how did I do? Did I beat it?" then, when Dr. Raskin sat down to score the polygrams, it would be very difficult for him to ignore this extra-polygraphic clue. When I was asked to comment on the report of this experiment by the editor of the journal to which it had been submitted, I urged that Dr. Raskin have the polygrams rescored by another polygrapher who had no extraneous cues as to which subjects were which. Dr. Raskin did not do this, however, so we shall never know how the real accuracy of the LCT on this occasion compared with that achieved in the Barland and Raskin study.

If we cannot take seriously the results of this experiment as an estimate of lie test accuracy in real life, can we at least learn something from the fact that the psychopaths tested performed no differently than the nonpsychopaths? However well the polygraph can do at detecting lying, does it do equally well with psychopathic subjects? We had predicted that psychopaths should be less disturbed and apprehensive than nonpsychopaths when being tested as criminal suspects, less fearful or remorseful while lying in response to the relevant questions. But, in the game-like context of this British Columbian experiment, there was no occasion for any of the subjects to be frightened or remorseful. The arousal responsible for the polygraphic reactions observed on these tests should not have been generated by such negative emotions but rather by the inmates' interest in the project, the challenge of the task, the desire to "beat the lie detector" and to win the $20. And there is no reason to expect the psychopath to be any less challenged or any less interested in winning: "When the felon's not engaged in his employment, or pursuing his felonious little plans, his capacity for innocent enjoyment is just as great as any honest man's."[20] This is, of course, precisely why the laboratory lie test, in which the subjects are motivated by curiosity or the offer of prizes, is a poor simulation of the real-life situation in which the subject is motivated by fear or guilt.

Dr. Raskin conducted the experiment we have been analyzing while the guest of Professor Robert Hare at the University of British Columbia. Dr. Hare is one of the leading authorities on the psychopathic personality. After considering the criticisms evoked by the report of this experiment, Dr. Hare concluded that the original thesis —that the psychopath may be better able than the normal subject to "beat" a lie detector test administered in the course of real-life criminal investigation—remains to be disproven.[21] We can only agree.

The Polygraph in Criminal Investigation

Nothing we have said so far militates against the use of polygraphic interrogation as an aid in criminal investigation under police auspices. If lie test results are not as accurate as some have claimed, they may still be useful in setting investigative priorities. If Pat passes the lie test while Mike shows a classic Deceptive result, focus your inquiry first on Mike's comings and goings—but don't let Pat leave town. With the polygraph in action, as many as 25% of crimes may be solved neatly and efficiently by means of a confession—but make sure that the confession can be verified. There is reason to believe that the Guilty Knowledge Test, discussed in Part IV of this book, could be of great value in police work, only in special cases to be sure, but possibly in many of those important and difficult cases where help is most needed.

The great problem in police polygraphy is in restraining the enthusiasm and credulity that these methods inspire in many police officers. A case in the news, as I write, concerns a priest accused of a series of robberies, recently cleared by the confession of another man who resembled the priest both in appearance and manner. But the priest had "failed" a lie detector test and the press quote the local police as still convinced that "we had the right man the first time." The lie test is seductive because it is so clear cut, no shadings of gray, no equivocating probabilities; the suspect either passes or he fails. It must seem a relief from the many uncertainties, often dangerous uncertainties, that characterize police work. But if police polygraphy is not to be abused, then police officers must learn to accept that the lie test is never certain either, that some villains pass, that many who fail will turn out to be innocent, that not even a confession should be accepted without verification.

Whether it would be in the interests of justice to present to a jury the results of a Guilty Knowledge Test is an intriguing question that will be taken up in Chapter 22. The considerations of the present chapter, in my view, combine to make a strong case against any use of Lie Detector Test findings in the courtroom. The lie test has modest validity at best and is biased against the truthful suspect—unless the test is administered by a "friendly" polygrapher. The test's validity will tend to be even lower on the selected set of cases that would be offered into evidence, due to the base rates phenomenon. The lie detector usurps from the trier of fact the central responsibility for determining credibility. If the lie test examiner is accredited as an expert witness, no other witnesses, expert or not, need apply. As we shall see in Chapter 18, it should not be difficult to teach most guilty suspects how to "beat" the standard lie test, and it seems probable that psychopaths and experienced criminals can often accomplish this without special training. If it has any legitimate role in the criminal justice system at all, the lie detector should be used exclusively—and circumspectly—in criminal investigation, aiding the search for the sorts of hard evidence traditionally admissible in court.

Notes

1. *Frye v. United States* (293 F.1013), 1924.
2. Burkey, L. Privacy, property, and the polygraph. *Labor Law Journal,* 1967, *18,* 79.
3. Jones, E. "Truth" when the polygraph operator sits as arbitrator (or judge). In J. Stern & B. Dennis (Eds.), *Truth, Lie Detectors, and Other Problems.* 31st Annual Proceedings, National Academy of Arbitrators, 1979, p. 151.
4. These studies are cited in the notes to Chapter 8.
5. For these calculations I have attributed to the polygraph screening test the same validity estimated for the Lie Control Test since there is no evidence at all as to the validity of the Relevant Control Test or the Positive Control Test, the only lie tests that can be used for screening purposes.
6. Orne, M. Implications of laboratory research for the detection of deception. *Polygraph.* 1975, *2,* 169–199.
7. The lure of witness fees can be compelling. In 1979, polygrapher David Raskin was charging $1,000 a day plus expenses.
8. Rosenthal, R. *Experimenter Effects in Behavioral Research,* New York: Appleton-Century-Crofts, 1966.
9. Jones, E. *op.cit.,* p. 78.
10. *People v. Kenny,* 167 Misc.51, 3 N.Y.S.2d 348 (Queens County Ct. 1938).
11. Koffler, R. The Lie Detector: A critical appraisal of the technique as a potential undermining factor in the judicial process. *New York Law Forum,* 1957, *3,* 123, 138–146.
12. Cavoukian, A. The effect of polygraph evidence on people's judge-

ments of guilt. Paper presented at the Meetings of the Canadian Psychological Association, June 13–15, 1979.

13. Carlson, S., Pasano, M., & Jannuzzo, J. The effect of lie detector evidence on jury deliberations: An empirical study. *Journal of Police Science and Administration*, 1977, *5*, 148–154.

14. Barnett, F. How does a jury view polygraph examination results? *Polygraph*, 1973, *2*, 275–277, p. 277.

15. Jones, E. *op.cit.*, p. 119.

16. Cleckley, H. *The Mask of Sanity*, 5th Ed. St. Louis: C.V. Mosby, 1976, p. 341.

17. Hare, R. *Psychopathy: Theory and Research*, New York: John Wiley, 1970. See also Lykken, D. A study of anxiety in the sociopathic personality. *Journal of Abnormal and Social Psychology*, 1957, *55*, 6–10.

18. Raskin, D. & Hare, R. Psychopathy and the detection of deception in a prison population. *Psychophysiology*, 1978, *15*, 126–136. For a critique of the above see Lykken, D. The psychopath and the lie detector. *Psychophysiology*, 1978, *15*, 137–142.

19. Barland, D. & Raskin, D. Detection of deception. In W. Prokasy & D. Raskin (Eds.), *Electrodermal Activity in Psychological Research*, New York: Academic Press, 1973, p. 445.

20. Gilbert & Sullivan's *The Pirates of Penzance*.

21. Letter from Professor Hare, May 25, 1978.

19

How To Beat The Lie Detector

Automatically and instinctively, we shun anything that is om-nipotent enough to threaten our safety. The polygraph must be placed in this category . . . it vests totalitarian God-like power in a single man—the polygraph examiner.

> —Marshall Houts, LL.B.,
> in Norman Ansley (Ed.),
> *Legal Admissibility of the Polygraph*, 1975.

This detestable machine, the polygraph (the etymology of which shows that the word means "to write much," which is about all that can be said for it). . . . It is such an American device, such a perfect example of our blind belief in "scientism" and the efficacy of gadgets; and . . . so American in the way it produces its benign but ruthless coercion.

> —William Styron, in his Introduction
> to *A Death in Canaan,*
> by Joan Barthel

A deceptive subject might try to beat the lie test by inhibiting his physiological reactions to the relevant questions. People can attenuate their responses even to very strong or painful stimuli if they know when the stimulus is coming.[1] Because the pattern of a control question lie test is fixed, a sophisticated subject should be able to tell when the relevant questions are about to be presented. Some persons have much better control of their reactions than others do. There are even ethnic differences. When Bedouin tribesmen of the Negev desert were examined on the polygraph, they were found to be far less reactive than Israeli Jews, whether of Near Eastern or European origin.[2] Moreover, most people will become habituated to any stimulus, like a question, that has been frequently repeated and then they will react less strongly to that stimulus than they did at first. A criminal suspect who has been extensively interrogated might, as a result of this habituating repetition, become less reactive to the relevant questions on a lie test administered later.

During the 1960s, my university accepted a secret research contract from the Air Force to study the effectiveness of countermeasures against lie detection. My job in this project was to train the experimental subjects. They practiced controlling their responses to my questions while observing their own reactions on the polygraph —the technique now known as "biofeedback." When I thought they were prepared, I would send them on to the chief of our university police department, a polygraph examiner of long experience, who would administer a formal lie test. This work had just gotten well under way when a new university president cancelled all secret research contracts, including ours. (I never understood why the Air Force insisted on the "secret" classification, since the only thing about our project that could really be kept secret was the source of the funding.) But we had gone far enough by then to convince me that some people could learn to attentuate their relevant responses and beat the lie detector in that fashion.

Thumbtacks and Muscle Tension

But the most dependable method of beating the lie detector is to augment one's reactions to the control questions. However disturbed one may be by the relevant questions, the scoring rules require that the examiner cannot diagnose "Deceptive" if the control reactions are just about as strong or even stronger. Knowing the principles of the method, a respondent could identify the control questions when the examiner goes over the list in the pretest interview. During the test, the respondent will try to sit calmly, breathing regularly, during the relevant questions. When a control question is presented, he will do something to augment his response, a different something each time so that the reactions do not appear suspiciously stereotyped. After the first control question, I might suspend breathing for a few seconds, then inhale deeply and sigh. While the second control is being asked, I might bite my tongue, hard, breathing rapidly through my nose. During the third control question, I might press my right forearm against the arm of the chair or tighten the gluteus muscles on which I sit. A thumbtack in one's sock can be used covertly to produce a good reaction on the polygraph.[3] So too can a thumbnail when dug under the nail of the forefinger.

Not knowing how to go about it, few respondents make any real effort to beat the lie detector or, when they do try, their efforts are easily detected. They cough or move in their chair or tighten their arm muscles under the blood pressure cuff. And these activities usually occur during or just after the relevant questions and, therefore, tend to augment the very responses that will lead to a Deceptive diagnosis. If he is not expecting a more sophisticated attempt at "beating the machine," the typical polygrapher might well be deceived by the approach outlined above. John Reid has recently denied my contention that criminals could beat the polygraph by self-induced reactions which, he says, "are so obvious and unnatural that they are a clear indication of guilt."[4] He has apparently forgotten that he proved my point himself years ago. Using muscular contraction or pressure, he found "that all the typical blood pressure responses of deception can be produced artifically at will" and that "the manner in which these blood pressure changes were effected was imperceptible to the operator."[5] Reid has since devised a special subject chair containing pressure sensors in the arms and seat, connected to auxiliary pens on the polygraph, for detecting such contractions or pressures but, since the vast majority of polygraphers do not use such equipment, pages 258 to 262 of the Reid and Inbau textbook provide a convenient guide to the criminal bent on defeating the polygraph.

Attorney F. Lee Bailey once offered a prize of $10,000 to "anyone who can beat the lie detector." I think Mr. Bailey's money is quite safe, in spite of the foregoing consideration. Imagine me showing up in John Reid's office saying, "Hook me up to your polygraph. I want to win Bailey's $10,000." Under these circumstances, one can be sure that I would be seated in Reid's custom-made "muscular movement chair." Certainly an examiner of Mr. Reid's experience would have his eyes peeled for the slightest twitch or movement. More importantly, under the conditions, any twitch or movement would be interpreted as a deliberate countermeasure rather than as an involuntary symptom of nervousness. Finally, if I did manage somehow the covert self-stimulation—biting my tongue, perhaps, which Reid's special chair cannot detect—what professional polygrapher could score a polygraph chart obtained under such circumstances as Truthful? There is no doubt that it would be hard to beat a lie test when the examiner expects you to try and knows how you mean to do it.

Yet, just as the polygrapher depends upon the respondent's naivete for the lie test to work in the first place—exaggerating the test's accuracy, deceiving him with the "stim test," misleading him about the function of the control questions—so too might the sophisticated respondent capitalize on the fact that most examiners do not expect skillful countermeasures and, not looking for them, may not see them. In the Horvath and the Barland and Raskin experiments discussed in Chapter 8, the LCT was quite successful in detecting lying —about 88% accurate on the average—although it did no better than chance in detecting truthful responding in both studies. If, unbeknownst to the experimentors, guilty suspects in these studies had attempted skillfully to beat the lie detector by the methods discussed above, then the frequency of false-negative errors might also have approached 50%.

(I have recently received some interesting data on this point. I insert it parenthetically because, while I believe that it is valid, it can hardly be called scientific evidence. I have been corresponding with an inmate of a Midwestern prison, convicted in 1976 of murder. His conviction resulted in large part from testimony by a polygrapher that this defendant had failed a stipulated lie test. At his request, I had sent this man some information about polygraphic interrogation, including an article of my own which explains how one might attempt to "beat" the Lie Control Test. My correspondent, who must remain nameless, writes to me as follows:

Since reading the article that you sent me . . . I have been running my own experiment. The prison that I am in forces anyone that is suspected of violating a prison regulation into taking a polygraph. I have been able to get to nine of these people prior to their taking a test. Out of the nine that I

KNOW were guilty of the "offense" that they were accused of, nine have beat the test! I realize that this is a small group to work with, but the 100% "hit rate" is nothing to laugh at. All I have done is have them read the article that you have sent me and then explain exactly what you were saying and they have all beat the test.

It would be difficult for a researcher to set up a controlled study to determine whether guilty suspects, to be tested under real-life conditions, could be trained to beat the lie test. My friend does not claim to be a scientist but I think he has helped to illuminate an inaccessible corner. As he remarks, nine out of nine is nothing to laugh at.

Legislative Intervention

No good social purpose can be served by inventing ways of beating the lie detector or deceiving polygraphers. As the example above shows, the most avid students of such developments would be professional criminals rather than the innocent suspects and the truthful job applicants who now fall victim to the trust that we Americans invest in this technology. In the preceding chapters, I have tried to show that no test based on the polygraph can distinguish truthful from deceptive responding with high validity, and that it is unlikely that a real lie detector will ever be invented.

Similarly, I have tried to show that there are no behavioral cues that an experienced observer could employ so as to become a "human lie detector" of such accuracy that courts, employers, and the rest of us should defer to his expert judgment. We have seen that polygraph tests and honesty questionnaires are being increasingly used in the United States to decide which job applicants should be hired and which employees should keep the jobs they have. And we have noted that this trend has continued in the absence of any evidence at all that either test actually differentiates between the trustworthy and the dishonest. We have discovered that American businesses, like the ancient nobility, maintain their own private police, armed with lie detectors rather than with clubs, and that employees suspected of crimes against the company are tried by polygraph and punished by dismissal, without the protection of due process.

Turning to the official criminal justice system, we have discovered that the lie test is finding its way more frequently into the courtroom.

We have acknowledged that, if the lie test were as accurate as its proponents claim, then in the interests of justice we should not only admit lie test evidence at trial but we should base the trial verdict directly on the lie test findings. But, perhaps thankfully, we have noted that in fact the lie test is not nearly so accurate as its advocates contend, that its validity is likely to be even lower on the selected cases in which it is now admitted by some courts, and that the consideration of such evidence is likely to impair, rather than facilitate, findings of fact in the traditional way. The use of the lie detector by the police as an investigative tool, while subject to abuse like any other tool, is not inherently objectionable and may improve the efficiency of the administration of justice through its effectiveness in inducing confessions. But we have learned that such confessions may not be valid and must always be carefully checked for authenticity.

For all these reasons, then, it seems apparent that the truth technology must be regarded as a growing menace in American life, a trend to be resisted and, it may be hoped, beaten by measures more dependable and lasting than secreting a tack in one's sock. At least 15 states prohibit employers from requiring workers or job applicants to take lie detector tests. But most of these statutes are easily circumvented. An employee can be coerced without being formally "required" to submit to the test. Even where the statute prohibits "requesting" or "soliciting" an employee or applicant to take a lie test, the practice persists because the prescribed penalties are small and, most important, few employers and even fewer employees are aware that such laws exist. The victims of these practices, in their thousands, are often young and powerless. Even when innocent of any actual wrongdoing, they feel shamed, under a cloud of doubt and suspicion. They rarely make a fight of it. Federal legislation, like the bill introduced by Senator Bayh of Indiana, should prove more effective if it can be passed over the strong opposition mounted by the lie detector industry and supported by their business clients who have persuaded themselves, for reasons not discernable to me, that lie detector screening saves them money. I believe, however, that the only safe solution, the only way to truly beat the lie detector, is to demythologize it. If lawyers, employers, judges, and ordinary citizens knew what you know now about the lie test, then the menace would be manageable. The first purpose of this book is to contribute to that end.

Some polygraphers are merely greedy opportunists. One would not regret their having to move into some more useful line of work.

But many polygraphers are honorable people, firmly convinced that they are building a respectable profession that will benefit society. One must regret having to turn one's face against this group, advocating reforms that would put them out of business. I agree that, if they could distinguish truth from falsehood with great accuracy, then professional polygraphers would eventually sit at every crossroad of American life, passing the virtuous and forestalling the malefactors. I accept the sincerity of those who believe that their judgments are accurate 95% or 99% of the time—but I believe that they are wrong. These claims are implausible and the available evidence denies them. This one critique will not dismantle a flourishing, multimillion dollar industry. I only hope to shift the burden of proof, which polygraphers have always shirked, back where it belongs—on the shoulders of the "truth" merchants themselves.

Notes

1.   Lykken, D., Macindoe, I. & Tellegen, A. Perception: Autonomic response to shock as a function of predictability in time and locus. *Psychophysiology*, 1972, *9*, 318–333. Lykken, D. & Tellegen, A. On the validity of the preception hypothesis. *Psychophysiology*, 1974, *11*, 125–132.

2.   Kugelmas, S. & Lieblich, I. Relation between ethnic origin and GSR reactivity in psychophysiological detection. *Journal of Applied Psychology*, 1968, *52*, 158–162.

3.   Reid, J. & Inbau, F. *Truth and Deception*, 2nd Ed. Baltimore: Williams & Wilkins, 1977, p. 207. The examples of "respiration deception responses," on pp. 61–66 of this text, provide useful hints for persons hoping to beat the lie test. Self-induced during the control questions, such reactions will lead most examiners astray.

4.   Letter to the Editor of *Student Lawyer*, October 1979, responding to an article critical of polygraphy, "Bloodless Executioners," by John Jenkins, in May 1979, issue of that journal.

5.   Reid, J. Simulated blood pressure responses in lie-detector tests and a method for their detection. *American Journal of Police Science*, 1945, *36*, 201–204, pp. 202–203. It should be admitted that the clinical lie test will be much harder to beat than the polygraphic lie test since examiners like Reid put greater weight on their clinical impressions, suspicions, and intuitions than on the polygraph records themselves.

DETECTING GUILTY KNOWLEDGE

And the whole secret, power, and knowledge
of their own discovery is locked within them
—they know it, feel it, have the whole thing in them.

—Thomas Wolfe
The Web and the Rock, 1939

The types of polygraphic interrogation we have been concerned with so far have all been designed for lie detection. We have seen that the validity of these various methods is generally unproven and that the limited evidence available indicates that this validity is only modest. I have explained why I believe that no amount of future research and development is likely to improve much on the present, rather bleak, situation. The prospects may be better for another and fundamentally different method of polygraphic interrogation that is intended to detect, not lying, but the presence of guilty knowledge. In Chapter 20, I describe my own initial experiences with the Guilty Knowledge Test and explain why this method seems to me to have promise as a tool of criminal investigation. Because this method is not well understood even by many polygraphers, I illustrate its application by means of a detective story in Chapter 21, a fictional account but written with methodological (if not literary) verisimilitude. Chapter 22 presents the theory of the Guilty Knowledge Test and the possibilities for its future development in a more sober expository format.

CHAPTER

20

Origins Of The Guilty Knowledge Test

The real use of [psychophysiological measurements] is therefore probably confined to those cases in which it is to be found out whether a suspected person knows anything about a certain place or man or thing.

—Hugo Munsterberg,
On the Witness Stand, 1908

In 1958 I agreed to supervise two freshman medical students who had been awarded summer fellowships. Bright and full of energy, they made short shrift of the project with which I had thought to keep them busy for three months. I needed a new experiment to last us through July and August. Intrigued by the polygraphic equipment in my laboratory, my two assistants had asked if I did any lie detector work and I had been forced to admit that I knew nothing about the subject. Equipped as we were with time, facilities, and ignorance, we resolved to do an experiment on lie detection.

The Experiment

Using student volunteers as our experimental subjects, we would have them enact mock crimes and then try to separate the "guilty" from the "innocent" by means of their physiological reactions during a standardized interrogation. For simplicity, we elected to use just one physiological measure, the electrodermal response (EDR), a wavelike change in the electrical resistance of the palms and soles, associated with imperceptible sweating in those regions. The EDR is an exceedingly sensitive indicator; almost any stimulus will elicit the response and, as a general rule, the stronger the stimulus—the greater its arousal value for the subject—the larger the resulting EDR will be.

We decided to use two mock crimes, a "theft" and a "murder." Our student subjects were assigned at random to one of four groups. A subject in the theft group, for example, was met at the lab by Assistant A and given the following instructions: He was to lurk outside a certain office in the building until the occupant departed. Then he would slip into the office and go through the drawers of the desk, seeking the object specified for him to steal. He would remove this prize and hide it in an empty locker in the corridor. A subject assigned to the murder group went to a different office where he played a hand of poker with the occupant, losing heavily. He then pretended to kill this opponent, using a weapon provided by Assistant A. After the victim had enacted his death throes, the student "murderer" was to hide the weapon in a predetermined place and then flee. A third group was assigned both of these crimes, hence these subjects were doubly guilty. Those in Group 4 were merely told to imagine that they had been picked up for questioning with regard to two matters that they knew nothing about. After completing this first phase with Assistant A, each subject was then taken to the polygraph room and handed over to Assistant B who, of course, was kept ignorant of the group to which the subject belonged. B's job was to conduct the interrogation and to determine from the EDR reactions whether the subject was guilty of theft or of murder, or guilty of both or of neither.

When it came to designing the actual interrogation, my then-ignorance of the lie detector field proved invaluable. I assumed then that "lie detector" was mere journalistic sensationalism. For the common-sense reasons discussed earlier in this book, I believed that actual lie detection was probably impossible. But we were interested (as are the police) in guilt rather than in lying; Assistant B's task was to distinguish the guilty from the innocent. And the important psychological difference between the guilty suspect and one who is innocent is that one was present at the scene of the crime; he knows what happened there; his mind contains images that are not available to an innocent person.

But how could we detect such guilty knowledge? Because of this knowledge, the guilty suspect will recognize people, objects, and events associated with the crime. There is no way to observe recognition directly, no distinctive "recognition response" just as there is no specific "lie response." But when we show a murderer a photograph of his victim, his recogniton will stimulate and arouse him in a way that a picture of stranger would not normally do. If we show him five pictures in sequence, including the one of his victim, then we might expect to see one large physiological reaction and four smaller ones. To the innocent suspect, all five persons pictured are equally strangers and he has no reason to react differently to the "correct" alternative than to any other.

Suppose you were a subject in Group 1 of our experiment, having enacted the mock theft. During the interrogation, Assistant B asks you the following:

The thief hid what he stole. Where did he hide it? Just sit quietly and repeat the names of these places as I say them. Where did the thief hide what he stole? Was it . . . In the bathroom? . . . On the coat rack? . . . In the locker? . . . On the window sill? . . . In the office?

You will probably show an electrodermal response to each of these five alternatives even though this is a make-believe situation and nothing important is at stake. But you know that the thief hid the stolen billfold in the locker, because you are he and you remember doing it. Therefore, your EDR to the alternative "In the locker?" will likely be larger than your responses to the other alternatives. If you were innocent of the theft, the five locations might seem equally plausible and only chance would determine whether your EDR to "locker?" would turn out to be the largest or smallest or somewhere in between.

In our experiment there were six multiple-choice questions for each of the two crimes. Some questions related directly to the criminal act while others referred to incidental matters. For example:

If you are the murderer, you will know that there was an unusual object present in the office where the murder took place. Just repeat the name of the object. Was it . . . A phonograph record? . . . An artist's easel? . . . A candy box? . . . A chess set? . . . A baseball glove?

For half of the questions, Assistant B did not know himself which alternative was correct until after he had finished the test; sometimes there was an easel in the murder room, sometimes a candy box or a baseball glove. We scored the tests by awarding two points if the EDR produced by the correct alternative was the largest, one point if it was the second-largest of the five associated with each question. Thus, with a six-item test, the guiltiest score would be 12 and the most innocent-appearing score would be zero.

The Results

The experiment was a great success. We had decided to classify as Innocent anyone scoring 6 or less; 48 innocent suspects were tested and all of them scored in this range. Of the 50 guilty suspects tested, 44 received scores of 7 or higher and were correctly classified as Guilty. One of our volunteers had been a resistance courier during the 1956 rebellion in Hungary, twice caught and intensively interrogated by the MKVD. On both occasions he had successfully maintained his cover and had been released. This man happened to be assigned to our Group 3, guilty of both crimes, and he was correctly classified by Assistant B without any need for beatings or electrical stimulation of his soft tissues. He concluded that he had defected to a technologically superior society. Using our objective scoring system and only the briefest of interrogations, we correctly identified who was guilty (or innocent) of which crime with 94% accuracy. Not one innocent subject was misclassified.[1]

I began reading the polygraphy literature at this point in preparation for writing up this experiment for publication. It turned out that our basic idea had been familiar to polygraphers since the early days, embodied in a method known as the Peak of Tension Test, which is rather like a single item of a Guilty Knowledge Test. Reid and Inbau describe a number of instances in which this method was used to encourage a confession. One striking example concerns a presser who had stolen a substantial sum of cash found in the pockets of a customer's trousers. As the polygrapher named various sums, this subject showed a peak of tension at "$765?" He was so impressed by the examiner's ability to pin-point the exact amount that he confessed and made restitution.

On the other hand, a one-item multiple-choice test is not very useful when the respondent fails to confess. My reading revealed that polygraphic interrogation in practice consisted almost exclusively of attempts at actual lie detection of the sort already described. I was persuaded that the Guilty Knowledge procedure rested on sounder psychological principles (even if my claim to its invention was arguable) and that the GKT should be considerably more dependable than any method of lie detection—especially for the exoneration of the innocent.

We quickly set up a second experiment. In this one, 20 sophisticated subjects—psychology graduate students, psychiatrists—were offered a money prize if they could "beat" the test, either by inhibiting their responses to the correct alternatives (which is difficult) or by producing artificial responses through self-stimulation (which is easier). These subjects were attached to the EDR apparatus and given time before the test to practice whatever technique they had decided to use, watching the pen trace out their EDRs as they experimented. Since the prizes were to be paid out of my own pocket, I used 20 items on this test instead of only 6, and I also used a more elaborate scoring system. All twenty subjects were correctly classified by this improved version of the GKT.[2]

In spite of these promising indications, professional polygraphers still have not taken up the Guilty Knowledge Test for use in criminal investigation. The reason given for this neglect is that the examiner seldom has available to him the necessary "keys," the items of information that only a guilty suspect would recognize and that could be turned into GKT items. The lie test, in contrast, is easy to set up. All the examiner needs to know to prepare the usual lie-test question list he can learn in a few minutes' conversation with the investigator, nor does it matter if the suspect has already been extensively interrogated. And there are crimes that simply do not lend themselves to the GKT approach at all. A recent news item refers to a former Green Beret officer, for example, accused of killing his wife and children. He claims that his family was attacked by a gang of "long-haired hippies" and that he somehow escaped. Since—guilty or innocent—he was present at the crime scene and is familiar with all its gruesome details, it seems unlikely that a Guilty Knowledge Test could have been constructed for use with this suspect. The Peter Reilly case would not have been suitable for the GKT, either, and for similar reasons.

But many crimes that are the subject of well-publicized trials could have been illuminated through the use of a Guilty Knowledge Test, provided that the person responsible for constructing the test items was able to participate in the investigation from the outset. The real reason why this method is not used, I believe, is that police polygraphers are not investigators and the detectives who actually conduct the investigations do not know much about polygraphic interrogation. If the potential of the GKT is to be realized, the test constructor must be early at the crime scene, camera and notebook in hand, looking as with the eyes of the perpetrator for those keys from which good test items could be contrived. The most efficient arrangement would be for the person responsible for the test to be the same person who is responsible for the investigation itself. This combining of responsibilities should ensure that the identification of keys will get appropriate priority and also that these keys will not be vitiated later by careless questioning of suspects. This does not mean that all detectives would have to learn how to run a polygraph or read charts; the actual test administration would be done as it is now by a specialist. The detectives would learn only the psychological principles of the GKT and how to construct good items.

The best way to illustrate the Guilty Knowledge Test in action would be to describe an actual case in which the method was competently used. For reasons already given, however, no such real case is available to me. Not being in the detecting business myself, therefore, I have had to resort to fiction. While I was working on this manuscript, there occurred in Minnesota two notorious crimes. Both of these incidents led to protracted investigations culminating in lengthy and expensive trials. It seemed apparent from the news reports that the GKT could have been used in both cases and that its use would have contributed to the efficiency of the investigations and to the certainty of just results. One of these crimes involved the kidnapping of a locally prominent citizen; any kidnapping should provide abundant keys for good guilty knowledge items. In the other case, an elderly invalid and her nurse were found murdered in a great house on Duluth's London Road. The wealthy victim had two adopted daughters, one of whom, together with her husband, was eventually prosecuted. The husband was found guilty of the murder, but his wife was exonerated. I know nothing more about the facts, real or alleged, of the actual case; all other details in the following account are of my own invention. All other details are imaginary save one—in that big house on the London Road there was found one morning a body, on the stairs.

Notes

1. Lykken, D. The GSR in the detection of guilt. *Journal of Applied Psychology*, 1959, *43*, 385–388.
2. Lykken, D. The validity of the guilty knowledge technique: The effects of faking. *Journal of Applied Psychology*, 1960, *44*, 258–262.

CHAPTER 21

The Body On The Stairs: A Pedagogical Detective Story

It will be clearer when you have heard the story.

—Hercule Poirot

The tale must be about dead bodies or very wicked people, preferably both, before the tired Business Man can feel really happy.

—Dorothy Sayers

Perched on its bluffs looking down on Lake Superior, Duluth might have been a handsome city, but its pioneers had more mundane ideas. The money was in shipping, steamers carrying iron ore and grain to the East and returning with coal and heavy machinery. The city is separated from the cold, blue water by a maze of docks and railroad yards, warehouses and smoky factories. The magnates and the managers built east of the city a row of mansions fronting on the (then) unpolluted lake. The most imposing of these great houses are almost invisible from London Road, a broad, shaded avenue that, further east, becomes the North Shore Highway, houses separated from its hurly-burly by great wrought-iron gates and impenetrable plantings of exotic evergreens.

Marion Rorcheck's salt-corroded Vega looked a bit incongruous as it turned, blinking, out of the early Monday traffic and pulled up before the finest pair of gates of all. Mrs. Rorcheck, wearing a heavy cardigan against the spring breeze that struck chill off the lake, stepped out long enough to insert a key in the switchbox on the left gatepost. The heavy gates swung open. After stopping once more on the other side to close the gates, Mrs. Rorcheck followed the curving drive some 200 feet to the side of the house. Another modest vehicle was already parked there, a middle-aged Ford, its windshield opaque with dew. Sarah Hanson, the night nurse, hadn't left yet, of course; Mrs. Rorcheck always made a point of being a few minutes early so that Sarah could get away by 7:00 sharp. The big Cadillac, lying in state behind the 30-foot doors of the garage, had not been used for months. Old Mrs. Haverstock, querulous and bedridden, wasn't going anywhere.

At the side entrance, Mrs. Rorcheck was a little surprised not to find Sarah with the door open, happy to greet her replacement once again and to share a quick cup of coffee before returning to her small house on the west side of town where, more than likely, she would have plans for a morning in the garden. The clean dirt, the vigorous young plants, the rich harvest to look forward to, all had become increasingly important to Mrs. Hanson since her husband died two years before and she had begun her nightly vigils with the old woman. Mrs. Haverstock seemed never to really sleep at all. She would doze for a while, sometimes as much as an hour, but then she would wake with a start, often appearing not to know where she was or who Sarah was, and would need to be soothed and coddled. And there were several trips to the bathroom, leaning heavily on the nurse's arm, and at least one change of bedding. Mrs. Haverstock was ready for bed—often already dozing—when Mrs. Hanson came on duty at eleven, and since she had no meals to prepare, errands to run, or house cleaning to supervise, the women on the other shifts had rather envied her at first. But now, after nearly two years, there had been enough trading off on shifts for them all to know that Mrs. Hanson earned her salary through the long nights, and a prompt relief in the morning.

Marion Rorcheck opened the door with her own key and went in. Except for the hum of the big refrigerator in the kitchen to her right, the house was silent. The entrance she had used opened into an octagonal breakfast room on the east side of the house, a pleasant airy room in the morning because four of its walls looked east and south through many windows mullioned in light oak. The wall opposite the patio entrance was all built-in china cabinet full of colorful pieces set off by beveled glass in doors hung on brass fittings. Centered in the angled wall on the left was a carved oak door that opened into the main dining room. The table in the center of the room had six, instead of eight, sides and this conflict of angles, along with the bright print upholstery of the six chairs, softened the elegance and made the room inviting. Mrs. Rorcheck took her lunch at that table almost every day. She had expected to see three grass mats on this table with a coffee pot and a plate of hot rolls on the mat in the center, cups and small clean plates at two place settings facing the windows. But the table was bare. Circling to the right, Mrs. Rorcheck pushed through the papered swinging door into the kitchen to see what was keeping Sarah.

The kitchen was empty and now even the refrigerator fell silent. There was no welcome aroma of brewing coffee; the coffeemaker top full of the cold grounds from the night before lay in the sink. The bottom or coffeepot section was missing, probably upstairs where Mrs. Hanson used it to sustain herself through the small hours. Unbuttoning her sweater, Mrs. Rorcheck started up the kitchen stairway. Mrs. Haverstock must be having problems—or making them, more likely, since if she had taken a serious turn, Mrs. Rorcheck would have expected to see the doctor's Buick, or even an ambulance, in the drive. Of course, they might be on their way right now. She hurried up the steep steps and opened the door to the landing where the kitchen staircase unobtrusively connected with the main stairway, the sweeping lower part of which curved grandly down and out of sight to the main hall below.

The landing was nearly 10 feet square and almost in its center, upside down and surrounded by an ugly brown stain, nearly dry, in the deep blue of the carpet, was the coffee pot. Its stainless steel and plastic presence in that outlandish circumstance riveted Mrs. Rorcheck and, at the back of her neck, she felt a faint movement as the muscles of a hundred hair follicles contracted. Still staring at the pot, in an oddly hushed voice, she called, "Sarah?" Raising her eyes to the right, she surveyed the empty lower stairway. Then, as with a deliberate act of will she turned both head and body to the left, she saw Sarah looking at her. Lying there, looking at her. At least the one eye that was partly open seemed to be looking her way, over her shoulder. The other eye, the left one, was obscured by the blood, blood that had stained the blue carpet to a kind of purple-brown, on the step where Sarah's head lay and on the step below that. Mrs. Rorcheck moved slowly backwards until her shoulders felt the intersection of the walls at the corner of the landing; then she whispered, "Help!" People do not often scream when they're alone. Screams are for times when someone might hear you and come, when a friend might hear and come to help. When one is alone, the throat constricts and cuts off screaming, screaming that would echo through the empty place and summon only panic, if nothing worse. And Mrs. Rorcheck, staring at the dead slit of Sarah Hanson's eye, knew that she was alone—hoped she was alone—in that big house that Monday morning.

Slowly, at first she sidled sideways, then, turning her head to watch where she was going, she almost ran down the main stairs, clutching the banister, did run then across the hall into the dining room, into the breakfast room where she had entered, opened the door to the patio—then stopped. All her muscles tight, Mrs. Rorcheck breathed deep of the cold air, turned back again, walked quickly back to close the door to the dining room, then dashed to the little writing desk under the window and picked up the phone. She stared dumbly at the rows of buttons for a moment, looking for a dial, then pressed 0 and waited anxiously, twisting about so she could keep her eyes on the two closed doors inside.

"Operator?"

"Operator, get me the police. Emergency!"

Squad 17 had passed 2040 London Road only moments before the dispatcher's call came on the radio and they nosed up to the Haverstock gates, red lights flashing, within two or three minutes. Her joints unlocked by the relief of seeing them, Mrs. Rorcheck sprang to the gate switch by the door, then hurried outside to the drive to await the policemen. In good control now, she gave her name and briefly explained the situation.

"Can you show us, Ma'am?"

Marion Rorcheck re-entered the house with the two tall patrolmen, through the dining room, up the stairway. Sarah Hanson's body looked quite different now, pathetic, a reason to feel sadness rather than the cold horror that had possessed Mrs. Rorcheck just a few minutes earlier. Patrolman Edstrom reached down and lifted Sarah's right hand gently from where it lay sprawled behind her hip. It was cold and beginning to stiffen. Her cheek, too, where he lay the backs of his fingers, felt cold, dead. Edstrom straightened up.

"Where did you say the old lady is, Ma'am?"

"Her room's up there, to the right."

"Okay, we'll have a look. Try not to touch the banister or anything."

It was a wide staircase and even the awkward sprawl of Sarah's body left a full two feet of unstained carpet on the right side. The three of them filed up to the large master bedroom, 24 feet square, its south and east walls mostly windows bright behind the lowered shades. Mrs. Haverstock's bed was centered on the west wall and, on either side of the wide headboard there were doors to the two master bathrooms. The one on the far side had been her husband's and had not been used perhaps for years. In the near bathroom the lights were on, revealing a number of coin-sized spots—they were bloodstains—on the tiled floor. One of the spots had been smeared, as if by a shoe. But the three people just inside the doorway were staring at the bed. The foot that projected from the bedclothes, a right foot, was bare; it was thin and white, old-looking. The toenails, neatly trimmed, appeared yellow against the pallid flesh. A hand was also visible, cuffed in white lace, a rather puffy old hand, palm up, with bands of rings on the third and fourth fingers. They were platinum bands and the stones, presently obscured by the supine position of the hand, were an old-fashioned diamond cluster and, on the middle finger, a fine large ruby surrounded by small diamonds. There was a pillow over the face.

Officer Edstrom stepped up beside the bed, grasped a fold of the pillow slip between his right thumb and forefinger and lifted the pillow gingerly aside. The startling thing about the face was the mouth, until one realized that she had been wearing her dentures and the upper plate had slipped and was protruding slightly. The left eye was open wide and surveyed the ceiling; the right lid drooped, half closed. After touching the cold cheek, Edstrom set the pillow back again where he had found it.

"You'd better call in, Marv. Use the phone this lady used. Tell them we've got what looks like a double homicide. And they can cancel that ambulance."

But as Mrs. Rorcheck and Patrolman Marvin Swaline descended the long staircase, the siren of the ambulance marked its arrival in the long drive. Swaline stepped outside to greet the driver and his paramedic colleague.

"We won't be needing you guys after all, Eddie. We've got two dead ones in there, looks like homicide. The old lady and her night nurse."

"Want us to take a look, Marv?"

"Better not. They're dead all right, already getting stiff. And the lieutenant has this thing about a crime scene—no unnecessary witnesses. I've got to call in now; see you guys later."

After making his call, Officer Swaline made a cursory, and gingerly, tour of the first floor, followed by Mrs. Rorcheck. They were careful where they stepped and Swaline opened doorknobs with his handkerchief. The only thing they noticed that was out of the ordinary was the walnut desk in the library. Three of its drawers stood open and several papers that looked like bills, normally kept in a leather folder on the desk, were scattered about on the floor. Officer Edstrom was making a similar tour of the second floor. With no one to watch him, he had his service revolver in his hand. In his five years on the DPD, Willard Edstrom hadn't seen that many murder victims and he was more rattled than he cared to admit.

Another siren announced the arrival of Detective Lieutenant George Catlin. The dispatcher had found him at home having breakfast and had been told to call Detective Sergeant Poehls at his home and to tell him to stand by. Catlin looked like everyone's stereotype of an FBI agent, trim, dark-haired, wearing a neat navy-blue blazer, a blue-checked shirt, and a dark tie. He was about 30. Catlin had attended the University of Minnesota, the main campus in Minneapolis, not the Duluth Branch, and had majored in Criminal Justice. During his last two years, he had worked on the University's police force, of a size appropriate to the community of more than 60,000 people within its jurisdiction, which was regarded as sort of an elite corps by most police officials in the state, although some of the roughneck element of the St. Paul and Minneapolis PD's thought they were a bunch of overeducated sissies. Catlin stayed on with the UPD for four years after he graduated, taking several FBI courses and spending as much time as he could in the department's well-equipped polygraphic interrogation laboratory, the best-run unit of its kind in the five-state area. When Duluth's mayor decided to upgrade the professional level of his police department, Catlin, a hometown boy, came on board as detective sergeant and now, five years later, was head of the Detective Division. Sergeant Poehls, taller, heavier, and rapidly balding, looked older than Catlin, although he was only 27. Arny Poehls was a graduate of the University's Duluth

Branch, a friendly, talkative bear of a man, smarter than he looked, a kind of protege of Catlin's.

The two detectives got out of Catlin's car and conferred with Officer Swaline on the patio where they were shortly joined by Officer Edstrom. Mrs. Rorchek, suffering a bit of aftershock from the previous half-hour, slumped down on a redwood bench at one end of the patio where she could feel the sun. Catlin went over and introduced himself and his partner and asked Mrs. Rorchek to wait there with Officer Swaline while he looked around inside. Then Catlin and Poehls followed Edstrom into the house. They looked at the two dead women, noticed a jewel box on its side and empty on Mrs. Haverstock's dresser (Edstrom had missed that but saw no need to call attention to the fact), and retraced Edstrom's fruitless search of the second floor. They started up to the third floor but, near the top of the stairs, Catlin stopped and put out an arm. The wood floor in front of them showed a layer of dust in the slanting morning sunlight and the dust was undisturbed. On the first floor they rediscovered the spilled papers in the library, the coffee grounds in the kitchen sink, and a broken latch on the French doors of the sunroom on the west side of the house. Brass sliding bolts were fitted top and bottom on both doors but none had been locked in place. The doors had apparently been kicked open from the outside—mudstains on the white paint suggested the sole of a shoe—and the simple central latch had given way easily with just a slight splintering of wood. The doors had apparently been closed again from the inside after the intruder entered.

Search of the large basement, the L-shaped game room with bar and billiard table, the laundry, and the big furnace room—Catlin remembered from sixth grade watching the school janitor tending a furnace just about that size—the many storerooms, the garage, all were unrevealing. Poehls spotted the switch that caused the big garage door to roll up with a solid rumble and they rejoined Mrs. Rorcheck on the patio. She had recovered her composure fully in the interim and was able to give Catlin a concise and complete account of her experiences that morning. She also provided some background on Mrs. Haverstock.

As the bride of a middle-aged mining executive 50 years earlier, it had been hoped that she would provide him the heirs that his deceased first wife had not. But this second marriage, too, was barren and, after 10 years, Haverstock died. His widow, in her late thirties, also wanted a child and, unlike her dead husband, she was not insist-ent that the child should be either male or biologically her own. So Victoria Haverstock adopted a female infant, a flesh-and-blood doll to whom she gave the doll-like name of Merry Bell, and proceeded to provide her new toy with every indulgence the Haverstock fortune could buy. Merry Bell Haverstock Garnett Michaelson Plunkett now, at 43, was on her third husband and, with the help of Numbers 1 and 2, had produced four grandchildren at a cost to Victoria, prorated over 24 years, of nearly half a million dollars each. Henry and Patricia Garnett, aged 24 and 22, were good-looking like their daddy and as self-centered and willful as their mother.

Erik and Hans Michaelson were the legacy of her second union. Erik, now 19, was a schemer like his father but lacked his charm; Hans, 17, kept his own counsel and no one yet seemed to have figured him out.

John Martin Plunkett, Victoria's third and present son-in-law, was neither aristocratically handsome, like Garnett, nor dynamic and cosmopolitan, like Michaelson. In spite of their failings, one might reasonably say of her two previous husbands, that Merry Bell had married rather above herself. Plunkett was quite an ordinary fellow, happy-go-lucky, enjoyed a good time, had no deep interests or high principles. Merry Bell seemed comfortable with Plunkett, not really satisfied, but then Merry Bell had never been really satisfied. She knew that she deserved something special in life, for Victoria had raised her to think, vaguely, that *she* was something special, but that special something always had eluded her. Plunkett wasn't the answer, but then perhaps a man wasn't the solution to her particular riddle in any case.

Not that Lieutenant Catlin got all this history from Mrs. Rorchek in their conversation on the bench that Monday morning. He got names and ages and, with the aid of an address book in the library, addresses and phone numbers. The younger Michaelson boy, Hans, attended a prep school in Minneapolis. Erik was at the University, living with much indignation in a freshman dormitory, but insisting on his own apartment next year. Pat Garnett lived in New York City "studying art." Henry Garnett had a swinging singles pad in Minneapolis. His mother and John Plunkett had a townhouse in Minneapolis, a posh summer home on the North Shore, 20 miles up the lake from the Haverstock place, and a sporty casa in Puerto Peñasca, on the Sea of Cortez. They were in Minneapolis the last Mrs. Rorchek knew. Catlin telephoned downtown for the "scientists": the medical examiner, the police photographer, and two fingerprint men. He also got Edstrom and Swaline relieved of their regular patrol duties for the rest of the morning so they could stay and help. He stationed Edstrom at the entrance gate and Officer Swaline at the opposite corner of the house by the sunroom, so that the two men, between them, could survey all sides of the property. Then Catlin called Mr. Rorchek, who was employed at a local lumber yard and, after appropriate reassurances, asked him to get off work long enough to come pick up his wife and take her home. When Rorcheck arrived, looking worried, Catlin held a formal meeting in the breakfast room.

"Folks, this is a serious matter, as you know, and I want to impose an unusual kind of security here until we get this case solved. Mrs. Rorchek, I couldn't expect you not to tell your husband about an upsetting experience like you had this morning, but I'm going to ask both of you to give me your solemn word of honor not to talk to anybody else about it, not to reporters, not to your other relatives, not to your best friends. You came here for work as usual, you found the two women shot to death and you called the police. You can't say anything more than that until the case goes to trial. Agreed?"

"Were they both shot, Lieutenant?" asked Mrs. Rorchek. "Is that what happened?"

"That's the way it looks to us, but we'll know for sure when the Medical Examiner gets here."

"Why all the secrecy, Lieutenant?" asked Mr. Rorchek. "What's going on?"

"Let me explain that to you, Mr. Rorchek, because I want to be sure you understand the reasons for it and won't think I'm just trying to throw my weight around. Whoever killed those two women knows what happened here last night. He knows what he did in this house, where he left the bodies, how they looked when he left them there. If he walked into the house right now, he wouldn't see anything that would surprise him—everything would fit with the pictures in his mind that he went away with last night, and they should be pretty vivid pictures. Now we have methods, sort of like lie detector tests, for finding out what pictures a person has in his mind. That is, when we get a suspect in this case, we'll be able to find out if he knows what happened in this house, whether he recognizes the way things look in there right now, whether he can tell the difference between the true story and some made-up stories that we'll try out on him. If he can't tell the difference, our polygraph machine will show that and then we'll know he's innocent. If he does recognize the true story, then the machine will tell us that and we'll know we have our man.

But this will only work if we can be sure that the police working on the case and you two folks—and the murderer—are the only ones who know what happened here. So that's the reason for asking you not to talk about this. I know it's hard, I know this may be the most frightening experience you've ever gone through, Mrs. Rorchek, and it's very difficult not to discuss something like that with the people you're close to or with people who press you with questions. But I also know that one little slip, telling just one friend next door or at work, can be the leak that breaks the dike. So will you do it?"

The Rorcheks, suitably impressed by this explanation, promised to maintain security and took their leave. Collecting Edstrom at the gate, Catlin walked with him around to Swaline's post and gave the two patrolmen a supplementary cautioning.

"Now you men know that neither of these bodies look like gunshot wounds; I'm not certain yet about the nurse. But, in any case, the public information from now on is that they were both shot. We're going to set up a Guilty Knowledge Test on this case and I will have the hide *and* the badge of any officer who talks to his wife or his mother or his buddies about anything at all he saw in that house. If there's an item in the paper about 'Nurse found on stairs' or 'Heiress murdered in her bed', then I'm going to stop investigating this case until I've found the blabbermouth and have him up by his thumbs. Okay, I want you men to stay in position until the print men are finished and then we'll give this house a proper going over."

Catlin then huddled with Sergeant Poehls.

"This looks like a good case for a GKT, Arny. We'll let it out that the women were both shot and, if that holds up, we'll be able to use manner of death as two keys. Then, we can use where each body was found, what they were wearing, and we ought to be able to get a couple of keys out of that coffee pot. And, listen, Arny, let's photograph those bodies in different positions. There's Billy Wister coming in now; have him get some pictures before the M.E. moves them and then we'll pose both bodies in four or five different ways and get some more pictures."

"Okay, George. What about talking to the neighbors?—and that nurse's family? And shouldn't we really look the house over? That bastard might still be hiding under a bed somewhere."

Catlin grinned a little sheepishly. "Are you suggesting, Arny, that I won't be able to use my GKT if we don't catch us a suspect first? Okay, Sarge, you're right. You organize the detecting and I'll organize Billy."

Billy Wister, the police photographer, and the two fingerprint technicians followed Lieutenant Catlin into the house. After setting the print men to work on the first floor, Catlin helped Wister carry his equipment to the stairway. The inverted coffee pot on the landing was photographed from above as someone standing by Nurse Hanson's body might have seen it, and also from the head of the staircase. Mrs. Hanson's body was photographed both from the head of the stairs and from the landing. In the master bedroom, pictures were taken of the bed as it appeared from the doorway, pillow still in place over the old woman's face, and of that dead face from the vantage point of someone standing over the body, and of the bloodstains on the bathroom floor. The dressing table with the emptied jewel box was photographed, as was the study with the apparently rifled desk and papers scattered about. The French doors in the sunroom were pictured from the outside, closed and open, and from the inside.

When the medical examiner had come and gone, Catlin had in hand these facts and speculations: Both women probably died between midnight and 2 A.M. Sarah Hanson received a heavy blow, most likely from behind, from a penetrating instrument which had fractured her skull in the left occipital-parietal region. She had been struck also on the left shoulder, probably preceding the fatal head wound. This, too, was a heavy blow, breaking the clavicle, and the appearance of the injury suggested a narrow pipe or bar, either a different weapon than that which caused the skull wound, or else the straight shaft of the same instrument. The scientists were already studying the wrought iron tools found neatly in place beside the bedroom fireplace. Victoria Haverstock had probably been smothered with the pillow, although cardiac arrest or a cerebrovascular accident, brought on by fear and stress, would have to be ruled out at autopsy. With some reluctance, the M.E. had agreed to sustain Catlin's public fiction that the "preliminary indications are that both victims died of gunshot wounds." But he insisted that, after his autopsy, he could no longer be a party to a deliberately false report and that the furthest he would go at that stage would be to withhold his findings "at the request of the police."

The fingerprint men finished their sweep with a rather pessimistic prognosis. They had a small collection of prints, but there was a lot of smearing on the desk, on the bannister, on the handle of the poker, that suggested gloved hands. With some show of disgust, the two technicians were drafted next to help in posing the bodies for more photographs. Mrs. Hanson was rotated where she lay so that her head pointed downstairs and then photographed from both above and below. The coffee pot was removed from its position in the center of the landing and the nurse's body posed as though she had been struck while on the last step above the landing and then fallen forward. A fourth pose made it appear that she had been struck just as she began to descend the lower flight of stairs and had fallen backwards onto the landing. Two more poses located the body on the lower, curving portion of the staircase, one with her head pointing upwards and the other down. This macabre activity then moved to the bedroom. The old woman's body was gently accommodated to two different but plausible positions on the bed and three positions on the floor and photographed in each position. The aim of all this was to provide six photographs of each body, with one of each six corresponding to the picture that must almost certainly be vividly imprinted in the mind of the murderer. But, to an innocent suspect with no such recollections of the actual scene, the other five positions of each corpse would appear equally plausible, equally horrifying.

Finally, this penultimate indignity completed, the mortal remains of Victoria Haverstock and Sarah Hanson were dispatched to the morgue. Sergeant Poehls, who had returned from an unrevealing round of visits with the neighbors, had never been inside a mansion the size of the Haverstock place before. He continued to feel a nagging concern that last night's intruder might still be hiding on the premises; unlikely certainly, but intolerably embarrassing if it were true and they hadn't looked to find him. So Poehls and the two print men worked their way methodically from basement to third floor. As in so many aspects of policework, the yield was nothing more than another base touched, one possibility ruled out.

Catlin and his photographer were contemplating the coffeepot.

"He must have noticed what the nurse was carrying when he clubbed her. Or else he must have seen that pot on the landing when he went down the stairs."

"How do you know she was carrying it, Lieutenant? Maybe she threw the thing at the guy when she heard him coming up the stairs."

"Nope, the M.E. says he got her from behind, probably from the head of the stairs while she was walking down, maybe six or seven steps down. I think he used that poker with the point on the side and then washed the blood off later in the bathroom. He broke her left shoulder first, the pot flew forward, she was sort of swung around to the left like this, then he got her in the head. She fell backwards. I wonder if he was left-handed? The M.E. can maybe tell from the wounds if he was swinging left to right. I'll tell you, Billy, this guy has to be someone they knew. Nurse lets him in, he goes up to talk to the old lady, nurse takes the coffee pot down to the kitchen, maybe he's poking the fire when she leaves the room and he just steps out the door and brains her. If he'd broken in and slipped upstairs, waited for the nurse to leave the bedroom, he'd have had to dart in the room and grab the poker and dart out again before she got away. How would he know there was a poker there? And the old lady would have yelled when she saw him; how would he get the nurse from behind? I think this one's friends or family, Billy."

It did seem very certain that Mrs. Hanson had indeed been carrying the coffee pot when struck from behind; the cup or two of liquid left in the pot would have splattered more widely if the pot had been thrown with any force. What else might a night nurse be carrying from a sickroom? What other fallen object would seem at least as plausible to an innocent suspect, to someone whose mind bore no image of that stainless steel pot on the landing? Catlin and Billy Wister found the evening paper folded neatly on a kitchen table. Catlin, standing half way up from the landing, tossed the paper forward several times until it landed, rumpled and partly open, in what seemed to be a suitable position in the middle of the landing, covering the coffee stain. Billy photographed it then, from the same angles he had used for the coffee pot. In the bathroom, they found a bottle of mineral oil, nearly empty. Dumping the residue in the toilet, the bottle was put in place of the paper and photographed; the nurse might have been carrying a medicine bottle. A couple of magazines, from the bedroom, were next. Then, waxing more inventive, a tray with a plate and cup and saucer were tumbled on the Landing. Finally, a vase from the kitchen with some flowers, found in the breakfast room, were strewn there to have their picture taken.

Wister then proceeded to photograph the house's interiors more generally, views that an intruder coming in through the sunroom would have seen on his way upstairs. If Catlin's conjecture was correct and the murderer was a previous visitor to the house, then these pictures might not be used. But should they ever have a suspect who claimed not to have seen the house or been inside, then they could use these shots to test him. They would get some interiors from other big Duluth houses and see whether their suspect reacted selectively to those from the Haverstock house. In the library, Poehls picked up the scattered papers.

"Billy, we'll base an item on the appearance of this room. Something like, 'How did the library look when the murderer was through with it?' Let's get a shot from the door with the room looking neat first. Then we'll get one with that chair tipped over, another with the rug rolled back and, let's see, what else?"

"How about stacks of books on the floor, like he was looking for something in a book or behind the books?"

"Okay," said Poehls. "And look here, Billy my boy, here's an honest-to-God wall safe behind the picture. I've never seen one before. We'll get the boys to dust it for prints and then we'll get a shot with the safe open. Somebody must know the combination."

Catlin, meanwhile, was looking through Mrs. Haverstock's bureau drawers. She had been wearing a distinctive long-sleeved nightgown with lacy cuffs and a blue ribbon at the neck. As Catlin had expected, the wealthy invalid had quite an assortment of distinctive nightgowns and from these he selected five, as different from each other as they were from the one found on the body. The murderer's palms should sweat when he sees that blue ribbon and the lace cuffs again, revealing that he recognizes that one of the six gowns.

When Poehls and his helpers completed their search of the house, Catlin made his security speech to Wister and the two print men and sent them back to their respective labs. It was high time to start contacting next of kin. This part was never easy, but Sarah Hanson was simplest to start with. According to Mrs. Rorchek, Sarah had been a widow and now lived with her brother, a one-time Great Lakes seaman who, Mrs. Rorchek thought, had lately gone to seed, maybe a drinker. Leaving the two uniformed officers on guard, Catlin and Poehls headed for the Hanson house on the west side. There was no answer when they rang the bell so they made use also of the brass knocker. Finally, through an open window above them, a thick, drunken voice demanded, "What s' want?" William Foster, Sarah's 57-year-old brother, was very drunk indeed. He had been sick on the floor of his bedroom and the rich stink of the upstairs hall contained a definite trace of juniper and gin. Foster didn't know where he'd been the night before, couldn't seem to register what they had to tell him about his sister, and was alternately belligerent and comatose. Catlin decided to take him in on suspicion. He had an idea of questioning Foster closely while his wits were still addled by alcohol but, at the jail, it was obvious that there would be no legal way of questioning Foster at all for hours.

Using separate phones, Catlin and Poehls began tracking down the Haverstock relatives, the Plunketts and Michaelsons and Garnetts. A maid at the Plunketts' Minneapolis house said that Merry Bell and John had left the day before (Sunday) to drive to Mexico. Both Erik and Hans were eventually located at their respective schools, both seemed rather stimulated to hear about the excitement in Duluth, and neither had known of their mother's plans to head for Mexico. But neither boy seemed surprised at the sudden departure. There was no answer at Henry Garnett's Minneapolis apartment but, when Poehls called the North Shore beachhouse, there was an unexpected answer after the fifth ring. It was Garnett. He'd been there with a couple of friends—three, in fact, one male—since Friday. There was a very long silence after Poehls told him the news about his grandmother.

"Well, I'm sorry to hear that, Inspector." ("Inspector!" thought Poehls. "Is he trying to be smart or does he read English detective stories?")

"Be sure and let me know if there's anything I can do," Garnett continued.

"We'd like to talk to you this afternoon, Mr. Garnett. The lieutenant and I could be out at your place in about half an hour. Would that be all right?"

There was another lengthy silence. Then, "Yes, I guess that's all right, half an hour. I'll be looking for you." Garnett hung up.

"I thought you'd want to run out and see this one, Lieutenant," explained Poehls. "He called me, 'Inspector,' on the phone. Maybe he'll call you, 'Chief Superintendent.'"

Mrs. Haverstock gave her adopted daughter the Beach House at the time of Merry Bell's first marriage. It was one of the few places along the North Shore with natural protection for a small boat landing, a rocky promentory shielding the entrance to a small, sandy cove. The house itself was built of Norway pine logs, each log hand fitted to the one beneath. There was a vast fireplace at one end of the two-story, vaulted main room, thousands of dollars worth of double-glazed windows looking out over the lake. In the cove bobbed a trim sloop, able to sleep four, and a cruiser with a flying bridge was tied at the dock. Lake Superior is too cold for swimming; one needs beach toys to keep amused. Catlin perceived that he might have difficulty liking anyone who lived in such a place, a place that he would give his soul—well, Arny's soul—to own himself. But as it turned out, he could have disliked Henry Garnett for himself alone. The 24-year-old was handsome, smooth, self-assured. He wore a terry-cloth jacket with his bathing trunks and had too good a tan for so early in the spring. He got the titles right, after Catlin had introduced himself and his partner—"Lieutenant, Sergeant"—and thereafter addressed himself exclusively to Catlin. While those two talked, Poehls slipped out to the cantilevered deck where Garnett's three friends, also in beach attire, watched him approach with lively interest.

"We had dinner here last night, Lieutenant," Garnett was saying. "Then we played backgammon for a while, listened to some music, went to bed early. I'd guess we were all in bed before midnight."

Poehls learned that the man and one of the two girls had visited the beach house with Garnett previously. "Henry often bops into town to play with his Duluth buddies when he's here, Sergeant," said the self-possessed little blonde. "He was out for a while last weekend on his own. But not last night. We'd been on the lake all day and were pooped. I think Harry went beddy-bye about eleven."

It wasn't until Tuesday that Catlin located and interviewed Marion Rorchek's weekend replacement, a semiretired R.N. named Edith Garmoly. From Mrs. Garmoly he learned that Henry Garnett had visited his invalid grandmother late Saturday night, a week earlier, just dropped in about 11:30 for a chat with the old woman. Since he had never paid a call on his grandmother that way on his own initiative before, certainly never in the middle of the night, both Sarah Hanson and old Mrs. Haverstock had been sufficiently impressed by his visit to mention it to Mrs. Garmoly the next morning. And Henry Garnett was left-handed; Catlin had had him write out his Minneapolis address and phone number in Catlin's notebook. The M.E. couldn't be sure that Nurse Hanson had been killed by a left-handed blow, but it seemed plausible. Garnett's friends couldn't have known if he had slipped out again late Sunday night; they were asleep. Like his sister, Pat, Garnett stood to inherit a million dollars when Victoria Haverstock died. A similar sum would be held in trust for his two younger half-brothers until they came of age. Catlin and Poehls had their second suspect.

Sarah Hanson's brother, their first suspect, was considerably subdued when he finally woke up in his jail cell. William Foster said he'd "had a few drinks" the night before and then gone home to bed before midnight. Acquaintances in three of his usual sleazy haunts remembered seeing him during the evening, drinking alone, less talkative than usual although he was known to be moody and unpredictable. Nobody remembered his carrying a bottle, and the liquor stores close in Duluth at 8 P.M. on Sundays. Foster usually drank beer or bar bourbon. Sarah Hanson didn't drink at all. But the empty bottle in Foster's room had a Bombay Gin label, expensive stuff. In the well-appointed bar at the Haverstock house, in the cupboard where the stores were kept, were three unopened bottles of Bombay Gin. Sarah Hanson's neighbor, Mrs. Prochaska, was quite sure she'd heard "that drunken brother" coming home late, well after midnight, "swearing and slamming around the way he always does. I wouldn't be at all surprised if that bum didn't go out there to get more liquor money from poor Sarah or to rob the house even. He was a devil when he was drinking and he was all the time drinking!" waggled Mrs. Prochaska, also a devoted gardener, whose only complaint about Sarah Hanson had been that Sarah had never really confided in her about her tribulations with that awful drunken brother. Did Foster visit the Haverstock house late that Sunday night to get money or liquor? Did he brain his sister in a fit of rage and then, because she would be able to identify him, did he smother the old woman?

When he was first brought into Catlin's office, Foster sat slumped in his chair, blinking at the floor. "I have some bad news, Foster," Catlin said. "It's about your sister, Sarah." The rheumy eyes looked up. "I'm afraid she's dead." The eyes blinked as Foster took in a deep breath, then he sighed and his gaze once again sought the floor. He sat quietly, expressionless, but the blinking became more rapid and the eyes were wet. There was no visible reaction to the news that his sister and Mrs. Haverstock had apparently been murdered. Nor did he look up when Catlin asked him about his movements of the night before. His answers were brief and barely audible and they were punctuated by long pauses.

"Where did you get the gin, Foster? That bottle of gin you drank last night—where did it come from?"

"Got it at home." Foster seemed to be working something out in his mind. "It was at home there. On the table. Must have been Sarah's."

"Did Sarah drink gin?" asked Catlin. A long pause here. "No," said Foster, "No, Sarah don't drink nothing." Foster looked puzzled. "It was on the table."

Catlin read Foster his rights, the *Miranda* formula, explaining that he was not required to answer questions and that he had the right to be represented by cousel. Then he said, "Now listen, Foster, didn't you go out to see your sister at the Haverstock house Sunday night?"

"No. Why should I? I never been to that place at all."

"You've never been inside the house? Inside the gate, even?"

"No. Why should I be?" Foster looked up briefly, as if genuinely unable to see any sense in such questions. "I see Sarah enough at home."

Catlin leaned forward, elbows on his knees. "Look, Foster, we've got two women killed and you can't account for your whereabouts Sunday night. I mean there's no way to prove you went home like you say you did and stayed there. And you can't account for that bottle of gin. That's expensive stuff, Foster. They have gin like that at the Haverstock's. You didn't buy it. Sarah didn't buy it, did she? Did Sarah buy expensive booze for you to drink?"

The wet and haggard eyes surfaced and sank again and Foster shook his head. "It was on the table," he mumbled. "I was sleeping and then I come down and it was on the table there. The front room."

Catlin recalled the layout of the Hanson cottage. An enclosed front porch, the storm windows not yet replaced with summer screens, the door opening into the small living room, an old library table against the front wall with a TV set and a few framed photographs, the narrow stairway against the right wall as one entered. "Was the bottle there when you came home?"

"Didn't see it."

"Well, when did you see it? You say you were upstairs, asleep. Why did you come down?" Catlin pressed him.

Foster peered at the floor as if trying to see through a haze. "I come down. Woke up for some reason, a noise, something downstairs. I come down to see. Then I seen the bottle on the table."

Catlin sat back in his chair and contemplated the apathetic, hopeless looking old derelict. "Would you be willing to take a polygraph test, Foster? If you can't explain how that bottle came to be there, we're going to have to hold you on suspicion. Maybe if you take a polygraph test we can clear this up. How about it?"

Another brief glimpse of the reddened, wet eyes. "Sure, I don't care. Maybe Sarah brought it home. It was there on the table."

This interview took place Tuesday morning. Foster was returned to his cell with the understanding that the polygraph test would be given the next day. Billy Wister had made enlargements of the photographs taken at the crime scene Monday and he brought them into Catlin later Tuesday morning. Sergeant Poehls also was called in. Catlin went through the stack of photographs, selected a shot of the basement game room with its bar in the background, one of the library taken after the scattered papers had been replaced in the folder on the desk, and an exterior view of the closed French doors. The lieutenant handed these three photographs to Sergeant Poehls. "Arny, you and Billy run over and see if you can get five of the neighbors there on London Road to let you take some pictures. I want five back doors, five rooms like this library, and five to go with this game room. I guess what we want is either bars or liquor cabinets; they don't have to be in the basement."

By 3 P.M. on Tuesday, Catlin and Poehls were ready to lay out the Guilty Knowledge Test that would be administered to William Foster Wednesday morning. By 4:30 P.M. they were finished and Catlin called for Sergeant Reedy, who was to be the polygraph examiner in this case, to meet them down in the interrogation room. Reedy had been deliberately kept out of the Haverstock investigation so that he would know nothing more than any other local citizen might know about the details of the case. Catlin's standard procedure was for the investigating detectives to design the questions to be used in the GKT and then to administer those questions first to another detective who, like Reedy, was ignorant of the case facts and thus could serve as a "known-innocent suspect." If Reedy's score on the test did not unequivocally identify him as being without guilty knowledge, then this would indicate that one or more items had been poorly designed and would have to be reworked. Assuming that the test proved out on this trial run, still ignorant of which alternatives on each question were actually "correct"—i.e., which answers or exhibits or photographs were actually part of the case materials and not equally plausible but incorrect alternatives—Reedy would administer the test to the suspect. This procedure both pretested the test and also ensured that Reedy would not inadvertently cue the correct alternatives by his manner of presenting them to the suspect.

Installed in the basement of the police building, the interrogation room had four windowless masonry walls to keep out extraneous noises. It was carpeted and the ceiling and the upper halves of the walls were acoustically tiled. An adjoining room contained the polygraph itself and an FM tape recorder, an instrument capable of recording all questions asked and answers given. This data recorder provided insurance against the possibility that a recording pen might fail during a test or the original charts might be lost or damaged; the complete record of the subject's physiological responses could always be rewritten, at the same or, for more detailed analysis, at a faster speed, merely by playing back the tape into the polygraph again. A standard stereophonic tape recorder completed the instrumentation. This was connected to two microphones suspended from the ceiling of the interrogation room, one directed toward the respondent's chair and the other toward a chair and table at the back of the room where the examiner would sit. When a criminal suspect was to be tested, this recorder was kept in operation throughout the period when the suspect was in the interrogation room, thus providing a complete audio record of both the formal questioning and of the informal conversation preceding and following the actual testing.

Set into the front wall of the interrogation room was a large rectangular aquarium containing a number of tropical fish. In addition to providing a point of interest for the subject's gaze as he sat some eight feet distant, facing that wall, this aquarium also served as a one-way mirror through which the subject and the testing procedure might be observed by the polygraph operator, sometimes accompanied by the respondent's attorney, sitting in the polygraph room on the other side of the fish tank. After Poehls had fastened the two respiration belts around his chest and abdomen, Reedy sat down in the padded armchair provided for the respondent. Using small adhesive discs, Poehls attached the electrodermal electrodes to the fingerprint area of Reedy's left index and ring fingers. A second pair were similarly attached to his right hand. A miniature photoplethysmograph sensor, used to measure heart rate and pulse amplitude, was then taped to the middle finger of Reedy's right hand. Thus instrumented and, of course, well acquainted with the drill, Reedy sat quietly, both feet on the floor, both arms on the padded armrests. Poehls retired to tend the polygraph next door.

"For the record," said Catlin, "this is a pretest of the GKT designed for William Foster. The date is Tuesday, May 26th, 1978. The time is 4:45 P.M. The subject to be tested is Sergeant Fred Reedy of the DPD. The GKT to be used here was constructed by Sergeant Arny Poehls and by me, Lieutenant George Catlin."

"Okay, Fred, we have the polygraph calibrated and the test will now begin. Have you ever been inside of or have you ever seen the rear entrance of the Haverstock home on London Road?"

"No," replied Reedy.

Catlin continued, "All right. I'm going to show you now six photographs, numbered one to six in order, showing the rear or lake-side entrances of six of the homes in that row which includes the Haverstock house. If you really have never seen the lake-side of the Haverstock house, you won't know which of these six pictures shows the Haverstock back door. On the other hand, if you *have* seen that rear entrance, you will recognize it in one of these pictures. I will show you the photographs one at a time, in sequence. I want you to just sit there quietly and look at the picture as long as I hold it in front of you. When I show you a picture, I want you to say out loud the number of that picture. I have marked the number in the upper lefthand corner. Just say the number and then study the picture. All right, here we go. Which picture shows the rear entrance of the Haverstock home? Is it Number 1?" Catlin held the first photograph in a comfortable position for Reedy to examine it.

"Number 1," said Reedy, looking at the picture.

After about 15 seconds, a dim red light, set in the wall behind the subject, came on indicating that Poehls, at the polygraph, was seeing a steady record with no spontaneous activity that might confuse measurement of the subject's response to the next alternative. Catlin placed the photograph face down on the table and held the next one in front of Sergeant Reedy. "Is it Number 2?" asked Catlin

"Number 2," Reedy replied.

So the process continued, with roughly 15-second intervals between each successive photograph.

Catlin then picked up another set of photographs. "Now, Fred, here are pictures of rooms from each of those six houses. If you were involved in this matter, you will recognize which picture shows a room in the Haverstock house. Here we go. Which photograph shows a room in the Haverstock home? Is it Number 1?"

"Number 1," said Sergeant Reedy.

On a clipboard situated on the table behind Reedy, but where Catlin could consult it, was a paper outlining the format of the Guilty Knowledge Test that Catlin and Poehls had drawn up. The outline looked like this.

GUILTY KNOWLEDGE TEST
RESPONDENT: *William Foster*   CASE: *Hanson/Haverstock murder*

ITEM 1.   Which photograph shows the rear or lake-side entrance to Haverstock home? (six photographs)

ITEM 2.   Which photograph shows a room in the Haverstock home? (six photographs)

ITEM 3.   Which photograph shows the liquor cabinet in the Haverstock house? (six photographs)

ITEM 4.   Where was Sarah Hanson's body found? Was it: (1) in the basement? (2) in the bathroom? (3) on the stairway? (4) in the kitchen? (5) on a sofa? (6) in a bedroom?

ITEM 5.   What clothes was Sarah Hanson wearing when she was killed? Was she wearing: (1) a pink bathrobe? (2) a white uniform? (3) a dark sweater and slacks? (4) a green sweater and a skirt? (5) a brown tweed skirt and jacket? (6) a yellow blouse and slacks?

ITEM 6.   Where were Mrs. Haverstock's false teeth after she was killed? Were they: (1) in the hallway? (2) in the bathroom? (3) in her mouth? (4) on the bedside table? (5) on the floor by the bed? (6) on the dresser?

ITEM 7.   Which nightgown was the old lady wearing? (six exhibits)

ITEM 8.   How did the nurse's body look when we found it? (six photographs)

ITEM 9.   What was Sarah Hanson carrying when she was hit? What did she drop when she fell? Was it: (1) a newspaper? (2) some magazines? (3) a vase of flowers? (4) a tray and dishes? (5) a medicine bottle? (6) a coffee pot?

ITEM 10.   How did the old lady's body look when we found it? (six photographs)

ITEM 11.   What weapon was used to club Sarah Hanson? Was it: (1) a wooden chair? (2) a blackjack? (3) a length of pipe? (4) a fireplace tool? (5) a baseball bat? (6) a brass table lamp?

ITEM 12.   What sort of coffee pot was on the landing? What did it look like? (six exhibits)

Whether the alternatives to a question were photographs or verbal statements or exhibits, such as an array of six different styles of coffee pot, each tagged with a large number from one to six, Catlin presented each alternative in the form of a question: "Was it . . . ?" However, his respondent never actually answered the question, but instead simply repeated the last word or two.

"Fred, if you did this murder, you'll know where you left the nurse's body. Now, where was Sarah Hanson's body found. Was it in the basement?"

And Fred would echo him stolidly, "Basement."

The first alternative for each item was never the correct one since people tend to react more strongly to the first alternative in any series. If alternatives two through six, some one of which *was* correct for that item, had been properly designed, they would all seem equally plausible to an innocent respondent who would, therefore, have about one chance in five of coincidentally producing his largest physiological response to that alternative. That is, excluding the first, the responses to the other four incorrect alternatives should provide an estimate of how strongly the subject ought to respond to the correct one if he does not know which one is correct. A respondent with guilty knowledge, however, should recognize the correct alternative and this recognition will engender a transitory physiological arousal, an "orienting reaction," which will appear on the polygraph chart as an augmented response to that alternative.

In a relaxed, deliberate fashion, Catlin worked his way down through the twelve items in slightly less than 25 minutes. Then, after a short rest, they began again, this time using a second outline in which the items appeared in the same order with the same first alternatives, but with the five scored alternatives for each item given this time in a different sequence. By 6 P.M. they were finished. Sergeant Reedy was sent home to dinner while Poehls and Catlin set about scoring the two tests. The two packets of Z-folded polygraph charts contained the parallel tracings of seven pens. Two of these showed chest and abdominal breathing movements and the next one represented changes in finger pulse volume. Pen 4 showed beat-to-beat changes in heart rate, obtained from the same finger plethysmograph sensor via an electronic device called a cardiotachometer. The next two pens recorded skin conductance, the electrodermal response, from the left and the right hand. At the bottom of the chart, an event marker pen indicated both when each question was being asked and also the brief intervals when the subject was uttering his echo "answers." Poehls had numbered the items on the charts with a felt pen as the tests were being run. Now each man took one of the packets and proceeded to locate, for each item, the alternative which produced the largest electrodermal reaction, separately for the two hands. The first alternative was always excluded from this scoring. An item was scored as a hit only if the correct alternative produced clearly the largest response of all five scored alternatives in both hands.

"I have him hitting on Number 3 and Number 7," said Catlin, who had scored the charts from the first test.

"Well, he only hit on Number 12 here," replied Poehls after rechecking the second chart.

"Okay, let's compare them item by item," said Catlin and, picking up his notebook in which he had transcribed the first test scores, he read them off in sequence as Poehls compared them with his list. Only on Item 10, involving the photographs of Mrs. Haverstock's body in its six different poses, none of them pretty, had Reedy given his largest response in both hands to the same incorrect alternative on both testings.

Catlin looked again at the charts for Item 10. "I think this is okay, Arny. His biggest responses were to number 2 on that 10th item, but they were just slightly bigger than the other ones. I don't think there's anything out of line with that picture. If Foster saw that body as it really was, I think he'll hit on this item, all right."

But in the test the next morning, Foster only hit on one item, Item 5. He hadn't known what his sister was wearing when she left for work that Sunday night, but he did know that Sarah never wore a nurse's uniform on this job and, when Reedy read the sixth alternative, "Was it a yellow blouse and slacks?", there was a long pause before Foster remembered to mumble, "Yellow," and the two electrodermal pens swept upward in a strong reaction. He responded strongly to the pictures of his sister's body, too, of course, but no more so to the true pose than to the others.

"I guess he just remembered that Sarah had a yellow outfit, Arny. Foster isn't our man after all. But he still may be lying about that bottle. While we've got him hooked up, I'm going to try to pump him a little about that."

Returning to the interrogation room, Catlin told Foster, "You passed the test, Foster. We believe now that you never went to the Haverstock house so you don't have to worry about that any more. We're going to let you go pretty soon, but first we have to find out where that gin bottle came from. If you can tell me about that, you can go home."

Foster showed no visible reaction to this news, his expression still slightly bleary, apathetic. In the next room the polygraph pens described a sluggish increase in arousal, falling away again like a sigh.

"I don't know about the damn bottle. Might have bought it sometime; Sarah might have brought it home." Foster spoke so softly, looking at the floor as usual, that Catlin wondered if the microphones would pick up his words. Then his eyes flickered up again as if the mists had parted for a moment. "It could have been delivered, a mistake or something while I was asleep upstairs. It was there on the table. I think I woulda seen it before otherwise." Resignation seeped back into the man, visibly, audibly. "Could ask the neighbors or something. Maybe somebody come in when I was sleeping. I don't know."

Catlin had been scribbling on his clipboard. "All right, look, Foster. We're going to do a regular lie detector test now. I will ask you some questions and you just sit there quietly and answer each question Yes or No. Do you understand? You answer Yes or No and our machine in the other room will show whether you're telling the truth or not. Have you got that?

"Yeah," said Foster. "Okay."

Walking to the table behind the suspect, Catlin assumed a more formal tone. "This is a control question lie test administered to William Foster on Wednesday, May 27, 1978. Lieutenant Catlin speaking. The time is 10:20 A.M. All right, Foster, the test will now begin. Sit quietly, listen to the question, then answer either Yes or No in a clear voice. Here we go. Is your name William Foster?"

"Yes," said Foster, clearing his throat and shifting in his chair.

"Try to sit quietly, Foster. Is today Wednesday?"

"Yes."

"Did you ever buy a bottle of Bombay brand gin?"

"No."

Catlin paused 10 or 15 seconds between questions to give Poehls time to make sure the pens were centered and ready.

"Are you what people call a drunk?"

A pause, and then Foster mumbled, "Okay."

Impersonally, Catlin reminded him, "Try to answer either Yes or No, Foster."

"Referring to last Sunday night, did you get drunk Sunday night?"

"Yes."

"Before a week ago, did you ever take liquor that didn't belong to you, without paying for it?"

"No." Foster always waited several seconds before answering, as if deliberating, trying to remember.

"Referring to Sunday night, do you know for sure where that gin came from—who brought it in the house?"

"No."

"Did you ever fight with your sister, Sarah—ever argue with her?"

"Yeah, sometimes."

"Do you know for sure that Sarah ever took things from the Haverstock house to give to you?"

"Naw."

"Have you told me everything you know about that gin bottle?"

"Yes."

"Do you know who killed your sister?"

"No."

"Okay, Foster, you can relax for a minute. I'll be right back."

Catlin made his way to the polygraph room where Sergeant Poehls was completing the labeling of the chart.

"He don't show much, Boss," said Poehls. "Reactions to four and eight, both controls, and a little smaller to the last question."

"Yes, he's really got the wino pattern, hasn't he? Long slow reactions to everything, as if somebody was twisting his arm or pinching him. He doesn't seem very interested in the gin bottle, does he? What do you think, Arny? Is he worth pushing any harder?"

"Christ, George, I don't think he knows anything. His brains are pickled."

But Catlin, returning to the interrogation room, decided to make one last attempt. "Foster, the machine says that you know more about that gin bottle than you're telling us. You can't beat the machine, Foster. Unless the polygraph says you're telling the truth, you can be in real trouble. All I want to know is where you got that gin. Now, how about it?"

But it was no use. Foster didn't seem to care what the machine said or whether Catlin believed him. He didn't seem to care much about anything. Poehls disconnected the polygraph leads and took him back to the jail side to collect his belt and belongings. Watching him shamble off into his now, more than ever, empty world, Poehls thought, "Poor old bastard. We aren't doing you much of a favor, are we?"

Arny Poehls' secret with women was that he treated them just as he treated men, easy, interested, but with no apparent awareness of sexual possibilities. If a flirtatious note was to be injected, they had to take the initiative. And frequently they did. Arny was sitting on the edge of the secretary's desk, smiling, chatting inconsequentially, when Catlin arrived for the 2 P.M. conference on the Haverstock case that Chief Walter Anderson had called for that afternoon. The post-mortem findings showed that Victoria Haverstock had been asphyxiated. Traces of starch like that in the pillow case had dissolved and then dried on her tongue. Sarah Hanson had died of massive brain hemmorrhage resulting from a blow inflicted by the fire tool in the bedroom. The penetrating head wound had been made by the pointed side projection at the end of that instrument, which had been found to be coated at that end by a faint film of new rust. A section of the shaft had been wetted and then allowed to stand overnight in the lab; the same degree of rusting appeared the next day on the shaft. No fingerprints had been found. The blood on the bathroom floor matched Sarah's. A tile under those bloodstains was freshly chipped.

"He grabbed the poker, went out and brained the nurse, then ran back to quiet the old woman. He tossed the poker on the bathroom floor as he ran by, chipping the tile. He smothered the old lady, then he rinsed the poker, maybe wiped the handle or else he had gloves on—probably gloves, since there were no prints on the jewel box or the banister or the desk downstairs. There were a few small drips of blood on the hall carpet that had been stepped on, but we don't know whether he did that or if it happened during the search afterwards," Catlin summarized.

"You're sure about the brother being out of it?", asked the Chief.

"Well, there's two things. He was full of booze the next morning and I can't say for certain that a long-time alcoholic like that can't wash his brain clean with a bottle of gin—retrograde amnesia like you might get from a blow on the head. But our man was sober and planful when he was doing the job and I can't see Foster operating that way. And we know he'd done quite a bit of drinking at his usual places early that evening. Then there's the gin bottle that he can't account for. But I don't think Foster knows where it came from either."

"George," Arny Poehls said, "I checked out the liquor stores like you said. None of them made any deliveries on that block Sunday night. None of them sold any Bombay Gin at all on Sunday. The Prochaska woman next door still claims she heard a door banging late that night but she never got out of bed and she's only guessing about the time; 'after midnight,' she says. But a guy named Walters, Leonard Walters lives across the street from the Hanson house. He was up going to the bathroom around 2 A.M.—says he wakes up about that time every night, has to pee—Walters says he heard a car pull up across the street, stop with the motor running, drive off again after a minute or so. He didn't look out the window or anything and can't swear it stopped at the Hanson house. But he thought it did at the time, thought he heard the porch door bang just before the car drove off, as if someone had come out of the house and he'd wondered if Sarah Hanson had been picked up for a late nursing job or something.

None of the other neighbors heard anything. It's mostly old folks around there, early to bed."

"Does Foster know anybody with a car who'd be driving him home?" Chief Anderson queried Catlin.

Poehls interjected, "It wasn't a cab, by the way, I checked on that."

"I don't know, Chief. We can round him up again and ask him, but he's probably drunk again by now."

"No, he was home, George, after lunch," Poehls explained. "He was broke, you know, when we turned him loose this morning. He was just sitting there in the living room. He'd made some coffee. Still claims he was home in bed by midnight because he ran out of money. I asked him again why he'd come downstairs later, when he says he found the bottle on the table. This time he said he thinks he heard a noise downstairs, like somebody was at the door, or the door slamming. I had the feeling he was telling the truth, George. Maybe some Santa Claus did deliver that bottle. Anyway, I asked Foster if I could have it. It was still on the floor upstairs. They're going over it for prints right now."

"You'll make lieutenant yet, Arny," the Chief congratulated him.

"Sure, as soon as this department can afford a captaincy," said Catlin. "Arny, we'd better find out this afternoon if anybody saw a car come in or out of that beach house after midnight Sunday. And let's talk to the Haverstock neighbors again. Maybe someone else had to get up to pee that night."

"Have you located the Haverstock daughter, yet, George?" asked the chief.

"Not yet," Catlin replied. "We've left a message at their place in Mexico. The trip down might take them four or five days."

But developments did not wait on word from Mexico. The gin bottle proved to be a treasury of prints, mostly smudged, mostly Foster's. But the clear imprints of two unidentified fingers were found on the bottom of the bottle, just where a man's index and middle fingers might fold around if he gripped the base of the bottle like a softball. An awkward way to pick up a bottle unless it were lying on its side, lying on the seat of a car possibly. And these two prints were made by Henry Garnett.

The pace quickened. A waterfront bartender remembered Foster talking to a "real fancy looking young dude" on the previous weekend. A plumbing contractor, nearest neighbor to the east of the beach house, had been walking his dog about midnight Sunday, waiting shivering in the lake breeze for the dog to do his business. He'd

seen a car pull out of the beach house drive and been intrigued by
the fact that the headlights came on only after the car pulled onto
the highway. Then he recognized Garnett's Porsche as it hummed
past him. Nurse Garmoly, questioned a second time, recalled more
details about Sarah Hanson's report of Garnett's late night visit. He'd
met her brother, she had said wonderingly, and he wanted to know
more about his drinking problem; did he drink at home?—did he
have blackouts, not able to remember where he'd been? Sarah disliked talking about her personal affairs, but Henry was persistent,
explaining that his girlfriend's father was an alcoholic and he needed
to know what it was like, living with someone like that.

"Ask her, then," Sarah had finally told him, terminating the discussion.

Garnett was still in bed when Catlin phoned him Thursday morning. After another of his characteristic pauses, he agreed to drive in
to police headquarters to answer some additional questions. They
talked in Catlin's office, Sergeant Poehls also present with his notebook. Asked about his activities on the Sunday prior to the murder
weekend, Garnett smoothly explained that he had driven into town
alone about 9:30. He had visited a few of the dives along the waterfront, drinking beer and enjoying the local color. He'd stopped by to
visit his grandmother on the way home, got home about midnight
and stayed up with his houseguests for some time, talking and listening to records. He said he hadn't left the beach house at all the night
of the murder and he denied any knowledge of Sarah Hanson's
family.

Lieutenant Catlin studied the self-possessed young man as he sat
there comfortably, his well-tailored legs negligently crossed, an arro-
gant fist in a grey flannel glove.

"Garnett, I have to tell you there are some discrepancies in your
story that will need checking out. I'm not going to put you under
arrest as long as you remain cooperative, but I think I'd better have
you read over this explanation of your rights before we go any further." Catlin handed Garnett a dog-eared copy of the Miranda statement. Garnett skimmed it quickly.

"Look, Lieutenant," he said, handing it back, "I don't know what
'discrepancies' you mean. I was home in bed Sunday night and I have
three witnesses to prove it. In fact, Ginnie Gabbay is what I'd call an
iron-clad alibi; she knows where I was all that night."

"Well, if you're telling the truth you have nothing to worry about,
Garnett. The quickest way to find that out would be for you to take

a polygraph test. If you come up clean on the polygraph, then we'll know we have to look somewhere else. Would you be willing to do that? This afternoon?"

Catlin was impressed by the way Garnett met his gaze during the long pause that followed this question. You could almost see the machinery ticking over behind the steady grey eyes.

"I want to be cooperative, Lieutenant, but I don't know much about this polygraph business. Is that what they call the 'lie detector'? How do I know if it's accurate?"

"No, it's not a lie detector," Catlin replied, "although we use the same sort of instrument, the polygraph. We use what we call the Guilty Knowledge Test. The idea is to find out whether you were at the crime scene, whether you recognize what we found when we went out there Monday morning, whether you know some things that only the murderer would know because he'd been there."

"Well, of course, I have been there you know; it's my grandmother's house. I was there just last week." Garnett's manner was deliberate, prudent. You could sense he would have more confidence in his own judgment than in a lawyer's advice.

"We understand that," said Catlin. "The test won't be concerned with whether you know what the layout of the house is like but with whether you know what things were like when the murderer left. Like the name implies, whether you have guilty knowledge."

Another series of calculations ran off behind the grey eyes and then Garnett put his head back. "Okay, Lieutenant. What time this afternoon?"

After checking with Sergeant Reedy's schedule, a date was made for 2 P.M. Garnett departed and Catlin huddled with Poehls. It was decided to retain the same question list that had been used with William Foster. Garnett ought to "hit" on the first three items, since he was familiar with the Haverstock house, but these would not be scored with the other nine items. Or ten items, because they decided to use Poehls' set of pictures of the library in various states of disarray:

ITEM 13.   How did the library look when the murderer left? (six photographs)

Finally they devised a separate set of questions relating to Garnett's possible connection with Foster and the mysterious gin bottle:

ITEM 14.   You say you're not acquainted with any of Sarah Hanson's family but we think you may have talked with one of them. If you did, you'll know which relative it was. Just repeat the last word I say. Which of Sarah Hanson's relatives have you talked to recently? Was it: (1) Her husband? (2) Her sister? (3) Her brother? (4) Her nephew?

ITEM 15. The relative we have in mind is her brother. If you've talked with him, you'll know what his name is. What is his name? Is it: (1) Thomas Hanson? (2) Walter Larson? (3) Robert Atkinson? (4) Herbert Betts? (5) Arnold Gordeen? (6) William Foster?

ITEM 16. We think you might also know where Sarah Hanson and her brother lived. What is the name of the street where Sarah's brother lives? Is it: (1) First Avenue? (2) Lakeview Road? (3) Fifth Street? (4) Maryland Avenue? (5) 16th Avenue? (6) Portland Avenue?

ITEM 17. We think you might have taken something over to Sarah Hanson's house on the night of the murder. If you did, you'll know what that something was. What did you leave at the Hanson house on the night of the murder? Was it: (1) Some clothes? (2) Some liquor? (3) Some tools? (4) Some papers? (5) Some money? (6) Some food?

ITEM 18. Somebody left a bottle of liquor at William Foster's house that night. If it was you, then you'll know what kind of liquor it was. What type of liquor was dropped off at Foster's house that night? Was it: (1) Rum? (2) Bourbon? (3) Vodka? (4) Brandy? (5) Gin? (6) Scotch?

ITEM 19. Somebody left a bottle of gin at William Foster's house that night. If you did it, you will know what brand of gin it was. What brand was left at the Foster house that night? Was it: (1) Seagrams gin? (2) House of Lords gin? (3) Booths gin? (4) Bombay gin? (5) Gilbeys gin? (6) Tanquerey gin?

ITEM 20. The person didn't give the bottle to Foster but just left it somewhere in the house. Where did he leave the bottle? Was it: (1) On the front porch? (2) On the kitchen counter? (3) On the living room table? (4) On the stairway? (5) On the dining room table? (6) On a kitchen chair?

Unlike Foster, Henry Garnett was an interested and attentive subject. He asked about everything, the microphones in the ceiling, the fish tank, each polygraph sensor as it was attached to his body. He was instructed to sit quietly throughout the test, to listen carefully to each question, to think about each alternative for about five seconds and then to either repeat the words, if it was a verbal alternative, or to give its number, if it was a picture or an exhibit. It was explained that he would be expected to recognize the correct alternative on the first three items and that these were being used as an added control. He was in fact an ideal subject, breathing easily, apparently relaxed, pausing a few seconds as instructed after each alternative, then giving his response in a clear voice.

After Item 3, Sergeant Reedy explained: "Now, Mr. Garnett, the rest of the items will be presented by means of a recording. I have a cassette recorder here and I'll turn it on and off so that the questions will sound very much as if we were doing it live."

"What's the idea of that, Sergeant?" Garnett asked. He was not a man to walk into anything blindly.

"It's to be fair to you, Mr. Garnett," explained Reedy. "On the items we've already done, I don't know what the correct answer is so I can't give it away by the way I ask the question. On these next items, I do know the correct alternative, but they had me make this recording before I knew so, that way, you're fully protected."

One way of handling items of this type, where the next item in the sequence reveals which alternative of a previous item was correct, is to type them on cards so that the examiner doesn't see, say, Item 15 until he's finished with Item 14. But Catlin and Poehls thought they might need to use these items again so they had Reedy record them from such a set of cards so that however many times the recording was used, his voice would continue to betray no tell-tale cues.

But when Reedy got to the question portion of Item 14, Garnett lost some of his composure. He sat up in the chair and cleared his throat.

Say, look, Sergeant, I thought this was supposed to be about what happened at my grandmother's house. I mean, what's the nurse's family got to do with it?"

"This whole test has to do with the murder of your grandmother, Mr. Garnett. Lieutenant Catlin made out the set of questions that he wanted asked. If you're innocent, you have nothing to worry about. But you will have to sit quietly now, just like you were doing before. I'm going to back up the tape now and we'll start this item over again."

Garnett somewhat reluctantly leaned back again and resumed his outward calm. On Item 16 he cleared his throat vigorously before responding to the first alternative and Reedy had to interject a caution.

"Mr. Garnett, if you think you have to cough or clear your throat, let me know at the start of a question and I'll just wait for you."

Garnett was looking grim by the time the test was finished. Lieutenant Catlin came in from the polygraph room.

"The test is looking good, Mr. Garnett, but I want to repeat some of the earlier questions, just to be sure. Is that all right with you?"

Garnett was visibly upset now, pale beneath his tan, and clearly reluctant to continue. Catlin went on to explain that the last set of questions would not be repeated, could not be since the later questions about the gin bottle had given away the correct answers to the earlier questions.

"So far, the test indicates that you did not murder either of those women, Garnett, and we just want to run through part of it again to make sure."

Items 8 through 13 were repeated and then Sergeant Reedy disconnected the polygraph sensors. He noticed that Garnett's well-manicured fingers as well as his hairline were slightly damp with perspiration. In the polygraph room, Catlin got out his pocket calculator.

"Okay, Arnie, he gave his biggest response from both hands to the correct alternative on all of the last seven items. If the probability of his hitting on one item by chance is 0.2, then the probability that he would hit on all seven is 0.2 raised to the seventh power which is . . . 0.000013. That's less than 1 chance in 50,000 that this is an accident. This son-of-a-bitch planted that gin bottle on Sarah Hanson's brother. Or, at least, he knows all about it. But he didn't kill the women! What in the hell do you make of that?"

Henry Garnett was not disposed to provide illumination. He had had enough of questions and tests and he wanted to talk to a lawyer. Based on the evidence of the fingerprints on the gin bottle and the witness who saw Garnett's Porsche leave the beach house about the time of the murders, the young man was placed formally under arrest. Catlin met with Chief Anderson later that afternoon and explained the situation.

"He hit on the first three items, but that's just because he knows the Haverstock house and doesn't mean anything. He hit on the last seven items and that proves he either delivered that gin bottle to Foster's house or else he knows all about it, talked to whoever did deliver it. But on the murder items proper, he hit on only two out of ten the first time through and on only one out of six the second time. So we don't think he was in the house during or after the killings. Now there's just one funny thing about the charts for these items. The first time through, he really hit on Item 13, the pictures of the library messed up in different ways. He showed a lot of activity when the question was first explained, as if that was the first question that really bothered him. Then, when we did the seven items about Foster and the gin bottle, he was excited throughout, he hit on every one, and there's some indication that he was trying to produce some phony responses. He cleared his throat after the first alternative on Item 17 and there's something funny on Items 19 and 20 as well. After both first alternatives there's a pause and he stops breathing and then shows a big, slow electrodermal response. We think he was biting his tongue or something at those points. Even so, he gave his biggest response to the correct alternative on all seven of those items and the odds are about 77,000 to 1 that he couldn't have done that without knowing about the gin bottle.

"Then when we repeated the first set of items again, he was still excited, his heart rate and pulse pressure were elevated and he's responding quite a bit stronger than he was the first time around. On the repeat, we couldn't use the first seven items; only 8 through 13 were still uncontaminated, and he hits on just one item. But it was Number 13 again and he shows that same funny business after the first alternative on 13, as if he was trying to give a phony reaction on that one item."

"So what does that add up to, George?", the Chief frowned.

"I think Garnett had a partner. Garnett's job was to plant the bottle on Foster while somebody else did the actual killing. And I think part of the plan was to mess up the desk in the library. Garnett hadn't actually seen what the library looked like when we found it, but he knew in advance what it was supposed to look like so he could pick out the right picture to respond to."

Chief Anderson looked dubious. "Why would Garnett want to be in Duluth at all on the night of the killing? He could have planted that bottle at Foster's house some other night and then have been safe at a Rotary Convention in Chicago or somewhere when the women were being killed. Why make it so elaborate, George? You've got the kid sneaking out of the beach house after midnight, lying about that. You've got him talking with Foster in local beer joints prior to the murders and then pretending he doesn't know him. You've got him planting the gin bottle at Foster's house. You've got him paying a late night visit to his grandmother the week before. Garnett just came back again last Sunday, killed the two women, delivered the gin and went home to bed. What's wrong with that?"

"What's wrong is that the polygraph says Garnett wasn't there when the women were killed. We ran that part twice with him. He hits nicely on the first three items where he knows the answer but on two runs through the other ten he only hit on three, three hits out of 20 chances. Well, call it three out of 16, since we could only use six items on the retest. He may have known the right answer for Item 13 so he hit on it both times but he sure didn't know the correct alternatives on the other items."

"I thought you said that test was less certain about detecting innocence than guilt," the Chief persisted. "You've got one test here that proves this kid knows about the brother and the bottle because otherwise how could he always react to just the right one of the five alternatives. But when he doesn't react to the right alternative, what does that prove? Maybe he got confused, didn't notice how the body was lying or what she was wearing. What's my secretary wearing right now, Arnie? You were just talking to her."

"Y'know, Chief, that little dolly was naked the last time I looked at her. I've got this problem with X-ray vision . . . ," replied Sergeant Poehls.

"No, you're right, Chief," Catlin said. "A negative test result is less convincing than a positive one because it all depends on judgment. Are these good questions? Would this guy have noticed these things if he'd been there? But we've got a little more than that in this case. I had Reedy and Poehls give the same test to the uniformed cops who answered the first call. They walked through the house and saw the bodies and I think they were pretty excited at the time. How did they score, Arnie?"

"Well, we just used the 10 murder items, numbers 4 through 13. Edstrom hit on all but 11 and 13 and Swaline hit on all of them. Item 13 was the pictures of the library and Edstrom never saw the library. Item 11 was the one about the murder weapon and neither of them officially knew about that. But Swaline remembered the fireplace in the bedroom and he'd thought about what he could see of the nurse's head wounds. He hit on 11 because he'd deduced already that she'd been hit with a poker."

"So you see, Chief," Catlin pressed on. "These two cops had less chance than the murderer did of picking up on these 10 keys and yet one hit on 8 and the other on all 10. So when Garnett only hits on 1 or 2 items, then I say he just wasn't in that house that night."

"What if he planted something else?", Sergeant Poehls interjected. "Hey, look, George, the Chief's right about the bottle. He could have planted that the night before the murders and been long gone with a solid alibi. That Garnett is too smart and too cool to be running around town here while some accomplice is wasting those two women. Unless he had a good reason. What if he was planting something else on old Foster besides the bottle? Like, where are the jewels out of that box on the old lady's dresser? Maybe the idea was to get something that night, whoever was in the house would pass it to Garnett and he'd plant it on Foster."

Chief Anderson turned back to Lieutenant Catlin with eyebrows raised in speculation.

"Hey, that's pretty clever, Arny," Catlin said. "Maybe we should buzz over to Foster's and really look around."

William Foster was at home and made no objection to the proposed search. In fact, he needed Catlin's advice. He was without funds and wanted to know, in view of his sister's death, whether it would be all right for him to cash her paycheck. That check, Catlin noted, was dated April 1; Sarah Hanson died May 24th. The check was signed by Mrs. Haverstock's accountant and a phone call to that gentleman revealed that he had prepared those checks early, that he usually visited Mrs. Haverstock during the first week of each month and left two sets of semimonthly paychecks in the folder on the library desk. The day nurse, Mrs. Rorchek, knew about this system and handed out the checks—that is, left them out to be collected—on each payday. Arny Poehls remembered that some of the litter picked up from the library floor that Monday morning had been checks of a similar appearance. Foster showed the two detectives where he'd found the check, rummaging in the drawer of the table in the living room.

The finding of this first apparent plant, corroborating Poehls' speculation, may have caused them to be more persistent in their search for the jewels than they might otherwise have been. They ransacked the porch, the first floor, the tiny basement. Although it seemed unlikely that Garnett would have risked going upstairs that night with Foster there in bed, they searched the second floor, all to no avail. Baffled, since finding the check had convinced them that the Haverstock jewels, whatever they might turn out to be, must also be somewhere on the premises, Poehls doggedly began sifting through the contents of the garbage can outside the kitchen door. Catlin felt himself getting unreasonably irritated at Foster, who was slouched in the living room, smoking incessantly, wiping his nose on his sleeve, looking pitiful and useless.

"Damn you, Foster, if you've taken or hidden that jewelry I'm gonna really bust your ass," he said, getting his topcoat out of the little closet under the stairs. Foster sputtered some sort of protest as Catlin settled the coat on his shoulders and felt in the pocket for his car keys. Then the detective walked back to the closet and scrutinized its contents. Foster's old navy pea jacket hung from a hook in front. Catlin remembered the jacket had been on a chair in Foster's bedroom when they'd picked up Foster that Monday morning. On hangers were Sarah's winter coat, a heavy, pile-lined garment, and a blue tailored raincoat. Catlin started going through the pockets.

"Now then! All *right!* Foster, go tell Sergeant Poehls to get in here. I've got a present for him."

There was a double string of pearls, cultured but numerous, an old-fashioned necklace of garnets set in gold, some matching earrings, a large dinner ring festooned with small rubies and diamonds. They'd been deep in the pocket of Sarah's storm coat which, as Catlin pointed out, could easily be confused with a man's coat, hanging in the dark closet. They were right. Garnett had been trying to set up the drunken old derelict for the murder of his sister and of Garnett's rich grandmother. But if Foster hadn't killed the women and if Garnett hadn't either, who had? Reinvigorated, Catlin called downtown to request that Garnett's three house guests be picked up at once for questioning. He also called Sergeant Reedy, who was home having his dinner, and told him that he might be needed later that night for additional polygraph tests. Then, not for the first time when they'd had a case "working," Catlin brought Arny Poehls home with him for dinner. Another call downtown revealed that the three people had been located at the beach house and were now in custody.

"We'll let them get a little hungrier, Arnie, and then maybe they'll be more eager to take the polygraph so they can be released before the restaurants close."

"What questions do you want to use?" asked Poehls.

"The whole set," said Catlin. "I want to know if they've been in that house, if they were there during the murders, and if they know anything about the plant. We'll do the girlfriend first, that little blonde, and then the man. I want to run them tonight before there's any chance of Garnett's talking to them."

Garnett's friends were less hungry than angry and a little scared. Catlin explained that Garnett would be arraigned on a murder charge the next day and that, under the circumstances, they all could be held at least as material witnesses. As an alternative to spending a night in jail, they each reluctantly agreed to take the polygraph test. By about 10 P.M. that evening, all three had passed the test and been released. Catlin and Poehls were sure that none of them had been involved either in the killings or in the planting of the evidence.

These were the last polygraph tests to be administered in connection with the Haverstock case, although the investigation was not yet over. Several other possible suspects were eliminated by telephone. The two Michaelson boys had spent the night of May 24th in their respective dormitories in Minneapolis. Pat Garnett had several friends able to confirm her presence that evening at a Greenwich Village loft party. Poehls' previous successes had inflated his confidence in his own policeman's instinct and, by Friday morning, that instinct had started whispering to Sergeant Poehls about Oscar Rorchek, whose wife had found the bodies. Rorchek was rather well known around the working men's taverns of Duluth, a big man and the undisputed left-handed arm wrestling champion. He was a sports enthusiast and a bit of a gambler. Arny Poehls initiated some quiet checking on where Oscar Rorchek had spent the previous Sunday night. To Poehls' chagrin, the answers came back readily and were incontrovertible. Rorchek's Sunday nights were regularly given over to bowling, followed by a rotating poker game with the members of his bowling team. Between 10 P.M. Sunday and 2 A.M. on Monday morning, Oscar Rorchek had been winning some $35 from five friends in his own living room.

The break in the case came nearly a week later after John and Merry Bell Plunkett had flown back from Mexico so that Merry Bell could muster legal assistance for her first-born son. As a matter of routine, Catlin obtained the itinerary of the Plunketts' trip south which had taken them five days. John Plunkett had signed the registration at motels in Kansas City, Albuquerque, and Phoenix, but at the first stop, a Holiday Inn in Des Moines, Merry Bell signed. The license plate number she listed was incorrect. A waitress at that motel remembered John Plunkett because she had served them a late breakfast Monday morning and Plunkett had told her he was from Minneapolis and left a $10 bill to cover less than $5 worth of food. But no one remembered Plunkett the night before. When Plunkett, who by this time had been able to communicate with

Henry Garnett, refused to take the same polygraph test that Garnett had been given, Catlin decided to operate on the hypothesis that Plunkett was the murderous confederate. That meant Merry Bell must have made her own way, presumably by airline, to Des Moines while Plunkett was driving the gray Cadillac toward Duluth. The Iowa police were set looking for the cab that might have taken Merry Bell from the Des Moines airport to the Holiday Inn on Interstate 35. And, visualizing that long wee hours drive from Duluth to Des Moines, Catlin asked the Highway Patrol to check the all night gas stations along the route where Plunkett might have filled that rather striking-looking car. And how would he know where to find Merry Bell once he got to that Holiday Inn? They had no prereserved room number. There must have been a phone call to Merry Bell after she had time to check in or from Merry Bell to Henry Garnett, possibly, at the beach house or perhaps even to the Haverstock house. Otherwise, Plunkett would have had to inquire his own room number at the motel desk or else his wife would have had to haunt the lobby in the early dawn, waiting for him to arrive.

The phone call was never established. But a gray Cadillac Seville had filled up on diesel fuel just north of Minneapolis around 4 A.M. that Monday morning—and John Plunkett's Seville had a diesel engine. And a Drake University student was located who, returning from a visit home to St. Paul, had sat next to a furred and jeweled woman who had smelled like $100 an ounce when the plane took off, but more like a double martini when it landed. This observant young woman had no difficulty selecting a picture of Merry Bell Plunkett from a set of ten alternatives offered to her. The taxi driver also was located. Merry Bell had directed him to the SaveMore Motel across the street but, after maneuvering to reverse direction and head back into town, he had seen her scurrying across the highway toward the Holiday Inn and that peculiarity had stuck in his mind.

At the trial, Plunkett's able and expensive lawyer took the best course open to him. There was circumstantial evidence against his client but there was evidence also against William Foster. Given this other plausible suspect, the jury must find reasonable doubt of Plunkett's guilt. In rebuttal, the State introduced the evidence of Foster's Guilty Knowledge Test, the fact that Officers Edstrom and Swaline had "failed" the test after their visit to the crime scene, while Foster had clearly "passed" it. Over the objections of the defense, the results of Henry Garnett's test were explained to the jury with their obvious implication that Garnett had been involved in planting the gin bottle at Foster's home but had not been at the murder scene. With the jury absent from the courtroom, Plunkett was again formally requested to submit to the same GKT and, after heated argument, the Court ruled that his refusal was material information that might properly be communicated to the jury.

In the event, John Martin Plunkett, Merry Bell Plunkett, and Henry Garnett were successively tried and convicted of conspiracy and murder in the first degree.

CHAPTER 22

Analysis Of The
Guilty Knowledge Test

A little [knowledge] is a dangerous thing.

—Alexander Pope

Because it is still poorly understood, even by polygraphers, and because it is to some extent my own brainchild, I have introduced the guilty knowledge method gently, its best foot forward. In this chapter, I will try to examine the assumptions of the GKT and the evidence concerning its validity as critically as I did the lie detection methods in Part II.

It should be remembered that the GKT has not yet been systematically tested in the field. Until it has, it should only be regarded as an interesting possibility.

Validity of the GKT in the Laboratory

When psychological experiments are repeated, by different investigators in different laboratories, all too often they do not come out the way they did the first time. There are many reasons for this, chief

297

among them being that psychology is an inexact science attempting to comprehend the most difficult of subject matter. I was greatly relieved, therefore, when another researcher first repeated my guilty knowledge work and got similar results.[1] A number of additional studies of the GKT have subsequently appeared; the method always works but some of these later experiments have not obtained as good a discrimination as I did between "guilty" and "innocent" subjects (none of these experiments have used actual criminal suspects as subjects).[2] A virtue of the GKT method is that, at least in theory, the discrimination of guilty from innocent suspects can be made as complete as one wishes, simply by increasing the number of good items. With 10 good items, for example, one might expect to identify 97% of guilty suspects if persons scoring 5 or higher are classified as guilty. The odds against an innocent suspect scoring so high would be more than 100 to 1. This suggests that the experiments that failed to achieve good discrimination either had too few items or else items that were not good enough.

Before explaining what is meant by a "good" item, let me define a few terms. The GKT items illustrated in the detective story each had 6 alternatives. The first alternative in each set is called a "buffer"; it is incorrect and does not figure in the scoring. The purpose of the buffer is to dissipate the subject's tendency to react more strongly to the first item in any series. One of the other alternatives is correct or *relevant;* the relevant alternative refers to the "key," the bit of guilty knowledge on which that item depends. The remaining 4 incorrect alternatives are called *controls.* Unlike the usage of this term in lie detection, the control alternatives in a GKT item are genuine controls in the sense that the responses they elicit provide an estimate of how strongly an innocent person should react to the relevant alternative.

There are several methods of scoring the GKT. The simplest is to award one point for each item on which the relevant alternative produced a larger response than did any of the controls. The respondent is then said to have "hit" on that item. With ten (good) items, the typical innocent suspect will hit on fewer than 3 items while more than half of the guilty suspects should hit on at least 8 items. The *cutting score* is the highest score that will be classified as indicating innocence. In the previous example, the cutting score was set at 5, in which case fewer than one innocent suspect in 100 would be expected to be erroneously classified as guilty. It will be recalled that this type of misclassification is called a *false-positive.* The *false-*

negative rate in this example—guilty suspects misclassified as innocent—would be about 3%.

Now that we have a working vocabulary, what do I mean by a "good" GKT item? An item with 5 scored alternatives will be "good" if (1) an innocent respondent has about 1 chance in 5 of hitting on that item, and (2) a guilty respondent has at least an 80% chance of hitting on that same item. The first condition will be realized if all 5 alternatives seem equally plausible to a person without guilty knowledge;—and if an unscored buffer is employed as the first alternative presented. The second condition, that most guilty suspects would hit on the item, will be realized if most guilty suspects unequivocally recognize the relevant alternative as part of their guilty knowledge. (This second condition also requires that the guilty suspect will not successfully self-stimulate on one or more of the control alternatives. I will return to the problem of counter-measures later.) Thus, the key bit of information on which the item is based must be something that the guilty person is likely to have noticed and remembered. The control alternatives should be easily distinguished from the relevant alternative (and from each other) so that the guilty suspect is not confused about which alternative he's seen before. For example, if the alternatives are photographs of six bank tellers and the relevant one pictures the teller that was robbed, the people chosen for these photographs should all be quite different in appearance so that the guilty suspect can know at once which faces are incorrect and which one he has seen before. This discrimination can be enhanced during the testing by requiring the subject to name each alternative in some fashion after it has been presented to him, as was done in the detective story. If instead he merely repeats some useless answer like "No," or "I don't know," after each alternative, or if he is not required to vocalize at all, then it will be easier for a guilty suspect to think of other matters and thus minimize the difference in impact between the relevant and control stimuli. Finally, the fact that he recognizes the relevant alternative must seem important to the guilty suspect if the item is to work as a good item. This condition should always be realized in a criminal investigation context but may not be in some laboratory experiments.

Various GKT studies have reported accuracies ranging from about 70% to 100%. In the less successful studies, one can readily see how the accuracies might have been raised, either by improving the quality of items or by increasing the number of good items. In one experiment, for example, the guilty knowledge keys were six "code

DETECTING GUILTY KNOWLEDGE

words"—like "blue, hat, window, day, air, north"—that all "guilty" subjects had memorized.[3] The purpose of the GKT was to determine who knew the code words. A typical test item would be, "Is one of these words a code word? Green. Yellow. Blue. Red. Brown. Pink." The subjects answered "No" after each alternative. There was no buffer alternative. Since all the alternatives in each item were of the same class—colors, articles of clothing, etc.—a "guilty" subject might respond to the first alternative because it is the first of a series; to the second alternative because it leads him to think that all the alternatives are going to be colors; to the third alternative because it is the key "blue"; to the fourth alternative because, expecting a color, he has predicted "red" and it is "red"; and so on. If that experiment were repeated using a buffer alternative, randomly chosen words as controls, requiring the subjects to echo each word instead of answering "No," and with 10 or 16 such items rather than only 6, then one would have to predict much better accuracy than the 77% found by these investigators. The accuracy that can be expected from GKTs containing from 5 to 16 "good" items is shown in Table 22–1.

TABLE 22–1. Accuracy of the GKT for tests of increasing length.

# of Items	Cutting Score	INNOCENT SUBJECTS		GUILTY SUBJECTS	
		True Negative	False Positive	True Positive	False Negative
5	3	99.4%	0.6%	87.2%	12.8%
6	3	98.3%	1.7%	90.1%	9.9%
10	5	99.4%	0.6%	96.8%	3.3%
12	6	99.6%	0.4%	98.1%	1.9%
16	8	99.9%	0.1%	99.3%	0.7%

NOTE: The table assumes all "good" items, i.e., that an innocent subject has a 20% chance—and a guilty subject about an 80% chance—of giving his largest response to the relevant alternative.

Two recent laboratory studies yielded results that fit reasonably well with the predictions of Table 22–1. Geison and Rollinson[4] required 20 Guilty subjects to enact a mock crime and then tested them, along with 20 Innocents, using 6 well-constructed GKT items.

According to Table 22–1, we should expect 98% of the Innocent subjects to pass and 90% of the Guilty to fail; the actual results were 100% and 95%, respectively. Podlesny and Raskin[5] used 5 reasonably "good" items and correctly identified 100% and 90% of the Innocent and Guilty. But Podlesny and Raskin also obtained high (laboratory) validities for the Lie Control Test; 95% of the Innocent passed while 80% of the Guilty were classified as Deceptive. We know from the Barland & Raskin study[6] (part of the same project but, curiously, never published in a scientific journal) that, when the LCT is administered to genuine criminal suspects in the field, about half of the innocent respondents will fail the test. This discrepancy illustrates the perils of estimating lie test validity from laboratory studies using volunteer subjects and mock crimes. Theoretically, the GKT should work as well in real life as it does in the laboratory—but that theory needs to be tested by experiment.

Scoring

The problem with the simple scoring scheme used above is that an item is scored as a miss unless the relevant response is larger than all four control responses. But plainly, if a subject always gave his second-largest response to the relevant alternative, this too would strongly suggest guilty knowledge. By chance or because of covert self-stimulation, one of the four control alternatives might produce the largest response but the reaction to the relevant alternative is consistently larger than average. A method of scoring the GKT that is sensitive to such possibilities is the method of *mean ranks*. One ranks the five responses for each item and then one averages the ranks of the relevant alternatives. The probability that an innocent suspect would produce such an average rank score can be determined from a table like Table 22–2.

In special situations where it is expected that the subject may try to conceal his guilt by deliberately augmenting his control responses, the GKT can be scored by the method of *expected ranks*. This requires a larger number of items or else several repetitions of the item list. Since the innocent suspect cannot distinguish the relevant from the control alternatives, one expects that the relevant responses of an innocent suspect will about equally often be ranked 5, 4, 3, 2, or 1. Any statistically reliable deviation from equal rank frequencies

TABLE 22–2. Probabilities of various mean-rank scores for an innocent subject on a 10-item GKT.

Mean Rank	Probability	Cumulative Probability
1.0	.0000001	.0000001
1.1	.000001	.0000011
1.2	.000006	.000007
1.3	.00002	.00003
1.4	.00007	.0001
1.5	.0002	.0003
1.6	.0005	.0008
1.7	.001	.0019
1.8	.002	.0042
1.9	.004	.008
2.0	.007	.016
2.1	.012	.03
2.2	.019	.05
2.3	.027	.08
2.4	.037	.12
2.5	.049	.17
2.6	.060	.23
2.7	.071	.30
2.8	.080	.37
2.9	.086	.46
3.0	.088	.55

NOTE: For example, there are about 16 chances in 1,000 that a subject without guilty knowledge would produce responses to the relevant alternatives having an average rank of 2.0 or higher.

will suggest that this suspect could in fact discriminate the relevant alternative—and that he has guilty knowledge. Normally, one would expect ranks of 1 or 2 for the relevant responses of a guilty suspect. Should he manage to strongly augment every control response, then the relevant responses may all rank 4 or 5. Even if every relevant response ranks exactly 3, the average of the control responses, we would be able to infer guilty knowledge. The suspect may have self-stimulated on two control alternatives for each item; how else could such a consistent result be achieved unless there was recognition of the relevant alternatives?

But I am letting myself get carried away. A policeman, eager for a conviction, could easily insure that his suspect will get a failing score on the GKT whether he is guilty or innocent. He could make sure that the only plausible alternatives are also the correct alternatives. Or he could read out the test questions in such a way as to emphasize the correct alternatives by his tone or inflection. We must reluctantly assume that any investigative technique that can be abused, will be abused sometimes. That is why, in the detective story, the GKT was routinely tested on persons known to be without guilty knowledge, and the questions were presented by someone ignorant of the correct answers and unable, even inadvertently, to cue the correct alternatives. These should be standard practices.

Counter-measures

The GKT will be susceptible to distortion by a guilty suspect who is skillfull enough to covertly augment his reactions to the controls. As is true also in lie detection, the best defense against such counter-measures is an observant examiner. Since the GKT is to be used only in criminal investigation, as a guide to the police, it does not much matter that a suspect invalidates the test in this way so long as his efforts are noticed. In lie detection, an innocent suspect might augment his control responses because of a justified fear of failing the test even though innocent. Only a guilty suspect would have reason to try to beat the GKT, the cardinal virtue of which is a vanishingly small likelihood of false-positive errors. More importantly, an innocent suspect *could not* systematically self-stimulate on the controls, since he would not know which alternatives are controls and which are relevant. Therefore, the police investigator learns just as much from the fact that a suspect tries to defeat the test as he would learn from a score in the guilty range. In both instances, he will focus his investigation on this suspect, searching for admissible evidence against him.

Under special circumstances, it may be worthwhile to attempt to get a valid GKT score in spite of obvious attempts by the respondent to defeat the test. This will require perhaps five presentations of a 10-item set in order that the method of expected ranks, described earlier, can be employed. When this technique was tested experimentally, 20 subjects were allowed to practise self-stimulation to produce misleading responses and they were offered a money prize if they could "beat" the test; none were successful.[7] Whether the method will work as well in real-life applications remains to be seen.

The GKT and the Polygraph

So far I have assumed that the GKT will be administered while the suspect is connected to a polygraph and that the only response variable used in scoring will be the electrodermal response, the EDR. The EDR is an extremely sensitive indicator of momentary arousal but, as we have seen, the EDR is also relatively easy to augment through self-stimulation. At least two other response variables might be used to supplement the EDR. One is the transitory change in heart rate that may follow each stimulus. This often takes the form of a brief acceleration, then a slowing, of the heart beat. Using heart rate, then, one could consider the *pattern* of the response as well as its amplitude. There is no reason why the pattern or the size of the relevant and control responses should differ if the subject does not know which alternative is correct.

Therefore, if Jones' heart slows, then hurries, after the control alternatives, but hurries, then slows, after the relevant alternatives, we might conclude that Jones has guilty knowledge. Smith might show the reverse pattern and yet still betray the damning fact that he recognizes which alternatives are relevant. Note the important difference between the GKT and any lie test: If Jones' heart rate response is consistently different to the control and relevant questions on a lie test, the interpretation is hopelessly ambiguous—because, on any lie test, the difference between the control and relevant questions is always apparent to guilty and innocent subjects alike.

A second response variable that may have potential for use with the GKT is the pupillary response, a minute but reliable change in the diameter of the pupil of the eye. Modern instruments, employing a TV or video camera, can measure pupil size with exquisite precision and trace the changes on a polygraph chart. As is true with heart rate, one cannot predict how recognition of the relevant alternative will affect the direction or size of the pupillary response—but that is no handicap for the GKT. As long as recognition makes a difference, any difference, then guilty knowledge can be demonstrated. For most subjects, it is doubtful that the electrodermal response can be improved upon in respect to sensitivity. The addition of heart rate or pupil size (or both), however, might provide a combination of variables that could defeat any counter-measure that would be successful against the EDR alone.

The GKT in the Courtroom

The guilty knowledge test is being advocated here as an investigative tool and not as a method of strengthening, in the eyes of a jury, the case for or against a criminal defendant. But a defense attorney who learned that a GKT had been administered to his client, and that the score attained had been as low as that produced by the known-innocent subject employed to calibrate the test, would be sorely tempted to have that fact brought into evidence. Similarly, a prosecutor, knowing that a defendant had scored higher than would be expected in 10,000 testings of innocent suspects, might reasonably feel that this information would assist the jury in its decision making. Since there are striking differences between the GKT and lie test evidence, both in respect to probable validity and also in the intrinsic nature of the evidence, it seems worthwhile to point out some of these distinguishing features.

In the first place, while any lie test requires the defendant to reply to the basic question at issue, "Did you do it?," the GKT requires no verbal testimony at all. The suspect is never asked if he "did it." The GKT alternatives are presented in the form of questions but those questions are not answered verbally; the only vocal response consists of echoing the question. The response from which guilty knowledge is to be inferred is nonverbal and involuntary. It can be argued that requiring a defendant to submit to a guilty knowledge test would be analogous to requiring him to show his face to a witness or to give a sample of his fingerprints. Requiring him to submit to a lie test, in contrast, is requiring him to testify against himself. Whether this difference makes a difference with respect to Fifth Amendment issues, my legal consultants have been uncertain about. It is, they have felt, "an interesting question."

Secondly, the examiner who would offer into evidence the results of a GKT would not be in the position of asking the court to accept his expert opinion. He would describe how the test was constructed, how it was calibrated on one or more known-innocent subjects. He would explain the score attained by the defendant and how that score was derived. Finally, he would explain the appropriate statistical interpretation of that score, the probability that such a score might be produced by a subject without guilty knowledge. The jury could be easily apprised of all the relevant facts and could as easily arrive at its own conclusions.

Future Prospects

It should be said again that the guilty knowledge test, as here described, has not been systematically studied in the context of real life criminal investigation. Questions remain that could be addressed in further laboratory work. But the important questions—Can the GKT be useful in criminal investigation? Can it be made as accurate, especially in exonerating innocent suspects, as the theory suggests?— will only be answered by adequate field trial. Such field research cannot be done by college professors or polygraphers working alone but will require the active participation of interested police detectives willing to try something new. If this book succeeds in fomenting a healthy scepticism about the flourishing industry of lie detection, honesty testing, and the private practice of police work generally, while at the same time generating a sceptical interest in the possibilities of guilt detection for use in criminal investigation by the duly constituted authorities, then it will have accomplished its objectives.

Notes

1. Davidson, P.O. Validity of the guilty knowledge technique: The effects of motivation. *Journal of Applied Psychology,* 1969, *53,* 399–403.
2. Ben Shakhar, G., *et al.* Guilty knowledge technique: Application of signal detection measures. *Journal of Applied Psychology,* 1970, *54,* 409–413. (20 items, 77% hits) Lieblich, I., *et al.* Efficiency of GSR detection of information with repeated presentation of series of stimuli in two motivational states. *Journal of Applied Psychology,* 1974, *59,* 113–115. (10 items, 93% to 100% hits) Waid, W.M., *et al.* Effects of attention, as indexed by subsequent memory, on electrodermal detection of information. *Journal of Applied Psychology,* 1978, *63,* 728–733. (5 items, 71%, 76%, & 77% hits)
3   Waid, W.M., *et al. op.cit.*
4. Giesen, M. & Rollison, M. Guilty knowledge versus innocent associa-

tions: Effects of trait anxiety and stimulus context on skin conductance. *Journal of Research in Personality,* 1980, *14,* 1–11.

5. Podlesny, J. & Raskin, D. Effectiveness of techniques and physiological measures in the detection of deception. *Psychophysiology,* 1978, *15,* 344–359.

6. Barland, G. & Raskin, D. *Validity and reliability of polygraph examinations of criminal suspects.* (Report No.76–1, Contract 75–NI–99–0001, U.S. Department of Justice, 1976)

7. Lykken, D. The validity of the guilty knowledge technique: The effects of faking. *Journal of Applied Psychology,* 1960, *44,* 258–262.

Jamais je n'ai menti;
entre nous, tout est fini.

—*Carmen,* Act IV

Index

Abrams, S., 44, 67–68
Accuracy:
    chance, 64
    of polygraph tests, 63–74
    (*See also* Reliability of poly-
        graph tests; Validity of poly-
        graph tests)
Alexander, Franz, 55
American Polygraph Association,
    44, 105, 192
American Psychological Associa-
    tion, 190
Ansley, N., 44
Anticlimax dampening concept,
    116–117
Anxiety IQ, 230
Aptitude tests, 68–69
Army Criminal Investigation Divi-
    sion, 75
Arther, Richard O., 31–34, 37–38,
    42, 65, 89–92, 94–96, 126, 219,
    225, 228
Ash, Philip, 123, 200, 202
Astrology, "proof" of validity, 67,
    123–124
Autonomic response to emotions,
    55–56
Ax, Albert, 55–56

Backster, Cleve, 31–35, 42, 92, 110,
    118
    anticlimax dampening concept,
        116–117
    Zone of Comparison method, 34,
        109, 111–112, 120
Bailey, F. Lee, 219, 222,
    239–240
Barland, Gordon, 44, 77, 97, 125,
    158, 222, 231, 232, 240, 301
Barthel, Joan, 93, 209
Base rates, 220–224
Bayh, Birch, 184, 188–189, 242
Beating the lie detector (*see* Coun-
    termeasures)
Behavior symptoms, 31–33, 39
    in clinical test, 95–97
    in Lie Control Test, 111
Bell, Allan, 35, 153
Bell Telephone Company, Has-
    kins Laboratory, 153
Bennett, Richard H., Jr.,
    159
Ben-Shakhar, G., 44
Benussi, Vittorio, 28, 60
Bersh, P., 75, 98–100
Biofeedback, 238
Bitterman, M. E., 107n.

Blood pressure:
  in countermeasures against lie
      detector, 239
    plethysmograph measurement
      of, 26
    in polygraph "cardio" tracings,
      60–61
    in polygraph tests, 16–18
Bok, Sissela, 54–55
Borchard, E., 209
Branscomb, H., 155, 158
Brenner, M., 154–155, 158
Buckley, J., 123
Burden of proof, 80–81
Burkey, Lee M., 41–42, 218, 222

Cannon, Walter, 56
Case examples:
  brother accused of raping sister,
      118–119
  Coker vs. Piggly Wiggly, 167–
      172, 190
  eating of polygraph charts, 21
  father accused of incest, 118
  Frye case, 218–219
  Galloway murder case, 116, 117,
      130
  Hanson and Haverstock mur-
      ders, fictitious, 254–255,
      257, 296
  John K., deputy sheriff, and bank
      robber, 176
  Ken Chiu murder case, 110–111,
      131–132
  Larson's shoplifting case, 28
  Linda K. vs. Kresge Company,
      175–176
  Mary St. Clare murder case,
      87–89
  Mendoza murder case, 116,
      226–228
  pants presser's theft, 252–253
  Peter Reilly case, 91, 93, 209–
      211, 214, 253–254

Case examples:
  sabotage in bakery, 173
  Sam K. and "rape" of Mary V.,
      119–121, 130
  Sister Terressa and honesty test,
      195–197, 201
  Walter K. and stolen camera,
      177–179
  Wayne K. and bank theft, 116,
      174–175
Central Intelligence Agency
      (CIA), 143–144
Chicago Police Department, 30
Children, tests of cheating and ly-
      ing, 198–199
Chimpanzees, communication
      studies of, 24–25
Cleckley, Hervey, 229
Clinical lie test, 31–33, 85,
      87–102
  assumptions of, 92–98
  behavior symptoms in, 95–97
  Bersh's study of, 98–100
  posttest interrogation, 91
  stimulation (stim) test, 93–95,
      106, 240
  validity of, 98–100
Confession:
  in clinical lie tests, 91,
      99–100
  coercion in obtaining, 213
  and courts, 212–215
  of crimes not committed, 75,
      209–211, 213–214
  in criminal investigation, 207–
      212
  as criterion measure, 75
  fourth degree in obtaining,
      211–212, 215
  in polygraph testing, 66, 205–
      215
  torture in obtaining, 25
Consent form, 16–17
Control question tests, 59, 105,
      109–111

Control questions, 3–32, 59
  in countermeasures against
      polygraph tests, 238–240
  general honesty, 13–14,
      19–20
  in Guilty Knowledge Test,
      281–282, 298, 301–303
  in Lie Control test, 109–121
  in Positive Control Test, 135,
      137–138
  in Truth Control Test, 129–133
Countermeasures:
  against Guilty Knowledge test,
      253, 303–304
  against polygraph tests, 232,
      237–243, 253, 303–304
Courts:
  confession in, 212–215
  Guilty Knowledge Test as evi-
      dence in, 305–306
  jury reactions in Mendoza case,
      226–228
  polygraph evidence in,
      217–235
  polygraphers as expert witnesses
      in, 218–220, 224–226
Covert lie detection, 151–160
Criminal investigation:
  clinical lie test in, 87–89
  confession in, 207–212
  criterion measure in, 74–75
  Guilty Knowledge Test in,
      253–255, 266, 275–282,
      286–291, 295–296
  Hanson and Haverstock ficti-
      tious case, 260–296
  in Lie Control Test, 109–126
  ordeals in, 25–26
  polygraph in, 2, 27, 31, 41,
      64–66, 233–234, 241–242
  with Psychological Stress
      Evaluator, 156–159
  in Searching Peak of Tension
      Test, 145–147
Criterion measures, 74–77

Dahm, A. E., 156
Damaging admissions, 206–207
Deception, confessions obtained
      by, 208–209
  (*See also* Lying)
Deception response, 59, 61
Defense, U.S. Department of,
      151–152
Dektor Counterintelligence and
      Security, Inc., 35, 153, 154, 156

Eden, G., 154, 158
Electrodermal response (EDR),
      158, 250–253, 304–305
Emotion:
  autonomic response to, 55–56
  bodily changes in, 56–58
  James's theory of, 56–57
Employee screening, 3–4, 183–
      194
  case against, 188–192
  case for, 185–188
  clinical lie test, 91–92
  cost/benefit ratios, 185–186,
      196–198
  honesty tests and question-
      naires, 36, 195–203
  legislation against, 184–185,
      188–189, 196, 242
  liberal viewpoint on, 197
  Lie Control Test, 174, 177, 187
  of police force applicants, 206–
      207
  polygraph tests, 3, 36, 45, 66–67,
      135, 183–194, 222
  postemployment, 184
  pre-employment, 184, 205–207,
      222
  Relevant Control Test, 139–144,
      187, 190
Employee theft, 172–177
  Coker case, 167–172
  Edna K., bookkeeper, 175–176
  extent of, 172

Employee theft:
  Lie Control Test, 174, 177, 187
  police investigation of, 180–181
  polygraph investigations of,
    172–177
  polygraphers in investigations
    of, 168–180, 199
  precautions against, 192–194
  rights of employees, 175, 177–
    180
  Walter K. and stolen camera,
    177–179
  Wayne K., bank employee, 116,
    174–175
Employment, fair opportunity
  legislation, 196
Error:
  false-positive and false-negative,
    198, 298–300, 303
  unbiased, 198
Exclusionary Rule, 212–213
Experimenter Expectancy Effect,
  223–224
Expert opinion, limitations of,
  64–68
Expert witnesses, polygraphers as,
  218–220, 224–226

Ferguson, R. J., 5, 38
Fidgetometer (wiggle seat), 152
Ford Motor Company, 191
Fourth degree, 211–212, 215
Frank, Jerome, 41

Galton, Sir Francis, 26
Geddes, L. A., 60
General honesty questions, 13–14,
  19–20
General Series Test, 105
Global scoring, 32–33, 73–74
Graybar Electric Corporation, 203
Guilt complex question, 31, 32,
  129–131, 133

Guilty feeling and lying, 55, 58
Guilty knowledge, 59, 146
Guilty Knowledge Test (Peak of
  Tension Test), 146, 158, 233,
  249–255
  accuracy of, 299, 301
  countermeasures against, 253,
    303–304
  as courtroom evidence,
    305–306
  experiment, 250–253
  in Hanson-Haverstock fictitious
    case, 266, 275–282, 286–
    291, 295–296
  polygraph in, 304–305
  scoring, 298–303
  validity in laboratory, 297–301
Gullibility, 25

Hagoth Corporation, 35, 159
Hare, Robert D., 61, 232
Hartshorn, H., 198–199
Hauptmann, Bruno Richard,
  27, 35
Heisse, John W., Jr., 156, 157
Henry, D., 155
Hohmann, G., 57
Holmes, Warren, 2
Honesty:
  of children, study of, 198–199
  general honesty questions,
    13–14, 19–20
  prediction of, 198–203
Honesty tests and questionnaires,
  36, 195–203
  assumptions in, 203
  validity of, 201–203
Horror Picture test, 155
Horvath, Frank, 44, 95, 122–125,
  158, 221, 222, 240
Hull, Clark L., 45
Human rights and polygraph tests,
  38–40, 46–47, 188
Hunter, F., 123

Inbar, G., 154, 158
Inbau, Fred, 27 –28, 30 –32, 42, 44, 64 –65, 90 –94, 111, 252
Independent chart evaluation, 73 –74
Informed consent right, of, 179
Infrared (IR) detectors, 152 – 153
Institute for Defense Analysis (IDA), 50
Irrelevant questions (*see* Relevant/ irrelevant questions)

James, William, 56 –57
Job applications (*see* Employee screening)
Jones, E. A., Jr., 39, 42, 96, 224, 228 –229

Keeler, Leonarde, 30 –31, 34, 42, 90, 94, 141, 225
    Peak of Tension test, 31, 145 – 146, 252
Keeler Polygraph, 30
Kennedy, John F., assassination of, 35, 153
Kinsey, Alfred C., 189
Known-lie control question, 111 – 115, 130, 131, 201, 241
Known-truth question, 130
Kradz, Lieutenant, 156
Kubis, J., 44, 96 –97, 157
Kugelmass, S., 44

Larson, John A., 25, 28 –30, 42, 105, 107, 141
Law Enforcement Associates, 35
Lee, C. D., 30, 42
Legislation against employee screening tests, 184 – 185, 188 – 189, 196, 242
Lie Control Test (LCT), 32, 109 – 127, 131, 133, 137, 140, 158, 219, 220, 231 –232, 240

Lie Control Test (LCT):
    assumptions of, 113 – 117
    base rates in, 221
    in employee theft, 174, 177, 187
    examples from life, 117 – 121
    known-lie control question, 111 – 115
    for rape victims, 113 – 114, 118 – 121
    validity of, 121 – 125, 301
Lie detector tests (*see* Polygraph tests)
Lie detectors:
    critical discussion of, 37 –42
    definition of, 27
    human, 25
    misconceptions on, 49 –50
    in national security, 50
    (*See also* Polygraph; Poly- graphers)
Lieblich, I., 44
Lindbergh kidnapping case, 27
Lippold O., 154
Lombroso, Cesare, 26
Long, Russell, 193
Luria, A. R., 26
Lying:
    in animals, 23 –24
    base rate of, 220 –224
    as bloodless violence, 54 –55
    frequency of, 55
    guilty feeling and, 55, 58
    ordeals for detection of, 25 –26
    physiological indications of, 26, 59 –60
    psychopathic, 228 –232
    signs of, describing by judges, 41
    specific lie response, 59 –62
Lykken's Law, 68 –70
Lynch, B., 155

McCoy, Judge, 218
Mackay, Charles, 26
McQuiston, Charles, 35, 153

Manufacturers Hanover Trust
Company, 191
Marañon, G., 56
Marcuse, F. L., 107n.
Mark II Voice Analyzer, 35
Marston, William Moulton, 27 –29,
43, 49 –50, 60, 218
May, M., 198 –199
Meehl, P., 34
Miller, A. L., 5, 38, 46
Miller Analogies Test (MAT), 69
Minnesota Multiphasic Personal-
ity Inventory (MMPI), 80
Montgomery Ward Company, 191
Morand, Donald R., 42, 96, 100 –
101, 126
Moss Committee, House Gov-
ernmental Operations Com-
mittee, 152
Münsterberg, Hugo, 27

Nachshon, I., 155, 158 –159
Newberg, D. C., 60
Northwestern University School of
Law, Scientific Crime Detec-
tion laboratory,, 30
Numerical scoring of charts, 34, 39

Ordeals, 25 –26
Orne, Martin, 44, 223
Oswald, Lee Harvey, 35, 153

Parkinson, C. Northcote, Parkin-
son's Law, 68
Pathometer, 60
Peak of Tension Test, 31, 145 –146,
252
(*See also* Guilty Knowledge
Test)
Penney, J. C., Corporation, 191
Personnel screening (*see*
Employee screening)

Personnel Security Inventory, 36,
199
Peter, L. J., Peter Principle, 68
Pius XII, Pope, 40
Plants, experiments with, 33
Plethysmograph, 26
Podlesny, J., 133, 301
Police force applicants, polygraph
examinations of, 206 –207
Police interrogations:
brutality alleged, 29, 211 –212
confessions in, 207 –212
of employee theft, 180 –181
Polygraph, 12, 16
"cardio" tracings, 60 –61
history and development of,
27 –35
Polygraph charts, 19 –21
global scoring, 32 –33, 73 –74
independent evaluating, 73 –74
numerical scoring, 34, 39
Polygraph tests:
accuracy of, 63 –74
American and European at-
titudes toward, 9
assumptions of, 92 –98
Backster's contributions to,
33 –35
base rates in, 220 –224
countermeasures against, 232,
237 –243, 253, 303 –304
in criminal investigation (*see*
Criminal investigation,
polygraph in)
critical discussion of, 37 –42
in employee screening (*see*
Employee screening, poly-
graph tests)
as evidence in courts, 217 –235
example of method, 11 –22
in foreign countries, 45
as fourth-degree investigations,
211 –212, 215
interrogations distinguished
from, 34 –35

Polygraph tests:
  literature on, 43–45
  opposition to, 38, 46–47
  in psychopathologic lying,
    228–232
  Reid's work with (*see* Reid,
    John E.)
  reliability (*see* Reliability of
    polygraph tests)
  science and, 42–45
  summary of, 148–150
  uses of, 1–4
  validity (*see* Validity of poly-
    graph tests)
  Voice stress Analyzer compared
    with, 157–158
  (*See also* Clinical lie test; Guilty
    Knowledge Test; Lie Con-
    trol Test; Positive Control
    Test; Relevant Control Test;
    Relevant/Irrelevant test;
    Searching Peak of Tension
    Test; Truth Control Test)
Polygraphers:
  in clinical lie test, 87–101
  in employee theft investigations,
    168–180, 199
  as expert witnesses, 218–220,
    224–226
  "friendly," 223–224
  judgment of reliability of tests,
    65–67
  number of, 1, 6
  as private detectives, 167–182
  training of, 1, 31
  work of, 1–3
Polygraphic Lie Test, 38, 75, 85,
  104
Positive Control Test (PCT),
  135–138, 140, 219
  assumptions of, 136–138
  example of, 136–137
Positron Tomography, 58
Posttest interrogation, 91, 207–208
Premack, Ann, 24

Premack, David, 24
Psychological reactions, 42
Psychological Stress Evaluator
  (PSE), 35, 153, 160
  commercial uses, 159–160
  lie detection with, 156–159
  stress measurement with, 154–
    155
  validity of, 159–160
Psychologists, 4–6, 42–45
Psychopathic lying, 228–232
Public opinion polls, 4

Rape:
  Lie Control Test for victims,
    113–114, 118–121
  polygraph tests for victims, 2
  Positive Control Test, example
    of, 136–137
Raskin, D. C., 44, 61, 77, 125, 133,
  222, 231–232, 240, 301
Reid, John E., 30–34, 42, 64–65,
  89–96, 109, 111, 118, 122–
  123, 126, 156, 219, 225, 228,
  239–240, 252
  clinical lie test, 31–33
  control question test, 59, 109–
    111
  guilt complex question, 31, 32,
    129–131, 133
Reid, John E., and Associates, 31,
  36, 65, 122–124, 194
Reid Polygraph, 30
Reid Report, 36, 195–197, 199,
  202
Relevant Control Test (RCT):
  assumptions of, 142–143
  in employee screening, 139–
    144, 187, 190
  example of, 140–141
  validity of, 143–144
Relevant/irrelevant questions, 13,
  28, 30–33, 39, 104–105
  in clinical lie test, 97–98

Relevant/irrelevant questions:
  in Guilty Knowledge Test, 298,
    301–303
  in Lie Control Test, 109–111,
    117–121
  in Relevant Control Test, 140–
    142
  "sacrifice relevant," 109–110
Relevant/Irrelevant test (R/I),
    103–108, 140, 141
  assumptions of, 104–106
  validity of, 106–107
Reliability of expert opinion,
    64–68
Reliability of polygraph tests,
    63–74
  examiner's judgment of, 65–67
  Lykken's Law of, 68–70
  studies of tests, 70–73
  vs. validity, 70, 74–80
Rights:
  of employees accused of theft,
    175, 177–181
  of employers, 177, 180
  human, and polygraph tests,
    38–40, 46–47, 188
  of informed consent, 179
Rockwell International, 191
Rorschach Inkblot Test, 220
Romig, C. A., 206

Sabotage, 173
Schachter, J., 56
Schizophrenia, 80
Schwartz, G., 155, 158
Science and polygraph tests,
    42–45
Searching Peak of Tension Test
    (SPOT), 145–147
Sears, Roebuck & Company, 191
Single-culprit paradigm, 78–79
Skinner, B. F., 207
Skolnick, Jerome H., 41–42
Slowick, S., 123

Smith, G., 155
Smith, Robert Ellis, 39
Snyder, LeMoyne, 208
Sociobiology, 24
South Bend Lathe Corporation,
    193
Soviet Union, relations with U.S.,
    50–51
Specific lie response, 59–62
Stage fright, 155
Stanton Survey, 36, 199
Steiner, George, 24
Stimulation test (stim test), 93–95,
    106, 240
Summers, Father Walter G., 60, 65
Suzuki, A., 44
Sweat box, 211

Theft by employees (*see* Employee
    theft)
Third degree, 211–212
Tobin, Y., 158
Torture, confessions obtained by,
    25
Tremor in voice, 153–154
Trials (*see* Courts)
Trustworthiness, 196
  (*See also* Honesty tests and ques-
    tionnaires)
Truth Control Test (TCT), 129–
    134, 219
  assumptions, 130–133
  example of, 131–132
Truth technology, 37–42
Truth Verifier, 49–62, 64, 219

Validity of polygraph tests:
  Barland and Raskin study,
    77–78
  burden of proof in, 80–81
  criterion measures in, 74–77
  as evidence in court, 219–220
  vs. reliability, 70, 74–80

Validity of polygraph tests:
    single-culprit paradigm, 78–79
    (*See also specific names of tests*)
Voice Stress Analyzers, 35–36,
      85–86, 151–161, 196
    (*See also* Psychological Stress
      Evaluator)
Vollmer, August, 28

Weir, R. J., Jr., 61
Wicklander, D., 123

Wiggle seat (fidgetometer), 152
Wigmore, John Henry, 53
Wiretaps, 39
Words, neutral and taboo, 155

Younger, I., 61

Zone of Comparison Test, 34, 109,
     111–112, 120
    (*See also* Lie Control Test)